C000224478

# *The Book of*
# NORTHLEW
# *with Ashbury*

*People of the Land*

THE NORTHLEW HISTORY GROUP

HALSGROVE

*This book is dedicated to the people of Northlew past, present and future.*

First published in Great Britain in 2002

Copyright © 2002 Northlew History Group.

Frontispiece photograph: *View of the church, taken in 1909.*

*All rights reserved. No part of this publication may be reproduced, stored in a retrieval system, or transmitted in any form or by any means without the prior permission of the copyright holder.*

**British Library Cataloguing-in-Publication Data**
A CIP record for this title is available from the British Library

ISBN 1 84114 197 6

**HALSGROVE**
PUBLISHING, MEDIA AND DISTRIBUTION

Halsgrove House
Lower Moor Way
Tiverton, Devon EX16 6SS
Tel: 01884 243242
Fax: 01884 243325
email: sales@halsgrove.com
website: www.halsgrove.com

Printed and bound by
Bookcraft Ltd., Midsomer Norton

*Whilst every care has been taken to ensure the accuracy of the information contained in this book, the authors disclaim responsibility for any mistakes which may have inadvertently been included.*

# PREFACE

The following text is taken from a book written by a Bible Christian minister, John Maynard, in 1900. John Maynard was born in 1820 and lived most of his life in Northlew. This text is still appropriate, as the village has changed very little since this was written and all the landmarks can be recognised. Northlew is still the beautiful village as described in the minister's book *Remarkable Incidents in the Life of John Maynard*:

*There is a rather pretty and very pleasantly situated village ensconced in the bosom of North Devon. Its figure is four square, and its sides nearly correspond to the cardinal points of the compass. The north side rises as a barricade against the cold winds of winter. The opposite side dips in a gentle gradient, so as to admit the genial sunshine and refreshing showers from the south.*

*As you stand at the top of the village with your back to the wall, some of the grandest hills of Dartmoor lift up their gigantic heads, and look you straight in the face. To strangers, who for the first time open their eyes upon this landscape, the scene is enchanting. One stands and gazes with commingling emotions of awe, admiration, and wonder, until his heart swells with delight. Withdrawing his attention from this charming view, and fixing it on objects immediately around him, he travels back in imagination to the time when this was literally the 'Village Green'.*

*At the north-eastern corner of the village is situated the Parish Church. Passing through the churchyard, you reach a stile over which you have a splendid view of the surrounding country. Looking across a rather deep valley, a fine expansion of land, with many green fields interspersed with some woods, and dotted with farm-steads and cottages, presents itself to your gaze, and fills you with a sense of beauty that greatly charms you.*

*Then, turning a little to the right, and looking in a south-easterly direction, there opens up a fine stretch of country, in which the beautiful is lost in the grand, and the grand rises up almost into the sublime. As the eye travels up the charming valley, and catches glimpses of its environment on the right hand and the left and then fixes itself on one of the hills of Dartmoor, which forms a splendid crown to the valley itself, one feels his heart swell with delight and almost imagines himself an inhabitant of Fairy Land.*

*Language utterly fails me to give an adequate description of the commingling beauty and grandeur and sublimity of this patch of landscape, this charming bit of scenery; it must be seen to be really appreciated.*

***The building to the right is the wheelwrighting shop, 1917. Note the shutters to the windows and the trees by the pump which were planted for the Coronation of George V.***

*The Lower Class at Northlew School, c.1910s.*

# CONTENTS

*The rood screen, before its renovation in Northlew Parish Church.*

# ACKNOWLEDGEMENTS

The History Group gratefully acknowledges the contributions that numerous people have made and without whose help the production of this book would not have been possible.

Dennis Adams, Percy Adams, Tom and Vera Andrew, Rita Bater, Jill Bennett, Mrs Brighton, Cecil Brooking, David Bourne, Bryan Haulage, Dorothy Cole, Brenda Curtis, Ivy Curtis, Percy Curtis, John and Frances Dufty, Pat Durston, Clem Early, Bill Elliott, Betty Friend, Pop and Kate Gay, Mrs M. Gerry, Lew and Lillian Gratton, Julian Gratton, Diane Grierson, Trixie Hannaford, Mrs M. Harrison, Laura Hawkin, Tony Hazell, Bill and Hilary Isaac, Mr R. Jordan, Stella Jordan, Nicola Lampe, Marlene McCafferty, Janet Millership, Revd John Peak, Nancy Pincombe-Docksai, Fred Rundle, Mrs E.C. Smale, Peter and Betty Spry, John and Lilian Spry, Freda Stratton, Phyllis Squire, Ruth Squire, Marcia Taylor, Chris Ware, Mrs M. Weeks, Muriel Woolsey, Mrs J. Worden, John Yelland, Brenda Zielinski.

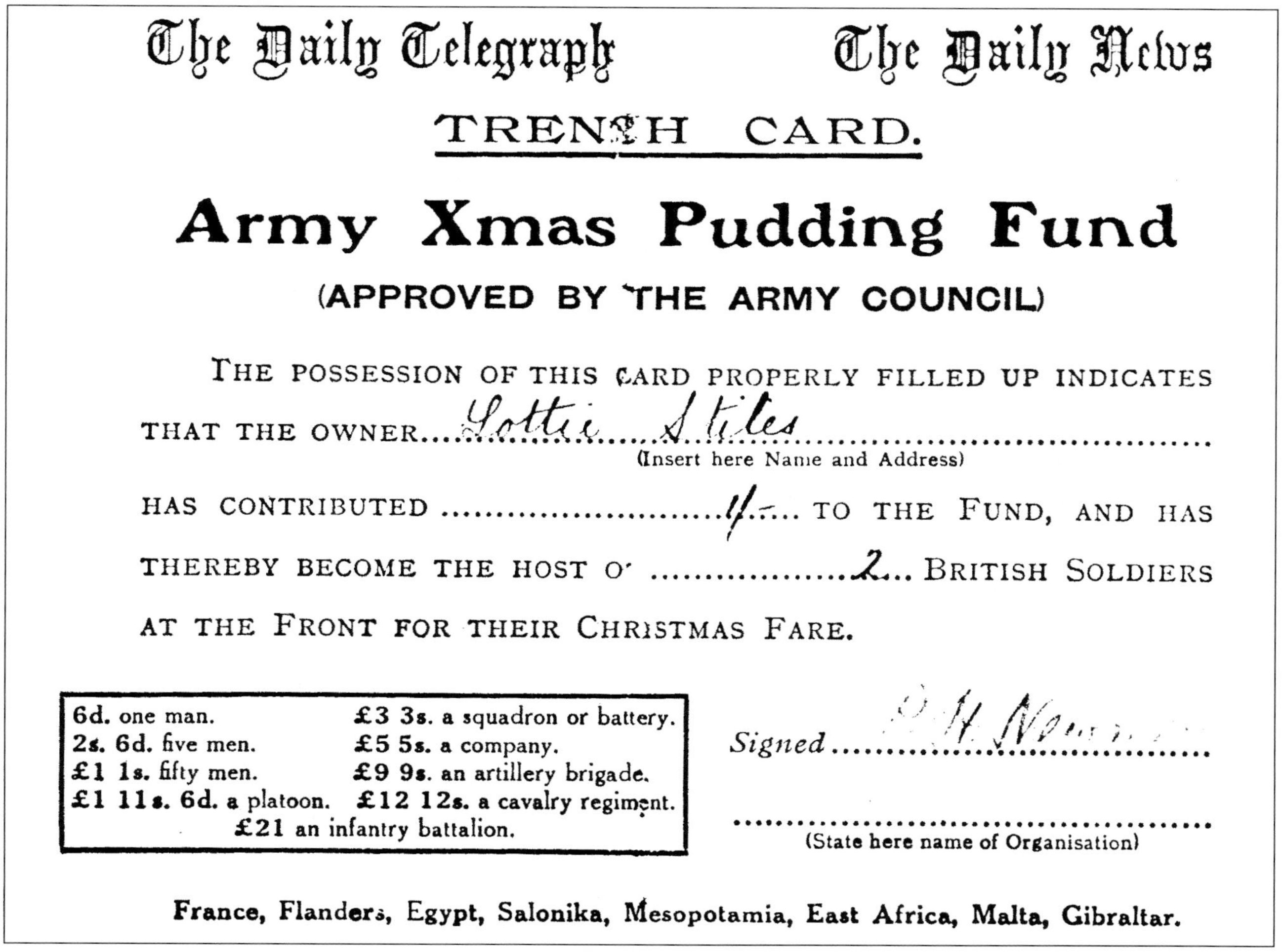

The Daily Telegraph — The Daily News

TRENCH CARD.

**Army Xmas Pudding Fund**

**(APPROVED BY THE ARMY COUNCIL)**

THE POSSESSION OF THIS CARD PROPERLY FILLED UP INDICATES THAT THE OWNER ......Lottie Stiles...... (Insert here Name and Address) HAS CONTRIBUTED ......1/-... TO THE FUND, AND HAS THEREBY BECOME THE HOST OF ......2... BRITISH SOLDIERS AT THE FRONT FOR THEIR CHRISTMAS FARE.

| | |
|---|---|
| 6d. one man. | £3 3s. a squadron or battery. |
| 2s. 6d. five men. | £5 5s. a company. |
| £1 1s. fifty men. | £9 9s. an artillery brigade. |
| £1 11s. 6d. a platoon. | £12 12s. a cavalry regiment. |
| £21 an infantry battalion. | |

Signed ......................

......................
(State here name of Organisation)

**France, Flanders, Egypt, Salonika, Mesopotamia, East Africa, Malta, Gibraltar.**

*Trench card: Schoolchildren contributed to soldiers' comforts and were awarded 'trench cards' throughout the war. This card was for a Christmas Pudding Fund.*

*Bible class.* Left to right, back row: *?, F. Maynard, ?, B. Vincent, Miss Harvey, ?;* centre: *Miss Harvey, D. Hortop;* front: *V. Perry, C. Smale, G. Adams.*

*Serving tea at one of the many social events in the Church Room.*
Left to right: *Marge Rundle, Eileen Wilson, Lilian Spry.*

# INTRODUCTION

## *The Northlew History Group*

Started by Jenny Voden, the Northlew History Group was formed to research information for an exhibition about Northlew and Ashbury in celebration of the millennium. The exhibition proved to be a great success, attracting both local people and visitors from all over Devon. Many of these requested that the material be collated into a permanent record.

There are seven members in the History Group: Molly Atkinson, Ros Eveleigh, Irene Oldale, Ron Oldale, Heather Richards, Lena Williams and Jenny Voden. These people have been involved in the writing of this book with valued and special help from Claude Smale and Marilyn Livingstone, together with significant contributions from Lew Gratton, Trixie Hannaford, Hilary Isaac, Fred Rundle and John Spry.

From these beginnings, the book gradually evolved as a community enterprise. Without the help of those living in the area and those from further afield who have kept in touch, the project would not have been completed. This unique and fascinating record stands as a tribute to them and the story of their community.

## *The People of the Land*

The earliest recorded reference to Devonshire is 'Defanascir' in the Anglo Saxon Chronicle under the year 851. The 'men of Devon' were first mentioned as 'Defnas' in 823. The word 'Defnas', which was a tribal name, came from earlier times probably from the original Celtic inhabitants, the British Dumnonii, who lived in the South West. Even though the Anglo Saxons conquered these people, the name Dumnonii continued, 'Dumno' meaning 'world' or 'land'. Thus the name Devon can be traced back to a Celtic word for 'people of the land' and for that reason, seemed to be a fitting tribute to Northlew as part of the title for this book.

*A view of Northlew taken from Kimber. The Kimber family held the manor of Kimber for many years – several members of the family appear in a list of those who paid for the repair of Northlew Church in 1613.*

*Chapter 1*

# EARLY HISTORY

When the Domesday Book was compiled in 1086, Northlew, a village in the hundred of Torrington, was divided into five manors: Ashbury, Gorhuish, Kimber, Lew and Rutleigh, each held by a different lord.

## The Manor of Ashbury

The estate extended to Durdon Cross, Cruft, Scobchester, Wadland and Ashbury Court. Before the Conquest, the lands of Ashbury were held by Wadel the Saxon. He paid tax on one virgate of land – about 30 acres. Wadland enshrines the name of its Saxon owner. Ashbury takes its name from the estate. The name 'bury' in Old English is burg, meaning to shelter. It is equivalent to the Latin 'villa' and means a country 'mansion' or 'estate'. In the Domesday Book Ashbury was recorded as Esseberie. There was arable land for five ploughs, ten acres of meadow and six acres of woodland. A church has stood here since at least the thirteenth century. In 1416 the church is named on the cathedral roll as Santa Marie de Ayschbyry.

## The Manor of Gorhuish

At Gorhuish one Bernard held all the land from Baldwin the Sheriff. Bernard's two unfree tenants held all land – one furlong in size, as well as half a plough. There was also one smallholder. Bernard owned 22 head of cattle, 11 sheep, 7 goats, 2 acres of coppice wood, 6 acres of meadow and 40 acres of pasture. The overlord of the manor of Gorhuish was the Earl of Devon in the fourteenth century, although its immediate landholder in 1377 was William Speke. The Newcombe family were resident at Gorhuish for much of the sixteenth and seventeenth centuries, as were the Tickle family. Alexander Newcombe of North Gorhuish was accused in the sixteenth century of cutting trees which belonged to Northlew manor. One Nicholas Tickle of Gorhuish was involved in a transfer of Northlew Moor in 1555, and members of the family appear in village records until the early-eighteenth century.

## The Manor of Kimber

According to Domesday the manor was sub-let to Roger the Fleming. It consisted of one virgate and two furlongs with one furlong held by unfree tenants. There are now three farmhouses at East Kimber and an old farmhouse lying back behind the avenue of trees at West Kimber but the site of the old Manor House has disappeared. In 1423 Robert Cary sold some land belonging to Northlew manor to John Bradeston of East Kimber, but most of the manor was held in the fourteenth century by Walter de Radeford as part of the Earl of Devon's estate. The land at Kimber which was owned by Northlew manor brought in annual rents of 33s.4d. A member of the Newcombe family held the farm of West Kimber for a time; he appears in the same list of subscribers to church repairs as members of the Kimber family.

## The Manor of Northlew

The largest of the manors was that of Lew. According to Domesday it comprised a hide, a virgate and a furlong which had been held by Brictric, as well as one virgate of land held by the King, and one hide of land held by 20 unfree tenants. There were also seven boardars (smallholders), and seven serfs (slaves). These numbers refer to heads of households; the actual population of this manor may have been as high as 120. In addition to the people, the king had on his land 7 broodmares, 50 head of cattle, 50 swine, 100 sheep and 15 goats, with 20 acres of woodland and 30 of meadow and pasture. The King's land was farmed by Goscelin for £9 per annum.

The lands of Brictric passed into the hands of Queen Mathilda after the Conquest, and after her death in 1083 William I gave Northlew manor to

*A church occasion at Northlew Manor before the First World War.*

Robert Fitzhamon, Count of Gloucester. His daughter married Robert de Clare in 1108 and Northlew was held as part of the Honour of Torrington by the de Clare Earls of Gloucester. After their lands were broken up in the early-fourteenth century the manor had a number of owners, including Hugh le Despenser and Guy de Brian. Although such men were the overlords of the manor, in reality it was controlled by sub-tenants. For example, in 1349 the manor was actually held by Henry Barry, who had Hugh le Despenser as his overlord. Barry would have been responsible for the day-to-day management of the manor and would have received its revenues.

### *Northlew Manor House*

The Manor House was owned by the family of Cary, from the time of John Cary who married Mary Holloway in 1386, for upwards of 200 years. The Manor House was later occupied as a farm-house and is mentioned on the Ordnance Survey Map of 1809 as North Holloway Farm. In 1823 John Bickle, the son of a yeoman farmer, married Catherine, daughter of John and Catherine Watkins of the Manor House.

*The gates of Northlew Manor. Northlew Manor has also been known as Holway Manor. The house now has a gabled roof, mullioned and latticed windows and is set at the end of a long drive. There are lawns in front and extensive views over pasture and of Dartmoor in the distance.*

The house was restored in 1883 by the owner Mr Borel. It was also altered under the direction of architect Mr Brynne when Mr S.J. Truman Lynch bought the property in 1901. In 1936 then owner Commander Fison brought to light old fireplaces, doorways and recesses and introduced an engine-house for electric light, pumping and other modern conveniences. Major and Mrs Vaux, who lived in the Manor House, were benefactors of the church in the latter half of the twentieth century.

Northlew Manor was a major employer for the area and kept a full retinue of servants: butler, cook, footmen and housemaids. There were extensive gardens which employed gardeners, grooms and other outside workers. The gardens were substantial with an orangery; the orange and lemon trees stood outside in summer and were brought inside in winter. There was also a mulberry tree and some villagers can remember a white sheet being spread under the tree, so that fruit could be collected when the branches were shaken.

## *The Manor of Rutleigh*

The manor of Rutleigh (called Redcliff in Domesday) was also held by Roger the Fleming. In the fourteenth century it was held by the same Walter de Radeford as held most of Kimber manor.

### *Rutleigh Manor House*

The Manor House was built in the fifteenth century and extended in the 1600s. At some time in its history it was used as a retreat by monks from Cornwall. Evidence of a ruined building has been found which may have been the family chapel. Further evidence of a building has also been discovered – was this the original house? The old Manor House has been converted into two farm dwelling-houses. The oak beams, old stonework and large rooms still survive.

The Kelly family were great benefactors of the church. The Arms on the porch are the Kelly and Trecarrell Arms; the Kelly Arms appear in glass preserved in the Rutleigh Chapel, on the pillar in the chancel and on a seat in the north aisle.

The manor was owned by the Revd Richard Phillips, the rector of Northlew in 1570, and by his son, the Revd Henry Phillips who succeeded him in 1607. The Revd Henry Phillips married a daughter of the Carpenter family, which afterwards became connected with the family of Garnier. There is an inscription on the outer porch 'A.D. 1648, W.G.' which would seem to refer to W. Carpenter Garnier as lord of the manor of Rutleigh.

*The door of the inner porch of old Rutleigh Manor House.*

*On the inner porch the name William Kelly is visible, above this is the letter 'P' with a cross through the tail. The Kelly family arms are on either side. The 'P' stands for the Latin 'par' or 'by' and the inscription shows that the porch was put up by William Kelly who married Jane, the daughter of Sir Henry Trecarrell, and who died in 1534.*

## Elsewhere in Medieval and Early-Modern Northlew

Throughout the medieval and early-modern period, landholding patterns in Northlew were complex and tracing the descent of the lands in the village is not straightforward. The village was not dominated by a single large landholder, although at times the influence of certain landlords was very strong. As well as the five major manors there were also small parcels of land in the parish which, like some of the manors, were held by people who did not live in the village. The Northlew lands were a small part of large landholdings held by these people elsewhere. For example, in the twelfth century, a parcel of land in Northlew was sold to William Brewer as part of a large sale of lands in Torrington, including the town of Great Torrington. Brewer was an important judge and courtier under both Richard the Lionheart and King John, and founded Torr, Mottisfont and Dunkeswell Abbeys.

By the fourteenth century another parcel of land described as the 'hamlet' of Northlew was held by William Martin (who also had lands in Holsworthy, Tackbere, Dartington and many other places in Devon and Somerset). Martin's property included a house, 80 acres of demesne arable land which was managed for him, a wood of 18 acres, pasture and part of a mill which could be rented at £1.6s.8d. per year. He had seven tenants who had smallholdings, and held a court for these tenants at which he levied fines of 3s.4d. Small parcels of land also changed hands. For example, in 1392 land at Netherdurdon was sold by John Heyne to John Columpberys.

Account rolls for the manor of Northlew in the fifteenth century list at least ten different tenants of that one manor. For example, William Ganvyle paid 4s.4d. for his land at Estecott, while 'William ate Worth' paid 40s. for Southdown, Westdown, West Holoway, Bredepark, Swynpart and 'le Northmede'. In the fifteenth century some land was arable, but cattle were much more important. The manor of Northlew was selling cattle and horses. Four horses were sold for 20s. in 1423/4, while cattle brought prices from 12s. for one oxen to an average of 7s. for each cow. There is no mention of sheep being farmed by the landlords of Northlew manor, but its tenants probably raised them.

*Northlew has always been dominated by agricultural activity. There were many small farmers as well as the larger landowners.*

Manorial tenants were required to attend a Manor Court. These courts dealt with land disputes, levied fines for sales of land between tenants, collected fines for the right to brew ale, and dealt with petty crimes such as assault and theft. The courts' jurors would have been manorial tenants, who would sit in judgement on their neighbours. The courts met as often as once a month, but sometimes only once or twice a year.

At a court held on Monday 18 October 1484, the jury was concerned with the rebuilding of a wall between Bolland and the lord's lake, a dispute which continued for some months. At the next court on Wednesday 8 December, three men were told that they were to repair the 'common way' at Holeford for 12 years, while Joanna Southcote was given the licence to brew ale. This court also dealt with a fight in the village between Richard Meder and John Proter. Richard hit John with a three-pronged fork, and when John retaliated with a stone, Richard stabbed John and drew blood. Two more men (John Juyll and Richard Growdon) joined in but only punched each other. The fight seems to have ended when Richard hit John with a stone. Participants in this scuffle paid fines totalling 3s.6d.; in addition the lord had the right to confiscate any weapons used in the fight.

At a court held in Northlew on Thursday 18 September 1516, Richard Glamvill of West Kimber was charged with breaking Will Hachyn's wall and also with stabbing Nicholas Tykell with a knife and drawing blood. At the same court two men, William Estcott and Thomas Tewel, were told to repair the road called the 'Lytelway'. Throughout the sixteenth century the court recorded fines for various misdemeanours, one of the most common being the pasturing of animals on the lord's moor. Such charges appear in many courts and were levied against a wide range of people, including the rector of the church. Another common complaint was that people were 'encroaching onto the King's highway east of Holoway'.

By the seventeenth century the Manor Court was not dealing with such local details but was a very formal affair held mainly to appoint local officials, although it did still issue licences to brew ale; in 1661 a licence was granted to Henry Turner.

The responsibilities of Northlew people did not end with their duties as tenants and jurors. They were also expected to help repair the church. More than 75 people contributed to repairs in 1613 and again in 1633. Contributions ranged from £2 to as little as 1d. These early-seventeenth-century contributors included a number of women, such as Jane Sprey who contributed 4d.

## America Bound

In the 1800s life in the countryside was hard, the living conditions were miserable and there was a chronic shortage of cottages. Most people were 'tied' to a particular farm. The 'tied cottage' meant that the farm worker and his family were completely at the mercy of the farmer who was the landlord. Most of the cottages were horrible damp places and rheumatism was rife. The farm labourers were paid between 7s. and 9s. a week, a sum rarely sufficient to support a family. The wives and children had to find work to keep the family going in order to avoid seeking help from the parish. This meant long hours for all with very little money.

*Bill and An Sindlinger with their children, Tucker and baby, 1993.*

In the second half of the nineteenth century, as transport began to improve, there was a general exodus from Devon villages to the towns. Some people left Northlew for towns such as Plymouth while others decided to sail to America.

Fairly recently the descendants of two families who emigrated have visited Northlew and struck up friendships with some of the villagers. The Sindlingers, who live near Chicago, are the descendants of the Hicks family and have visited Northlew three times, the most recent being in 1998. William and Betsy Hicks left Northlew in 1854. The Hicks' came from Northlew and another branch of the family, the Palmers, heralded from Ashbury. William and Betsy settled in Waterloo, Iowa.

## The Pincombe Family

Nancy and Ronald Pincombe-Docksai with Nancy's father, Stephen Pincombe, are another family who have recently visited Northlew. They have traced their direct line of the Pincombe family back to 1671. Some background is included because it links to many names which are present in Northlew today.

Stephen Pincombe married Maria Friend in 1820 and occupied the property of Waterhouse, which at that time was owned by the Revd William Kitson, the rector of Northlew. Stephen and Maria worked the mixed farm until Stephen died aged 38. He left Maria and six children. Maria remarried John Smale in 1837 and together they worked the land for many years. According to Northlew employment directories, descendants of the Friends and Smales still farmed the land until 1940.

Thomas Pincombe, a son of Stephen and Maria, married Elizabeth Sobey in 1846 and they lived in Fordatown. Thomas worked as a labourer and Elizabeth as a glover. Thomas died aged 32. The Census records of 1861 and 1881 show that Elizabeth was then living with her mother and mother-in-law at Pincombe's Cottage which is thought to have been a part of the present Rockey Cottage.

Stephen Pincombe, a son of Thomas and Elizabeth, left Northlew and married Beatrice Potts in Plymouth where Leonard, Nancy's grandfather, was born. Leonard married Kathleen Phelan on 14 May 1922 and four months later the newly-weds left their home in Plymouth to journey to America. They both left behind very large families and the security of family life for a new beginning in Chicago, Illinois. The excited couple, wearing new outfits which Kathleen had made, boarded the steam-powered ship, *The Zeeland,* at Southampton. It was a harrowing transatlantic journey for all 1,162 passengers due in part to the weather and the size of the ship which measured 580 feet by 60 feet. On 10 September 1922 *The Zeeland* entered New York harbour. Nancy says that her grandparents stood in awe upon being greeted by the towering Statue of Liberty, a symbol of freedom of speech and economic opportunity. They hugged and kissed each other while giving thanks to God. They had made it!

Leonard and Kathleen then headed off to Chicago where a job was awaiting Leonard in the famous Chicago stockyards. Kathleen's brother, Dan, who had emigrated to America earlier, had secured the position for his new brother-in-law. After a year in Chicago, Kathleen and Leonard left the windy city and settled in a suburb east of Cleveland where Nancy's father, Stephen, was

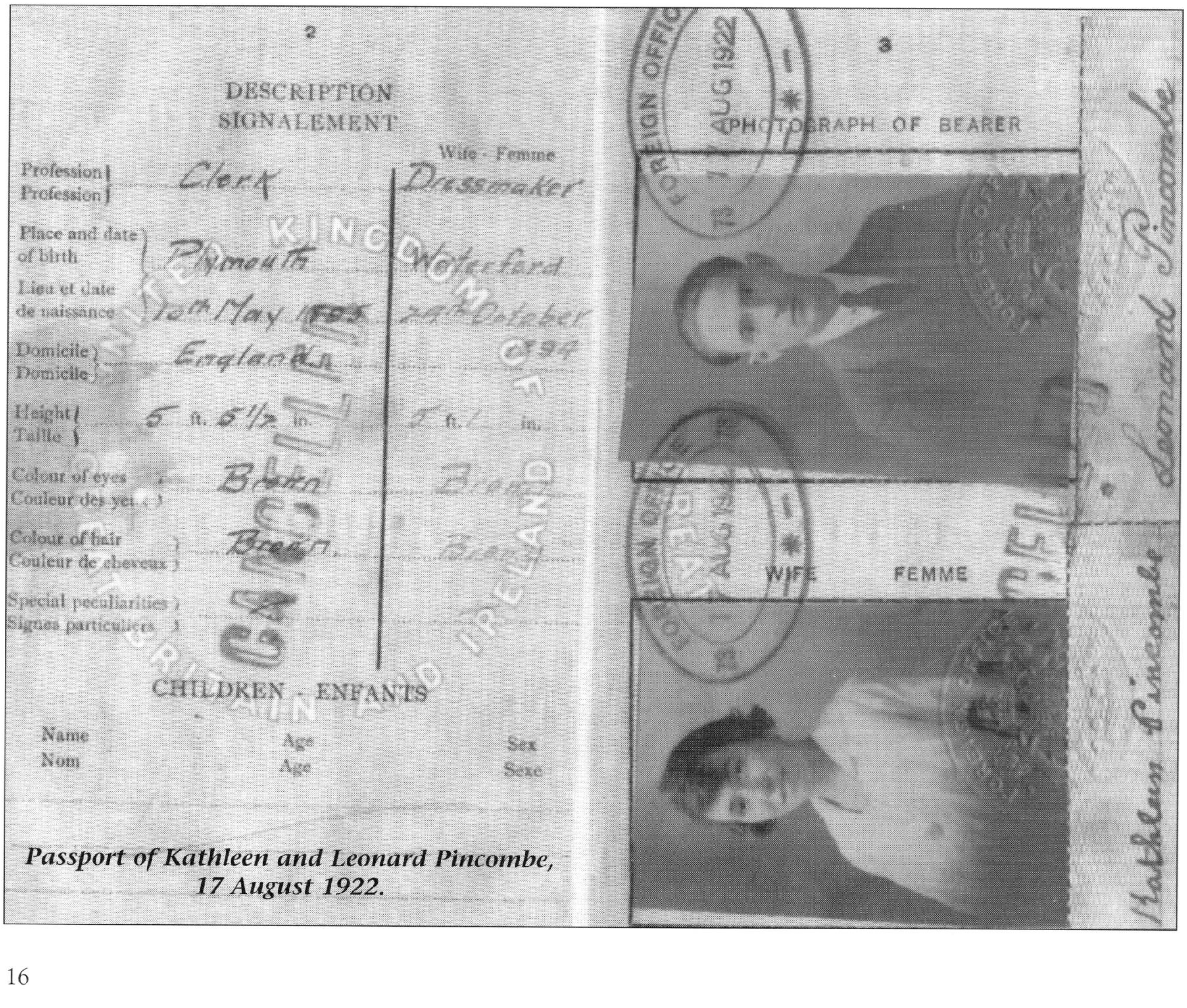

***Passport of Kathleen and Leonard Pincombe, 17 August 1922.***

born on 14 December 1927. Stephen met his future wife in the spring of 1952 and they married in November. Nancy is the middle of five children.

William and Betsy Hicks and Leonard and Kathleen Pincombe took risks when they left our shores for a new life in America. Their descendants are thrilled to visit Northlew and look up the old church registers, to find family headstones in the churchyard, to see some of the places where their ancestors lived and to track down distant relatives. Northlew certainly has ties with the United States.

Above: *The Pincombe family.* Back row, left to right: *Ann (sister), Ron (Nancy's husband);* front: *Dennis (brother), Nancy, Rick (Nancy and Ron's son), Mary Jane (mother), Stephen (father).*

Above: *Dallas McGinnis from Iowa outside the Post Office in 1991 (also a descendant of the Hicks').*

Above: *Great-grandparents Beatrice and Stephen Pincombe.*

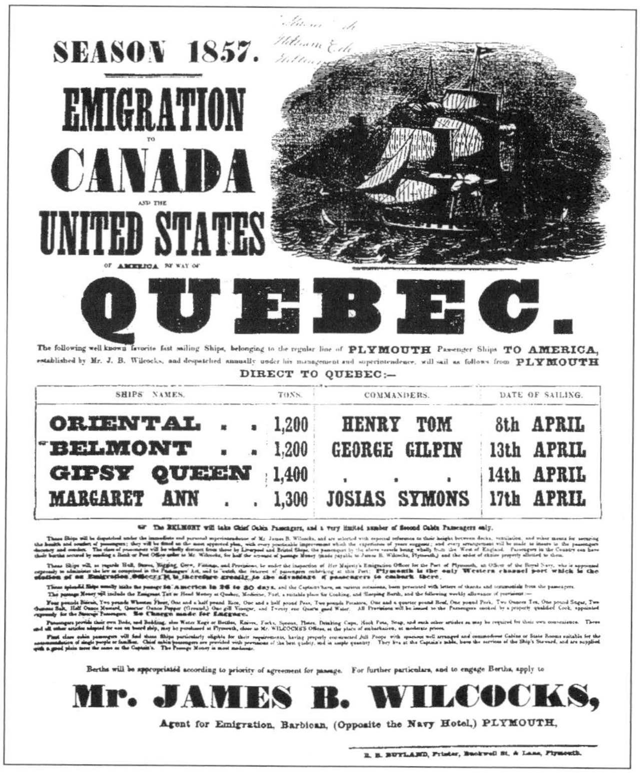

SEASON 1857.

EMIGRATION TO CANADA AND THE UNITED STATES OF AMERICA BY WAY OF QUEBEC.

The following well known favorite fast sailing Ships, belonging to the regular line of PLYMOUTH Passenger Ships TO AMERICA, established by Mr. J. B. Wilcocks, and despatched annually under his management and superintendence, will sail as follows from PLYMOUTH DIRECT TO QUEBEC:—

| SHIPS NAMES. | TONS. | COMMANDERS. | DATE OF SAILING. |
|---|---|---|---|
| ORIENTAL . . | 1,200 | HENRY TOM | 8th APRIL |
| BELMONT . . | 1,200 | GEORGE GILPIN | 13th APRIL |
| GIPSY QUEEN | 1,400 | . . . | 14th APRIL |
| MARGARET ANN . . | 1,300 | JOSIAS SYMONS | 17th APRIL |

The BELMONT will take Chief Cabin Passengers, and a very limited number of Second Cabin Passengers only.

These Ships will be dispatched under the immediate and personal superintendence of Mr. James B. Wilcocks, and are selected with especial reference to their height between decks, ventilation, and other means for securing the health and comfort of passengers; they will be fitted on the most approved plan, with every practicable improvement which the experience of years suggest; and every arrangement will be made to insure to the passengers decency and comfort. The class of passengers will be wholly distinct from those by Liverpool and Bristol Ships, the passengers by the above vessels being wholly from the West of England. Passengers in the Country can have their berths secured by sending a Bank or Post Office order to Mr. Wilcocks, for half the amount of passage Money (made payable to James B. Wilcocks, Plymouth,) and the order of choice properly allotted to them.

These Ships will, as regards Hull, Stores, Rigging, Crew, Fittings, and Provisions, be under the inspection of Her Majesty's Emigration Officer for the Port of Plymouth, an Officer of the Royal Navy, who is appointed expressly to administer the law as comprised in the Passengers' Act, and to watch the interest of passengers embarking at this Port. **Plymouth is the only Western channel port which is the station of an Emigration Officer; it is therefore greatly to the advantage of passengers to embark there.**

These splendid Ships usually make the passage **to America in 26 to 30 days**, and the Captains have, on various occasions, been presented with letters of thanks and testimonials from the passengers.

The passage Money will include the Emigrant Tax or Head Money at Quebec, Medicine, Fuel, a suitable place for Cooking, and Sleeping Berth, and the following weekly allowance of provisions:—

Four pounds Biscuit, Two pounds Wheaten Flour, One and a half pound Rice, One and a half pound Peas, Two pounds Potatoes, One and a quarter pound Beef, One pound Pork, Two Ounces Tea, One pound Sugar, Two Ounces Salt, Half Ounce Mustard, Quarter Ounce Pepper (Ground,) One gill Vinegar, and Twenty one Quarts good Water. All Provisions will be issued to the Passengers cooked by a properly qualified Cook, appointed expressly for the Steerage Passengers. **No Charge made for Luggage.**

Passengers provide their own Beds, and Bedding, also Water Kegs or Bottles, Knives, Forks, Spoons, Plates, Drinking Cups, Hook Pots, Soap, and such other articles as may be required for their own convenience. These and all other articles adapted for use on board ship, may be purchased at Plymouth, close to Mr. WILCOCKS'S Offices, at the place of embarkation, at moderate prices.

First class cabin passengers will find these Ships particularly eligible for their requirements, having properly constructed Full Poops with spacious well arranged and commodious Cabins or State Rooms suitable for the accommodation of single people or families. Chief cabin passengers are provided with provisions of the best quality, and in ample quantity. They live at the Captain's table, have the services of the Ship's Steward, and are supplied with a good plain meat the same as the Captain's. The Passage Money is most moderate.

Berths will be appropriated according to priority of agreement for passage. For further particulars, and to engage Berths, apply to

**Mr. JAMES B. WILCOCKS,**

Agent for Emigration, Barbican, (Opposite the Navy Hotel,) PLYMOUTH,

R. B. RUTLAND, Printer, Buckwell St. & Lane, Plymouth.

Above: *Shipping notice.*

# *A Poem by Betsy Hicks Palmer* (abridged)

**In 1983, Margaret Alice (Montgomery) Smith of Taverse City, Michigan found the following poem among papers saved by her mother, Ruth (Hicks) Montgomery, who was Betsy's niece.**

*This time is up for us to start,*
*Dear brothers and sisters we must part,*
*Farewell father and mother too*
*We feel it most to part from you.*

*I took my baby, eight weeks old,*
*This morning, it was rather cold.*
*We then got into Plymouth town*
*Before the sun was quite gone down.*

*We stayed at uncles' three days or more*
*Then together left the shore.*
The Oriental *was the name*
*Of the ship in which we came.*

*There an enclosed berth we had,*
*The open ones were rather bad.*
*Twenty-five, Captain, Doctor and the crew*
*Passengers, three hundred and forty-two.*

*In April, the eighteenth day*
*We had fair wind and sailed away.*
*We all lost sight of land so quick*
*And the passengers soon were very sick.*

*Provisions once a week we had,*
*And some of it was very bad.*
*Our friends for us did well provide*
*We did not want what the ship supplied.*

*We saw some icebergs very high*
*And some of them were rather nigh.*
*When we o'er the banks did flood*
*We saw men fishing in a boat.*

*We thought our passage would be quick*
*But then the fog came in so thick.*
*That the Captain could not take the sun*
*And we nearly into a vessel did run.*

*There were many vessels to be seen*
*But with the ice, they were all blocked in.*
*We saw a vessel venture through –*
*Then ours, and others, ventured too.*

*We soon did all the doctors pass*
*Then off again so very fast.*
*That evening anchored in the sound*
*There had a view of Quebec town.*

*Next, the boat to Monroe –*
*My husband he was sick.*
*Then took the cars for Chicago*
*And arrived there double quick.*

*We reached our destination,*
*The garden of the west,*
*And there we met the cholera*
*And every other pest.*

*Sickness and disappointment*
*Met us at every hand,*
*And even rich old Uncle Sam*
*Could not give us land.*

*Our baby took the cholera*
*And the doctor thought it best*
*For the sake of our darling's health*
*To still go further west.*

*With a sick baby in our arms*
*And not much in our purse,*
*We bade our city friends farewell*
*And prospects still grew worse.*

*We had been in Waterloo*
*Only two weeks and a day*
*When our earthly treasure*
*From us was called away.*

*No bridges spanned the Cedar then –*
*No churches met our view –*
*A few log cabins and two stores*
*Comprised all Waterloo.*

# *Ashbury House & the Woollcombe Family*

For centuries the Woollcombes provided distinguished members of the professions, the Church and the Services, many of them attaining high-ranking positions. Dame Jocelyn Woollcombe was Director of the Women's Royal Naval Service (the Wrens) from 1946–50 and was ADC to King George VI – the first woman to be so appointed. She was appointed CBE in 1944 and DBE in 1950. The Woollcombes were highly respected; as the village saw it, gentlefolk had their place in the order of things. They provided employment and in this case were generous benefactors to the community.

*Ashbury House and lawns in 1910.*

*Ashbury House in 1909. Ashbury was, for centuries, the seat of the Woollcombe family and remained in their possession until the 1930s when, following death duties and some injudicious management decisions, the estate was broken up and sold off.*

*William Blatchford, father of Jack Blatchford, was a gardener at Ashbury House. Tom Court of Malthouse at Harpers Hill was the butler. Mr Court had been completely deaf from birth. Both gave loyal and dedicated service to their employers.*

*A Woollcombe family photograph.* Left to right, back: *Sir Charles, R.S.W. (Bishop of Whitby), Gerald;* middle: *Mrs Gerald, Lady Charles, Arthur, ?;* front: *?, Richard, Mrs R.S.W., Charles' daughter.*

*A piece of a tiled floor in a field is all that is left of Ashbury Manor. All that remains of the gardens are a few rhododendrons and a flat area, once a tennis court, and part of the walls of the walled gardens. Ashbury Farm was at one time the laundry and the barns around the farm are the remaining outbuildings. The church, which stood next to the house, continued in use until the mid 1960s.*

*Aerial views of the village showing the Square. Taken about 1912 by a pilot friend of Canon Harvey who flew from Winkleigh airfield. Note, along the school wall the old skittle alley, old Tom Andrew's store sheds in the saw-pit and the buildings, now demolished, above Elmfield.*

*The Square in the early 1900s. To the left of the picture, at the corner of Crowden Road, is the shop. At the opposite side of the opening to Crowden Road is the chapel. The large white building behind the pump is the Green Dragon Hotel. At this time the Square was covered in stones.*

*Chapter 2*

# THE PARISH OF NORTHLEW WITH ASHBURY

## A Tour of the Parish

### Introduction

Northlew lies within a vast area of carboniferous rocks called Culm Measures, Culm being a word used in medieval times to denote poor-quality coal. This rock strata extends from the Atlantic coast in the west to Bampton in the east, and from Dartmoor to the south almost as far as Exmoor in the north. Locally around Northlew the rocks are part of the Crackington Formation – mainly shales and thin sandstones.

Together with high, flat-topped land, these rocks have given rise to thin, poorly-drained clay soils where rough, rush-covered pastures can be found. Deep valleys, too steep for arable cultivation, cut into these high areas offering shelter from strong winds, and producing thick woodland. Most farmhouses and villages have sought protection in such valleys or other sheltered areas created by dips in the high land. Northlew's situation is typical of this.

### Climate

It is said that 'the Devil died of cold at Northlew', indicating that the village receives more than its fair share of harsh weather. Indeed, the wind does pour for uninterrupted miles across high land bringing upwards of 50 inches (125 centimetres) of rain each year. Being part of the south-west peninsula means that these winds, though rain-bearing, are in fact relatively mild. Although an equable climate, extremes of temperature can occur. Many people recall harsh winters when the only means of getting about was to walk on 'top of the hedges' to avoid the deep snowdrifts of the lanes.

The high humidity and cleanliness of the air gives rise to an abundance of plant life, particularly lichens, mosses, ferns and, in spring and summer, wild flowers, which adorn the lanes. The many daffodils and snowdrops planted along the banks bordering these lanes also enhance this profusion of growth. The lanes around Northlew are a little-known delight in spring and can be attributed to Stan Percy of Waytown who, as a cattle farmer, would follow his stock along the main road with a pocketful of daffodil bulbs to plant. Trixie Hannaford rescued the snowdrops and daffodils that were planted in The Orchard before it became a housing development, replanting these bulbs along the lanes towards Shallowford and Crowden. There must have been many others involved as most lanes contain such plantings bringing delight to both passers-by and visitors.

### Northlew Village – The Square

The Square is the focal point of the village; it is a large area sloping steeply from north to south. All roads radiate from the Square. One of the earliest references to the Square was as a village green, crossed by footpaths. The Green filled the site of the present Square, an area in Milltown Lane, and included a broad strip of grass, which ran down the left-hand side of Harpers Hill. There are records of an old deed or lease, which gave the owner of one of the cottages the right to pasture two geese and a gander on the Village Green. The grass remained until the early 1900s when the Council decided to cover it over with stones.

The pump has stood in the Square for more years than is known. At one time it was very ornate, supporting a large curved handle about 6ft long. When idle, the handle rested on the ground at the side of the pump. The water supply for those living in the centre of the village came from this pump. When the pump ran dry, as once happened, the villagers used the well at the top of Harpers Hill, which is now hidden in the new vicarage garden. Near the pump is the seat presented to the village by the Women's Institute to commemorate the Queen's Jubilee on 16 June 1970.

### The Square – South

Half a century ago the village was self sufficient, with many shops and businesses, including three butchers. Food, clothing and machinery could be purchased locally. A shop has traded on the present site of the village store and Post Office for

*John and Kitty Brooking. Owners of the shop in the early 1900s.*

longer than anyone can remember; and the building is one of the Devon longhouses situated in the centre of the village. The business, recently taken over by Richard and Judith Clark, was previously owned by Mrs Pat Durston, and before that the Adams family. Originally this building was thatched, with a lean-to cart shed at one end, which was later turned into a butcher's shop by the Adams family. For many years the butcher was Mr Heathman. Mr Adams sold petrol from a pump situated on the forecourt of the shop.

Adjoining the east side of the shop building was Ern Adams' bakery, Lew Gratton being the delivery driver for several years. Between the school and the bakery, where the bungalow now stands, there once stood a long wall approximately 8ft high, of Devon stone construction. This was the front wall of a large square enclosure surrounding a saw-pit and carpenters' workshops. The workshops consisted of two large sheds, one very long, which at the time, being the largest building in the village, was used for Sunday school teas and other events. The teas were provided by Miss G.Woollcombe, of Morth Grange. There is a record of a Sunday school tea for the Methodist schoolchildren in 1848, when 84 children took part. At this time it must be remembered that most of the cottages in or around the Square housed families with 8 to 12 children.

Next to the saw-pit was the Poor House. The building was sold in 1865, pulled down, and a new school built on the site which was opened in January 1867.

At the western side of the shop is a driveway. This was originally the entrance to the old Rifle Butts, where men of the village would practise shooting. The Rifle Butts, and Northlew Rifle Club, disappeared many years ago. Next to the shop on the far side of the driveway is the Church Room, originally the Wesleyan Chapel, which was in use between 1860 and 1910 after which it became the Church Hall. The school also used the hall for practical lessons after 1931, and now it is used regularly for social events.

*Members of Northlew Rifle Club photographed in 'Broomfield', 1911.* Back row, left to right: *Bert Pascoe, G. Glass, Sid Stiles, Arthur Elliott, Will Tapp, Tom Lake;* front: *Col Edwards, Revd Barker (curate), ?.*

Attached to the garden wall at the front of the Church Room is the village notice-board, usually crammed full with notices and leaflets advertising the activities of a thriving village. This board was presented to the community in memory of Mrs Barbara Bostock-Smith, a respected member and President of the Women's Institute for many years.

A few yards past the Church Room, and discretely hidden behind laurel bushes, are the village toilets; built in the 1960s and opened by the Mayor of Okehampton. These toilets were built on a site once occupied by six very small cottages.

Opposite top left: *Opening of the new toilets in Northlew, 6 May 1975.* Left to right: *Harold Sanders, Bill Spry, Dennis Adams, John Dufty, John Spry, Fernley Bater, Mr Colton (Chief Executive of West Devon Borough Council), Mr Passmore (Mayor of Okehampton) and Mrs Passmore.*

## *The Square – North*

On the north-west corner of the Square stands the Bible Christian Chapel, a very interesting building, erected in 1814 and opened the following year. The new meeting-hall and kitchen were added in 1996. The two cottages to the right, originally one, also belonged to the chapel in the early 1900s.

Taking centre place at the north side of the Square is the Green Dragon Inn, an old Devon longhouse and an impressive building. The

*The Green Dragon Inn. Above the door is the stained-glass window with the green dragon.*

stained-glass window over the door, depicting the green dragon, is eye-catching when illuminated at night. The original cobbles can still be seen across the forecourt. Originally it was an hotel, and at one time a much more prestigous building than it is now. Upstairs at the back of the Green Dragon was a long room where, in the early 1900s, the Dairy School was held. There are also interesting wall paintings in the inn. Across the alleyway next to the Green Dragon is Pound Cottage. The Pound was called 'Black Chain Arms', and faced the Green Dragon Inn at the front and Milltown Lane at the rear. Stray cattle found on the roads would be impounded here by the police constable.

Adjoining Pound Cottage and fronting the Square is a large stone house which was originally the cobbler's shop, the cobbler being Mr Badcock. A few years ago the previous owners of the house unearthed cobbler's nails while renovating the yard behind the house. Church House, an architecturally interesting building on the corner of Milltown Road, was for a short time, between 1869 and 1910, a manse for the Wesleyan Chapel. The house, dating from about 1750, has an impressive columned entrance porch and ornate cobbled path. Church House was once the home of Grannie Watkins and family and also their lodger Jack Blatch, the chimney sweep. From time to time the travelling dentist used the house as a dental surgery.

The very narrow road at the front of Church House is called the Arcade. The small cottages clustered in the Arcade were at one time owned by the Church and housed the curates, who travelled around the neighbouring parishes. Over the years

*In 1996, Northlew Methodist Chapel's new extension was officially started with the laying of the foundation stone by life-long Methodist Mrs Rita Bater and the minister, Revd Brian Skutt. Little three-year-old Stacey Dufty presented Mrs Bater with a buttonhole. The new extension provided a new kitchen, meeting-hall and toilets for the chapel.*

*The first Post Office in the village was run by Mrs Gay and her daughter Eleanor.*

these cottages have provided premises for various local businesses, including a tailor, builder and undertaker and, at the time of writing, a painter and decorator and supplier of newspapers. The cottage at the church end of the Arcade was at one time a small Post Office run by Mrs Gay and her daughter Eleanor. A substantial house once stood at the Square end, but later this was altered and became Henry Andrew's wheelwrighting shop, which was always of interest to passers-by who would stop to watch the work. In the early days, the window openings were unglazed, wooden shutters were taken down at the start of the day and the front doors remained open. For years they had cleaned out their paintbrushes on the backs of the doors and paint had built up to a great thickness.

*The Cross was restored in 1850 under the direction of the rector, the Revd Thomas England. The stones were marked, taken down and placed in a circle. A solid core was built, around which were placed the ancient sculptured granite blocks in their original position. Through the efforts of the Revd John Worthington, the shaft of the Cross was restored after the design of G. Fellowes Prynne in 1900.*

At the church end of the Arcade the pathway opens out into a wide area. Here the Village Cross stands on the site of the old preaching cross and dates back to the fifteenth century. The old legend tells the tale that the Devil died of cold caught on Sourton Moor and was buried under the Village Cross. The Devil is said by some to have been a stag, which was hunted and died one hard winter in the Village Square. Others say that the Devil was a Cornish cock, which was brought to fight a Northlew cock and died in a mysterious way.

On the left is Church Gate Farm, again a Devon longhouse. Mr and Mrs Vincent lived at the farm and supplied milk to the village from their six cows. Villagers collected their milk 'at that time unpasteurised' in jugs. The farmhouse is one of the oldest in the village and can be traced back to Domesday. At the end of this open area stands the lych gate and the entrance to the churchyard of the fifteenth-century Parish Church of St Thomas of Canterbury. Inside the church porch are the old stocks. It is not known where they were originally sited. Opposite the church door is the War Memorial commemorating the fallen from Northlew.

### *The Square – East*

Returning along the Arcade to the eastern side of the Square, the row of three cottages has, over the years, been altered many times. In the early 1900s behind the middle cottage was the slaughterhouse, with buildings and pens at the rear. Parts of the slaughterhouse buildings are still visible. Slaughtering was a very grisly business, with the blood running down the road and on to the Square. At the front of the slaughterhouse stood the butcher's shop run by Ern Adams. The cottage at the northern Arcade end is now the home of Percy Adams. Path Cottage at the southern end of the row is where Granny Adams used to sell sweets and cakes. Path Cottage is a fine example of a local dwelling and is the only remaining thatched cottage in the row. Behind is Rectory Cottage, at one time a Post Office. A short road leads past this to the impressive gates of the former vicarage.

*A view of Rectory Cottage in 1912 when it was a Post Office, this is before the postbox was inserted in the end wall. There was already a telephone for use as a public telephone as the sign makes clear. In the distance, behind the Cross, Churchgate Farm is visible.*

This house was the original vicarage, an ornate building with stables and a walled garden. Eventually it became too large for modern living, the grounds were divided and a new modern vicarage built next door to it in the former vicarage gardens.

Situated behind the old slaughterhouse is Rose Cottage, a large cottage with a pretty garden and once the site of a milking shed where Peter Hutchins milked his cows.

### *The Square – West*

The properties at the southern end of the row have contributed considerably to the history of the village. Records show that the Major family lived here in 1812 although they were probably in residence there some time before that date. Henry Major was a local builder and carpenter of substance, and he rented the house and adjoining builders' yard. He also owned the saw-pit and carpenters' workshop on the south side of the Square. The Major family provided the money for, and built, the chapel, which was opened in 1815. The son Joseph later took over the business and bought the house. On his death his daughter Hannah inherited the property and opened a draper's shop in the front room. In 1903 the house became the manse for the Bible Christian Chapel. In 1966 it was sold and a new modern manse was build in the Kimber Road.

The houses at the northern end of the row were shops and local businesses, including at various times a grocery and Post Office. The end house, London House, was a well-known tailor's shop, and the tailor's son, a professional jockey, rode in the Grand National at some time before the Second World War.

Behind the houses fronting the western side of the Square is Queen Street, locally known as 'Back Street'. At the top end, behind London House, is Alma House which was the home of Fernley and Rita Bater. Rita's mother Eleanor Shobbrook originally owned the house and was an accomplished tailoress. Mrs Shobbrook was also one of Northlew's longest living residents; she died six months before her 100th birthday. From the early 1900s Rita and Fernley ran a substantial haulage business from their yard in Queen Street. Near the Bater's yard was the 'new' slaughterhouse which was moved from the eastern side of the Square. The slaughterhouse fell out of use in the thirties but there are memories of cattle being pole-axed; their heads were drawn down to a ring at floor level for this exercise. Les Vallance, a local doctor, was one of those who did the pole-axing, following which the carcasses were hung up for skinning and drawing.

Clome Cottage, a thatched 'picture-book' house, is next to the yard. This is thought to be the oldest house in Northlew, and is mentioned in the Domesday Book. Adjacent to this is Fingles Wood, where Eleanor Moore kept a small shop selling cigarettes and tobacco. There was no shop front; customers knocked on a door at the side.

*Clome Cottage, thought to be one of oldest houses in Northlew and mentioned in the Domesday Book.*

On the opposite side of Queen Street, the southern end is now a barn conversion. This was originally the Major family's builders' yard. Next door was originally one house, now divided into 1 and 2 Glen Cottage. No. 1 Glen Cottage is said to be haunted! The owner at the time of writing has experienced strange happenings, especially when work is carried out on the building.

No. 2 at the northern end had a small yard at the side with a deep well. This has now been built over and incorporated into the house, and the well is partly covered by the kitchen floor. The yard at one time went through to an alleyway at the back between the row on the Square and the Queen Street buildings. There was access from No. 2 to the grocery and Post Office fronting the Square, as the shop owners, Harold and Edna Sanders, and later Cecil Sanders, lived in Glen Cottage. At one time, before the school came into being, the upstairs room of No. 2 was one of the three dame schools in the village.

Many of the houses around the Square and Harpers Hill are 300 years old and were originally thatched and had dirt floors. These cottages were homes for large families and conditions were squalid. There were terrible outbreaks of typhus (traced to fleabites) in the village from December 1821 to April 1822 and again in 1825 to 1827. Since that time, improvements in personal cleanliness and hygiene have made this disease comparatively rare. There are also entries in the Parish Registers of deaths from smallpox as late as 1837.

### *Harpers Hill*

Up until 1820 the very steep Harpers Hill, which leads down to the river valley, was known as Harboror Hill. Standing at the top and looking down the hill, to the right is October Cottage, which in earlier years was run as a general store by Kit Shobbrook. Adjoining October Cottage is Honeychurch, originally the Honeychurch Arms. The Honeychurch family were landowners in Northlew and the inn was named in their honour. In the days of post riders, carriers of messages or letters, this establishment was a posting inn. This method of communication survived for a long time in outlying districts.

*Looking down Harpers Hill from the Square. To the right is October Cottage where Kit Shobbrook used to run a general store. Adjoining October Cottage is Honeychurch, once the Honeychurch Arms.*

Between 1777 and 1847 the inn was the centre of the early Revel and opened day and night. At this time Northlew was rough and lawless, with dancing, wrestling and noisy festivities, accompanied by drink, probably cider. In 1920 during quieter years, the landlady was Ellen Smale. Eventually the inn became the home of Nurse Dodds who nursed the sick in the village before Okehampton's hospital was built.

There were several shops and businesses in the Harpers Hill area. George Leach had a cobbler's shop adjoining Honeychurch and further down the hill at Church Path Cottage Jack Webber ran a variety of businesses. These included a cycle shop, a hair-cutting service, a shop selling rabbits and poultry, and a radio-repairs outlet.

Half way down the hill at Thatches live Tom and Vera Andrew, who before retirement ran a building and undertaking business from the Arcade. On the bend was the smithy run by Tom and John Baker. In time the shop was taken over by Bert Hucker who had a good line in garden gates. The last house at the bottom of the hill is Brook Cottage, originally known as Holbrook. Also at the bottom of the hill on the opposite side is Dingley, another house which has changed considerably over the years. The garden at one time was well known for its very tall monkey puzzle tree.

The terrace of properties at the bottom of the hill, on the left near the river, is the area known as Fordatown. Here Tom Woods ran a tailor's shop and employed workers who sat crossed legged on the floor to sew. The workshop also made ecclesiastical robes for Whipples of Exeter.

*Approaching Northlew from Okehampton. The cottage to the left is Holbrook and to the right is the area known as Fordatown. The famous monkey-puzzle tree at Dingley is situated in the centre at the end of the terrace. This view is now screened by trees and Fordatown is no longer visible.*

Across the bridge over the River Lew, which in earlier years was a ford, is Rockey Cottage. This is one of the oldest cottages in the village and has been depicted on many a picture postcard. The cottage was named after the Rocky family who once lived there. It was also the home of Mary

Bowden, a local woman of character. Originally two cottages but now one, the cottage is built into the rock face behind it. At one time it was said to be haunted, and after several distressing incidents, the family living there at the time decided to have the cottage exorcised.

To the right of Rockey Cottage is Shorts Lane where there are a few cottages and houses spread out along its length. The lane follows the river valley and eventually leads to Waterhouse Farm, now two barn conversions.

### *Crowden Road*

Making the steep climb to the top of Harpers Hill and crossing the Square diagonally, the narrow road between the chapel and London House is the start of Crowden Road. The first house next to the chapel is Brooklyn and was at one time the home of one of Northlew's most famous residents, Devereux Evance, and his sister Alice. He travelled widely in America, encountered Indians and became a Fellow of the Royal Geographical Society. In later years he also became a poet and most of his poems were composed at Brooklyn. On the opposite side of the road is The Orchard, a development of new houses where many younger families live. Crowden Road is a cross-section of houses and cottages. Number 6, the impressive double-fronted cream house in the centre of the row, was the home of Dick Gratton. The house is still occupied by the Gratton family. In 1886, at a time when the village was without a manse, the three cottages next to the schoolroom were purchased to house Methodist ministers, but these cottages were never used and were eventually sold off with the field next door. The end cottage was also the workroom of local bootmaker Mr W.J. Smale. Traditionally, boots and leggings were worn by all farm men until Wellington boots came in.

The Methodist schoolroom was built at the far end of Crowden Road in 1894. The adjoining field for the graveyard was purchased in 1904 and a further piece of land for an extention was purchased in 1914. Next to the chapel graveyard was Dick Gratton's cycle shop and carpenters' workshop. On the corner of the road junction, opposite the Methodist graveyard, is the entrance to the playing field.

The first house on the right down the narrow lane signposted Norley, is Kesterfield. It was a farm for many years but, at the time of writing, is the Devonshire Doll Company and Doll Museum. The museum is open to the public on certain days throughout the summer. Kesterfield was also the home of the Lambretta Museum and the Lambretta Preservation Society. Unfortunately the museum contents were sold in September 1994.

*Dick Gratton and his wife Florence in the 1920s. Dick Gratton, a local tradesman and preacher, was nicknamed 'Happy Dick'. He would walk to the chapels in the distict and take off his socks and shoes to cross the ford at Hollowmoor.*

*The playing-field was donated to the village by Mr Percy Adams for use as a children's playground and football field. The opening ceremony, on 28 May 1990, was performed by Mr Fred Baker. Also in the picture is Dennis Adams.*

### *Milltown Lane*

Travelling across the north of the Square and next to Church House is a narrow road called Milltown Lane. This is an unmade road eventually turning into a track. On the right is Fern Terrace, a terrace of three houses. The first house was at one time a Post Office and the home of Mr Fred Baker, church organist and choirmaster for many years. Miss Enid Baker, Fred's sister, was the Post Mistress for 29 years. For a long period the Post Office had the only phone in the village. In 1921 a public telephone was sited in the Square, but connected to Miss Baker's telephone, which meant the public telephone could not be used at the same time as Miss Baker's. The middle house in the terrace was the house always allocated to the schoolmaster. The third house in the terrace was the home of the local policeman. P.C. Toms lived in Milltown Lane before moving to the new police house in Station Road. Other local police officers were P.C. Greaves, who died of kidney failure; P.C. Loram and P.C. Knight of whom the village children were afraid. Next along the lane are Numbers 1 and 2 Bedford Cottages and then Rosemary Cottage.

After Rosemary Cottage the lane passes through open fields to two modern homes and then eventually to Milltown Farm. One of the village wells was situated in Milltown Lane. A mill was situated near the river at Milltown. The only access was via the fields, but there is no trace of the mill in modern times.

### *Station Road*

Diagonally across the Square from Milltown Lane on the south side is Station Road. Station Road is a mixture of the old and new. This is mainly the newer part of the village. The first property is Elmfield House. In 1840 Elmfield was known as Spreys Farm with a large farmyard which incorporated the land where the garage and the Victory Hall now stand, and also Bater's yard. The farm was the home farm of the Woollcombe family and part of the Ashbury estate. Now known as Elmfield House, it is a large impressive house which has changed hands many times. The house has fallen into disrepair and been rescued from dereliction several times. For a few years it was the home of Lt Col Guy Lawrence and his wife Dilys who contributed greatly to the village. The Lawrences supported the local church by opening their lovely garden annually for strawberry teas. Close to Elmfield House is Elmfield Barns. These barns were at one time part of the Ashbury estate and later became the Men's Club. In recent years the barns were converted into two homes with the old boundary walls and original ornate gates still in place.

Opposite Elmfield Barns is Clarke's garage, where three generations of the Clarke family have worked for many years. They are speciality motor engineers, working on old motor bikes and cars as well as modern vehicles. Next to the garage is the Victory Hall, home to many local events over the years. The foundation stone was laid by Lord Methuen on Wednesday 26 May 1920, and the ceremony was opened by Herbert Woollcombe, Esq. Next to the Village Hall is the old police house followed by two modern bungalows. Opposite the Victory Hall is another barn conversion, which was again once part of the Ashbury estate. This was also the site of an old village pond, probably lost due to the widening of the road over a period of time.

Further up the road, on the left, are the council-houses, now mostly privately owned. Further up the road again is a row of very old cottages, once thatched. These cottages were originally six, but over the years have been altered and are now three. The first cottage nearest the village has a deep well, with a pump, and this was used to pump up water for domestic use until quite recently. This cottage was also at one time a farrier's and the middle cottage a cobbler's shop. The records state that in 1840 there were four more cottages on this site running from the road back towards the fields.

The detached properties on the left, higher up Station Road, are called Elmfield Meadows and have taken their name from the fields they were built on. Village events, fêtes and teas were held in Elmfield Meadows. Higher up the road are modern houses and bungalows until the bend at Bolland. On the right-hand side is Voadens dairy farm, with very old cob barns. On the opposite side there once stood a smithy run by Mr Blackford. The narrow unmade lane leads to a small row of 300-year-old cottages.

Higher up Station Road past the farm at Bolland is Yellands' engineering business and the homes of the Yelland family, and further up the road again is the depot for Carmel Coaches.

*Tea in Elmfield Meadow, early 1900s.*

*(From the* Western Times *Friday 28 May 1920.) Wednesday was a proud day for Northlew for it was honoured by a visit from Field Marshal Lord Methuen, GC, GCMG, GCVO. The distinguished soldier came to lay the foundation stone of the Victory Hall, which is to be the War Memorial for the parishes of Northlew and Ashbury, and also to be present at the centenary meeting of the Northlew Friendly Society, the two functions being combined. The Right Hon. George Lambert, MP, was also present during the day, and there were notable visitors. The Victory Hall is to be a one-storey structure, with a main room 60ft by 30ft. This will be available for public and social functions. There will be an ante-room and offices. The cost is estimated at about 1,000 pounds, and of this sum about one-third has already been raised. The building is expected to be completed by the end of September. It is being erected by three local builders – Messrs J. Brooking, R. Putt and G. Wooldridge. Much of the hauling of the material is being done free of charge by farmers and a quantity of stone is also being given, while the site was the gratuitous gift of Mr T. Andrew. The Hall which is being erected in Station Road at the entrance to the village of Northlew, is to be under the control of a body of 15 trustees elected from the two parishes. Mr H.L. Woollcombe is chairman of the Memorial Committee. Mr Woollcombe presided at the stone-laying ceremony and about 30 ex-Servicemen acted as a Guard of Honour, one of these, Pte James Scout, was presented by the Field Marshal with the MSM. Lord Methuen, addressing the crowd, spoke about the horrors of war, which the men had endured, and the sorrows of the women who had pulled themselves through the war with patience and determination. An attractive programme of sports was carried out in a field close to the village, where tea was also provided.*

## Kimber Road

The turning to the right in Station Road, just past the old police house, is the Kimber Road. The new manse is on the right as you turn into the Kimber Road; just past the manse is Kimberlands, a development of new houses and bungalows housing local families and some of the older residents. On the left is a very old beech tree which has been a landmark of the village for at least 100 years.

The Kimber Road dips down to 'Tichy Brook' and then up to the site of Kimber Manor. All that remains of the manor and the old farmhouse is an avenue of trees across a field, which at one time lined the impressive entrance.

The Adams family of Kimber, Jean, Dennis, Jenny and Mike, ran a milk round, delivering to the village and district for 34 years. The Kimber Road eventually leads to West Kimber.

*The old beech tree situated in Frank Voaden's field where nearly all the young people over the years have carved their initials, or the initials of their sweethearts, onto its trunk.*

## The Outer Reaches of the Parish

Northlew is a large parish, and travelling along the Crowden Road, past the houses and out into the countryside, is a dip by the river called Shallowford. Here is a small collection of houses and council-houses known locally as the 'Costloes'. In the hedge opposite 'Costloes' was another of the village wells. After Shallowford is an area known locally as Marshgate, where post-war children enjoyed playing down 'Mash'. After Shallowford the road rises steeply and then descends into the hamlet of Crowden next to the West River Lew. Before dropping down into Crowden the road passes Rose Cottage, where at one time Fred Bater had a cycle shed for spares and repairs. Further down the hill is Sweetbriar Cottage, where a succession of owners have opened the lovely garden to the public. Crowden is a collection of farms and cottages, some of the farms being worked by the same families for generations. The area has always been very busy with many small businesses.

Crowden is also the site of one of the old water-powered corn-mills, once a feature of rural Devon.

The mill is a stone building constructed in 1721. The mill last functioned as a working mill in 1948, and has since been converted into a family home. Many of the mill's artifacts have been saved and restored to feature in the building. The river winds its way around Crowden and the mill. Many of the houses are built over the river which flows underneath the buildings.

Mr Evely worked Crowden Mill until after the war. Before the days of motor vehicles he delivered flour with a wagon and horses. Whenever he went down Baker's Hill there was a turn-out to watch. The 'dreg shoes' would first be fitted to the wheels; by restraining them, the wagon was braked. There was always much anxiety about the descent; sometimes the wagon would veer off and get stuck or the horses would panic. Frank Knight ran Crowden Mill for some time after the war. Horses and carts would travel along the lanes from Crowden Mill to load the trains at Ashbury Station. The lanes being narrow and steep, it was a tortuous journey.

Passing through the hamlet of Crowden and over the bridge is Lower Crowden Farm, a seventeenth-century farmhouse and one of the older houses in the area. There are also two barn conversions at Lower Crowden Farm and a registered site for five caravans. Stone from the quarry at Crowden was at one time used to construct local buildings.

Travelling further on from Crowden is the Holway Moor area where stands the imposing manor house, once known as Holway Manor, but later Northlew Manor. Holway Moor is a wetland area which regularly floods. Across country to the west of Holway is the small hamlet of Whiddon. Whiddon, set in a deep sheltered valley, is a collection of substantial farmhouses and once a small chapel. Unfortunately the chapel was demolished in 1998 and some of the stones moved to Northlew Church where they were used to lay a pathway in the cemetery. The tiny graveyard at Whiddon is still cared for by the Methodists. A Victorian postbox is still in use at Whiddon.

Moving westwards across lovely farmland towards Dartmoor the next site of interest is Ashbury Station. The station at one time played a large part in the community, transporting goods and passengers. Next to the station was Ashbury Court, standing at 234 metres, and now partly demolished, but once part of the Ashbury estate.

Leaving the station yard and turning right the road leads to Castle Cross. On approaching the crossroads the field to the left behind the modern communications mast is the site of a Roman fort. Nothing can be seen at ground level, but in dry weather, from the air, the fort is visible as markings in the ground. The straight road across the top of the crossroads leading to Halwill is a Roman road. Castle Cross is the highest point in the parish at 279 metres, with views to Bodmin Moor, Exmoor and Dartmoor. At one time it was common land, and one of the sites for the beacons situated at high points across England to warn of invasions or other dangers. It was also where the gibbet stood for hangings.

*The well-known beech avenue near Ashbury Station and looking towards Bogtown.*

Retracing the road from Castle Cross to Ashbury Station, towards Northlew, and passing Stoney Farm, there are some of the most extensive views of Dartmoor in the area on the right. There is an ancient burial mound recorded opposite Stoney Farm. The next turning to the right at Bogtown runs downhill to the small hamlet of Ashbury, a thriving community when Ashbury House was still standing. Ashbury House employed many local people, the Woollcombe family keeping a large retinue of servants inside and outside the house. The Ashbury Church of St Mary the Virgin is in the field next to where the house once stood. Sadly the church is no longer in use. All that remains of the house is a tiled floor and the old circular washing lines next to Ashbury Farm; the farm once being part of the laundry of Ashbury House. There is also a massive stone barn, parts of the walled garden and a few remaining rhododendrons. Ashbury is one of the prettiest areas in the parish.

Nestling in the valley at Ashbury is Wadland Barton, site of one of the oldest inhabited farms. Wadland, being the name taken from Wadal the Saxon, one of the first landowners in the area. Near Wadland Barton is Wigdon Mill, once a corn mill and part of the Ashbury estate. The smaller water-wheels are still attached to the house and the mill leats can be seen. The area around the mill is a flood plain and the water often covers the garden in winter. The mill was built in the 1700s and closed in the early 1900s and later became a private house.

Returning to Ashbury and turning right up the hill to Scobchester is the site of a medieval village. This could have been the site of the original Northlew. This village disappeared many years ago although another ancient burial site is recorded in this area.

Moving around the outer areas of the parish, close to Scobchester is Cruft. This was a substantial community at one time with a small chapel. In 1892 the farm at Cruft, owned by the Squires family was destroyed by fire and the occupants moved into the chapel. The house was eventually rebuilt but the chapel never reopened. The nearest chapel was then Bethany Chapel at Waytown but this was a journey of nearly three miles by road, or on a public footpath across fields. Even the Waytown chapel eventually closed and Mr and Mrs Squires decided to leave the farm to their son and moved to Elmfield House, Northlew. The Cruft chapel is now sadly an animal shed and Waytown is still standing but unused.

One of the features of Cruft is the very interesting Bronze-Age burial site behind Cruft Meadow bungalow which has been recorded by English Heritage.

There was also a small community at Kigbere with a mill and its own chapel, but this chapel also eventually closed being too expensive to run and only the farms remain.

Moving east across the countryside, but nearer to Northlew, is the area known as Gorhuish, and this must have been a sizeable hamlet or village at one time. Many of the houses and cottages have since disappeared, but there are traces of cottages, and records refer to properties long gone. The area was remote, and although only two miles from Northlew, in the 1800s the dirt-track roads made it very difficult for the people of Gorhuish to walk to Northlew for the shops and school. Men would wear the traditional hessian coverings over their shoulders and the women hessian aprons to keep the rain out. These coverings were locally known as 'Dartmoor Outfits'.

In 1938 it was decided to plant a forest near Howard's Farm, Gorhuish, but when war broke out planting ceased and the ground was tilled and planted with corn. German prisoners of war and Land Army girls came to harvest the corn.

Travelling eastwards towards Durdon Cross Farm, again one of the higher points on the landscape at 193 metres, at the junction one makes a left turn towards Northlew and the crossroads. Standing at the crossroads is the wayside cross; most of the signposts in the parish are still called crosses. The wayside crosses were not only signs to point the way to fords, bridges, towns and villages, but stood to remind the passer-by of the Redeemer's love and of the way to Heaven.

Turning right at the crossroads the road from Durdon travels down to the river valley, over Gribbleford Bridge and rises again to Rutleigh. Rutleigh is a collection of farms and cottages, once dominated by Rutleigh Manor. This is now a farm, but traces of the old house remain. The main door to the house is of medieval construction and there is a very interesting font in the sitting room. The River Lew winds its way around Rutleigh and the river banks are covered with wild daffodils in the spring. There is reference to the Lew Mill at Rutleigh, but this closed in the early part of the century to become a private house.

Returning towards Northlew over Corscombe Down there are several farms with medieval longhouses. The large house situated above the valley on the approach to Northlew is Morth Grange. This is an impressive Victorian house with views across the valley to the villages of Northlew and Ashbury. The house was built by the Woollcombe family of Ashbury Manor for Miss G. Woollcombe.

Near Morth Grange on the Okehampton Road is Cary Cottage where the village nurses were based. The nurses would be called out to assist with the delivery of babies and to deal with any other emergency in the village. In 1937 Dr Mitchell would have travelled all the way from Hatherleigh and would be assisted by Nurse Bray from Cary Cottage.

A few yards past Cary Cottage at the Eastacombe crossroads there stood another stone cross but unfortunately this disappeared in the 1960s. The parish is criss-crossed by many footpaths and bridleways. In the past, the only way for local people to travel was to walk. Only wealthy farmers and the gentry could afford to buy and keep a horse, and goods were moved on wooden sledges. These footpaths were shortcuts into the village to the church and shops. Years ago there were many more crossing places over the river. There are records of two wooden bridges, long since disappeared, and fords at Milltown. Ivy Curtis tells of how her mother would walk along the river bank from Rutleigh to Costloes, at Shallowford. This would have been about two miles by road, a distance which, at the time of writing, is six miles.

There are three church paths mentioned in parish records. One from Blackworthy to Worth; one from Harpers Hill to the lower gate of the churchyard; and one from Northlew village to Ashbury Church through Ashbury Woods. These footpaths would have involved considerably less mileage than travelling around by road.

*The head of the Durdon Cross was carried off one night by sacrilegious hands and thrown into the well at Durdon Moor. The members of the hunt, who were passing by and just happened to look in, found it many years later, at a time of drought. The cross was lifted out and laid by the well. The Durdon Cross meanwhile has been restored.*

*Stray sheep on the road at Eastacombe. On the left is the entrance to Morth Grange.*

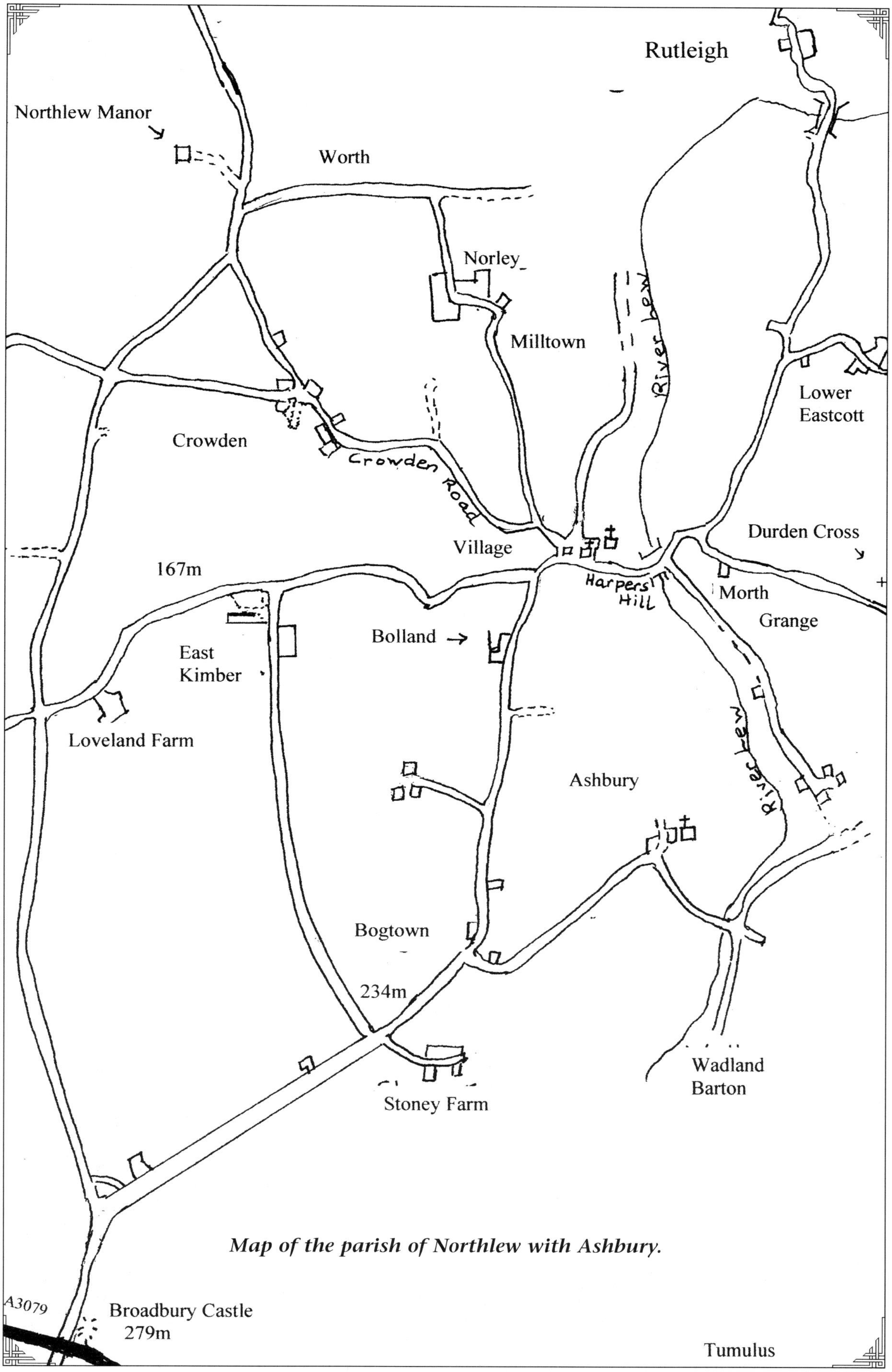


*Map of the parish of Northlew with Ashbury.*

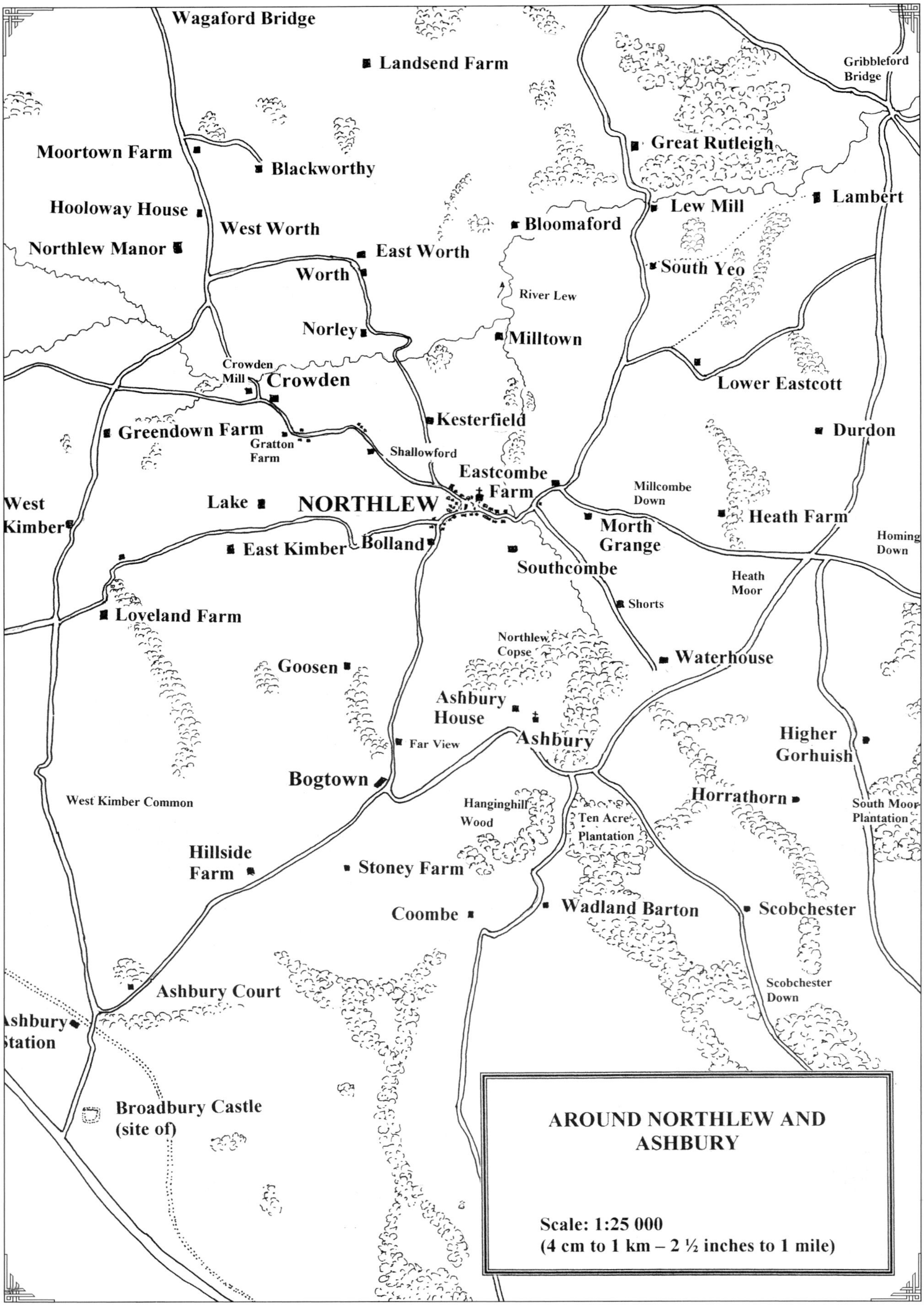
Wagaford Bridge
Landsend Farm
Gribbleford Bridge
Moortown Farm
Blackworthy
Great Rutleigh
Hooloway House
West Worth
Lew Mill
Lambert
Bloomaford
Northlew Manor
East Worth
South Yeo
Worth
River Lew
Norley
Milltown
Crowden Mill
Crowden
Lower Eastcott
Kesterfield
Greendown Farm
Gratton Farm
Shallowford
Durdon
Eastcombe Farm
Millcombe Down
West Kimber
Lake
NORTHLEW
Morth Grange
Heath Farm
East Kimber
Bolland
Southcombe
Homing Down
Heath Moor
Loveland Farm
Shorts
Northlew Copse
Waterhouse
Goosen
Ashbury House
Ashbury
Higher Gorhuish
Far View
Bogtown
West Kimber Common
Hanginghill Wood
Ten Acre Plantation
Horrathorn
South Moor Plantation
Hillside Farm
Stoney Farm
Coombe
Wadland Barton
Scobchester
Scobchester Down
Ashbury Court
Ashbury Station
Broadbury Castle (site of)
AROUND NORTHLEW AND ASHBURY
Scale: 1:25 000
(4 cm to 1 km – 2 ½ inches to 1 mile)

*Chapter 3*

# THE VILLAGE AT WORK, PAST & PRESENT

## *Past Trades and Industry*

Until the early-twentieth century, Northlew was a self-sufficient village. The major occupation was farming and the majority of other jobs were associated with it.

### *Devonshire Cream*

In the days when transport was slow and refrigerators were non-existent, the surplus milk was used to make cream. The fresh milk was set in pans in the dairy on slate slabs and the next morning was slowly scalded on the earthenware crock which was filled with burning coals. The cream was not allowed to boil, but was taken off the heat as soon as the ring or circle appeared in the pan. The cream was skimmed off the next morning.

### *Butter Making*

The butter, like the cream, was made by hand. The cream was placed in a large basin and stirred slowly round and round. The particles of butter gradually began to form and eventually gathered together to make a lump. The lump was then salted, washed and beaten again and again, until all the buttermilk was taken out. It was then made into pats ready to be sold. Butter making was a tedious process in the heat of summer and a painful task occasionally in winter time.

*The Dairy School, early 1900s. The school was held in the long extension at the rear of the Green Dragon Hotel. The proprietor was John Lake, pictured on the left.* Also included are: *Gertie Adams, Lillian Friend, Miss Ida Elliott, Mrs W. Sparke, Miss M. Friend, Mrs Littlejohns, Miss V. Gratton, Frances Friend, the Revd Worthington.*

At the beginning of the twentieth century the farms had their own separators but the butter was still made by hand. Many farmers however sold their milk to the patent factory at Lifton and bought butter for their own consumption from the shops.

### *Cider Making*

The cider apples were gathered in October and were left to mellow in a heap. The apples were picked over and all the black ones carefully removed. The apples were then taken to the mill where they were layered alternately with straw to make cider cheese. This went into the press, which was turned slowly down to extract the juice. The juice was drained through a funnel and was then poured into the cider casks. Yeast was added and the casks were left open for a while, to allow fermentation to take place. The casks were then closed and carried back to the farms by carts to be stored for future use.

### *Mead*

Mead is an alcoholic liquor made by fermenting a mixture of honey and water. Four pounds of honey were mixed with a gallon of water and boiled with spices. As the mixture cooled one ounce of brewer's yeast per gallon of liquid was added. The mixture was then left to stand for eight hours after which it was poured into a barrel to ferment. When fermentation ceased a small quantity of isinglas was added to clear the liquid. After bottling, the mead was stored for six months.

### *Brewing*

The farmers used to brew beer for themselves and their labourers. There was no tax to pay and no interference from the licensing authorities. The brewing tackle was kept clean and bright and went round from farm to farm. There was the great copper kettle for the boiling, the pans for cooling and the ladles for stirring. The reapers always looked forward to a special brew at harvest time.

### *Milling*

The three water-mills, Crowden, Wigdon and Lew, were a necessary feature of village life. The mills ground the wheat into flour for the community and the oats and barley into meal for the cattle, poultry and pigs. The farmers took the wheat, barley and oats to the mills in carts and the millers carried the flour in sacks to different farms on their donkeys.

### *The Smithy*

The village blacksmith made the blades for the harrows, the share and coulters for the ploughs,

*The Forge, Harpers Hill. Thomas Baker (blacksmith) on right.*
Left to right: *Jonas Kimber (holding horse), Sam Wood, George Kimber, Nicholas Tapson.*

DEVON 25·1·72

**This Indenture** made the Twenty fifth day of March Instant One thousand eight hundred and seventy five. Between George Andrew ~~James Blatchford~~ of the parish of Northlew in the county of Devon Labourer of the first part Thomas Andrew ~~James Blatchford~~ his son a minor of about fifteen ~~sixteen~~ years of the second part and Philip Andrew of the same parish Carpenter and Wheelwright of the third part **Witnesseth** that he the said Thomas Andrew ~~James Blatchford~~ by and with the consent and approbation of the said George Andrew ~~James Blatchford~~ his father doth put himself Apprentice to the said Philip Andrew to learn his Art and with him after the Manner of an Apprentice to serve from the date above written unto the full end and term of five years from thence next following to be fully completed and ended **During** which Term the said Apprentice his Master faithfully shall serve his secrets keep his lawful commands every where gladly do he shall do no damage to his said Master nor see to be done of others but to his Power shall tell or forthwith give warning to his said Master of the same he shall not waste the goods of his said Master nor lend them unlawfully to any he shall not commit fornication nor contract Matrimony within the said Term he shall not play at Cards Dice Tables or any other unlawful Games whereby his said Master may have any loss with his own Goods or others during the said Term without Licence of his said Master He shall

neither buy nor sell he shall not haunt Taverns
nor Playhouses nor absent himself from his said
Masters service day or night unlawfully But
in all things as a faithful Apprentice he shall
behave himself towards his said Master and
all his during the said Term And the said
Philip Andrew doth hereby for himself his
Heirs Executors and administrators covenant
promice and agree to and with the said ~~James~~ Thomas
~~Blatchford~~ Andrew his Executors and Administrators
that he the said Philip Andrew his said Apprentice
in the Art of a Carpenter and Wheelwright in
all its branches which he useth by the best means
that he can shall teach and instruct or cause
to be taught and instructed Finding unto the
said Apprentice sufficient Meat Drink and
Lodging and all other necessaries during the
last year of the said Term except Washing
Clothes Medicine and Medical attendence in
case of sickness and the said ~~James Blatchford~~ Thomas Andrew
hereby covenants with the said Philip Andrew
that he the said ~~James Blatchford~~ Thomas Andrew will find
and provide himself with Washing Clothes and
in case of sickness Medicine and Medical
attendence during the said Term And the said
Philip Andrew doth hereby for himself his Heirs
Executors and Administrators covenant promice
and agree to and with the said ~~James Blatchford~~ Thomas Andrew
his Executors and Administrators to pay to the
said ~~James Blatchford~~ Thomas Andrew six pounds of lawful
English money in the following payments
namely that is to say for the third year One

pound for the fourth year two pounds and
in the fifth and last year three pounds And
the said ~~James Blatchford~~ Thomas Andrew for himself his
Executors and Administrators doth hereby
covenant promise and agree to and with the
said Philip Andrew his Heirs Executors and
Administrators to find himself Meat Drink
Washing and Lodging from Saturday night
until Monday morning in each and every
year except the last year during the said Term
And for the true performance of all and every
the said Covenants and Agreements either of
the said Parties bindeth himself unto the other
by these Presents In Witness whereof the Parties
above named to these Indentures interchangeably
have put their Hands and Seals the Twenty fifth
day of March and in the Thirty ~~second~~ seventh year of
the Reign of our Sovereign Lady Victoria by the
Grace of God of the united Kingdom of Great
Britain and Ireland Queen Defender of
the Faith and in the Year of our Lord One
thousand eight hundred and seventy five

George andrew
Thomas Andrew

Mark of Philip X Andrew

Signed Sealed and delivered by the said
~~James Blatchford~~ George Andrew ~~James Blatchford~~ Thomas Andrew and
Philip Andrew in the presence of George William Gould

the shoes for the oxen and horses and nails and bolts. Mr Thomas Dart was for many years the village blacksmith and when he went to America Mr Baker, who had been his apprentice since 1841, bought the business.

### *The Wheelwright*

The wheelwright's shop, like the smithy, was a busy centre of activity in the village. The wheelwright made coffins, wagons, carts, wheels and yokes for the oxen, horses and donkeys. Handles for the scythes and reap hooks, the frames for the winnowing fans and harrows, the seedlips for the sowing, the eddish rakes and the wood chips for the ploughs were also made. Mr Edward Glass was a famous wheelwright in the mid 1800s.

### *Gloving*

The hand sewing of gloves was at one time a common occupation in the village. The unmade gloves, in cotton or silk, of different colours and sizes, were brought over from Sheepwash and afterwards collected and forwarded to London. The workers were paid from 1s.6d. to 2s.0d. per dozen and some were able to finish as many as five or six dozen pairs a week.

### *The Cordwainer*

The cordwainer was the village shoemaker. The name 'cordwainer' was derived from 'cordrovan', a leather from Cordova, a town in Spain, used in making shoes. The cordwainer made the half boots and the shoes. Zacchaeus Bickle was a cordwainer in 1709.

### *The Carrier*

The old carrier in the village was John Martin. He was a pork butcher and used to go to Tavistock every Thursday for the Friday market and then on to Plymouth for the market on Saturday. He drove a horse and covered wagon and always took his dog Nelson with him. He was willing to take passengers, to carry parcels and to do small commissions for friends and neighbours.

### *Tailoring*

The journeyman tailor used to travel around the villages and stay at a farm for a week at a time. He would make clothes for the men and women whom he visited. The householder provided the cloth and the tailor received 10d. a day plus board and lodging.

### *The Higgler*

Thomas Brooking of Churchgate Farm went to Hatherleigh on Tuesdays, to Holsworthy on Wednesdays, to Torquay on Thursdays, to Exeter on Fridays and on Saturdays he went to Okehampton. He would sell produce that cottagers brought to him in their baskets and eggs, butter and poultry that he collected from the farms.

### *The Pedlar*

There was a pedlar called Columbo of Okehampton who would come to the village to sell china cups, saucers, plates and basins. He would carry it all in a basket on his head. There was another pedlar named Honeychurch, who would come to the village in a wagon, to sell pans and pitchers. Pedlars also brought goods and sample patterns from the shops at Hatherleigh and Okehampton. They were called 'Johnny Fortnights'.

### *Roundsmen*

In the early 1930s, local deliveries by 'roundsmen' greatly helped the domestic supply. Stevie Blatch of Newhouse delivered milk with his trim milk

*Shop and Church Room, south of the Square.*

*Green Dragon Hotel, north of the Square.*

float. The float contained a large galvanised churn which had a long-handled pint measure hooked over the rim. Stevie was dextrous with his measure, he held it by the hook, high above the proffered milk jug, and tipped it without spilling a drop – one whole measure plus a little dip extra.

Ern Adams had a number of vans for his bakery and butchery business. Bill Crocker drove the weekly van from Westcotts of Okehampton and Bert Trenaman of Hatherleigh came to the village with his butcher's van. W.J. Smale travelled around the district with his Norton side-car outfit delivering boots and shoes.

### *The Village Postman*

There was no postman in the village in the early days. Squire Woollcombe paid a man called Durden to fetch the letters for the Hall from Okehampton. He would bring letters for the villagers and leave them to be called for at the Hall. It was not unusual for the squire to call to a passer-by, 'Hi! There is a letter for thee at my place, it has been there for a week.' It sometimes happened that the owner could not read his letter and was obliged to take it to the parson or the schoolmaster, who would read it to him. In 1854 the postal authorities promised a village Post Office and a collecting box was provided with delivery six days a week.

Between 1850 and the early 1900s there was an increase in mechanisation and most of the old village trades gradually died out. Transportation improved and goods were produced in factories. Even so, as late as 1954 the *Western Morning News* described Northlew as 'an independent and self-sufficient community with a larger number of craftsmen and tradesmen than one normally discovers in places of similar size in Devon.'

### *Other occupations*

Thatchers – Tom Maynard, Wilf Mitchel after 1945
Wheelwrights – J. Bater, T. Andrew
Dairymen – Polly Friend, B. Vincent, J. Hind
Eggs, butter, rabbits – Clem Andrew
Grave- and well-digger – Jim Mills
Water Diviner – Emmanuel Spry
Rabbit trappers – Jimmy Topp, Jim Ware, Alfred Worden
Haulage lorries – F.W. Bater after 1945
Millers – John Evely (Crowden Mill), John Glass (Lew Mill)
Hay cutter – Jimmy Symons
Dustmen, horse and cart – Steve Blachford, Harry Middleton, George Jordan
Garage – Dick Andrew, John and Fred Yelland, Robin Clarke

*Mr and Mrs Shobbrook.*

## *Businesses Today*

Mike Karslake was known to scooter fans as the 'Godfather of Lambrettas'. He moved his museum to Northlew from Southend purely as a retirement project, it was non-profit-making being supported by voluntary contributions and donations. Mike Karslake was a respected and popular larger-than-life character. His death, and the eventual closing of the museum and Lambretta Preservation Society, was a great loss to the village and to all who knew Mike personally.

*The scooter collection started with the first scooter bought in 1952. The collection, housed in a purpose-built barn, included a Lambretta-based, three-wheeled fire engine, a rickshaw, the first Lambretta made in 1947 and the last in 1978.*

Jed Dryden the local thatcher is usually seen standing on his biddle on a thatched roof. Jed uses traditional tools and thatching spars, which are made from split hazel and willow, and thatching crooks. These crooks were traditionally made by a blacksmith but are now mass-produced.

*The local thatcher, Jed Dryden, pictured using a mallet, also known as a bonker.*

Ben Dufty, who in the past has worked as a thatcher, is still making the split-willow thatching spars required by the trade by hand.

Dorothy Coles delivers milk around the Northlew area. Dorothy has provided a very good service to the village and her efforts are much appreciated, especially by those in remote areas and those unable to walk to the shop.

Rachel Karslake, of The Devonshire Doll Company and Doll Museum opened her museum and workshops many years ago. Rachel has a large collection of antique dolls, a business making new dolls and a repair service. Her workshop is full of surprises, not only are there wonderful collections of dolls, but also teddy bears, doll's tea sets and doll's prams. Rachel began making wax dolls in 1962 and progressed to china dolls in 1978. She has numerous teaching qualifications and her work has won many prestigious awards at fairs and contests around the globe.

Lew Gratton, a prominent Northlew resident, came to the village as a child at the age of seven. He worked for Mr Dufty, at Stoney Farm, (the present John Dufty's father) for 4s. a week, rising eventually to 11s. a week. He later moved on to work for Mr Eveleigh and during the war delivered groceries and paraffin and supplied poultry. There were 1,500 customers during the war, all using ration books. Lew always took his terrier 'Nick' with him as a guard dog. He joined the 'Dad's Army' and was on duty the night that bombs fell on Northlew. After the war he joined the local bakery, where coke ovens were used to make the best kind of bread. Later, when the local

*Lew Gratton (the Wonder Baker) delivered bread, cakes and groceries to the parish and surrounding district. He delivered to Maddaford Moor where TB patients were housed and to the nudist colony at Metherell. Others in the village have mentioned the knot holes in the high surrounding fence, which the locals used to push out to try and peep at what was going on inside.*

bakery closed, Lew joined another bakery and carried on as delivery man. Lew travelled around the district delivering bread for over 50 years until his well-earned retirement in 1988. He was honoured by the British Legion in June 1997 for his services as a poppy worker and was presented with a 'For Merit' badge in recognition of the outstanding service given to the poppy appeal over many years.

*Unloading at Northlew Haulage.* On the lorry: *Tom Maynard, Gat Perry;* standing: *Mr Hedley (sales rep. for Silcocks), Fernley Bater, Colin Taberet.*

Fernley and Rita Bater of Northlew Haulage lived at Alma House and ran a very successful business, Fernley overseeing the yard and haulage side and Rita working on the accounts. They expanded the business from one to six lorries. Both Rita and Fernley were lifelong Methodists, as were Mr Bater's father, William Bater, and his grandfather William Shobbrook. All were lay preachers and Fernley Bater was a Steward of Northlew Methodist Church. Rita was especially known for her wonderful handicrafts and cleverly knitted toys made each year for the toy service. Fernley Bater's great interest was music and until illness intervened he was a playing member of the Northlew Silver Band, also holding the positions of chairman, treasurer and a trustee of the band room. The band-room building, once part of the haulage business, is still in use for practice and storing of instruments. For a number of years Fernley was a member of Northlew Parish Council and for four years a member of West Devon Borough Council. He was also a trustee of Northlew Men's Social Club. Bryan Haulage grew from a small business with a second-hand van delivering to local farmers into a large company with 80 articulated vehicles which now employs well over 100 people. The company moved into the chilled-food sector and became very successful. It is now one of the largest independent chilled-food hauliers. The group includes an employment agency, a high-tech training facility and a commercial advertising arm offering third-party companies advertising on its trailers.

Although public transport is in rapid decline in many areas, in the locality of Northlew the reverse is true. Carmel Coaches provide services for both senior citizens and the younger generation by covering many 'school runs' in the Okehampton area. Carmel also run regular bus services to and from Okehampton. Tony Hazel and family provide an excellent service and are much appreciated by the local community.

R.E. Clarke of The Garage, Northlew, are well-known motor engineers. Over the years the garage has been worked by three generations of the Clarke family, offering engineering expertise for older vehicles and vintage motorcycles. They can also perform iron and sheet-metal work, turning and surface grinding as well as the more common motor repairs.

J & J Services is an established motor-repair business on the outskirts of Northlew. The company, run by John Millership, offers a reliable and dependable personal service. Not only does he repair vehicles but can supply tyres, exhausts and batteries and undertake MOT work. Steve Wood of Crowden works as a self-employed Machine Tool Service Engineer.

In the year 2001 F.W. Yelland & Sons celebrated their 50th year based in Northlew. In 1951, Fred Yelland purchased garage premises next to the Village Hall from Dick Andrew. Mr Yelland employed Bill Elliott as a mechanic for 13 years. Regent petrol was on sale for motor vehicles from two pumps. John joined his father in 1956 and the business traded as F.W. Yelland & Son. The firm also supplied farm machinery in the area after a newly-planned workshop, stores and offices were completed on the outskirts of Northlew in May 1971. John eventually took over the running of the business and was joined by his sons, Philip, Michael and Colin. In 1974 the demand for the erection of farm sheds and barns became apparent. This resulted in phasing out the agricultural machinery side of the business in 1986.

Doris Spry, a postlady for many years, delivered the mail on her bicycle. Mrs Spry's post round was along the Crowden Road up to Greendown and Kimber, returning along the Kimber Road to the village. There was no postal uniform at that time, only a badge. Not only was Mrs Spry busy with the post delivery and bringing up a family, she was also a very keen gardener. Renting a plot next to the chapel (where the Methodist Hall is now), she grew a selection of admired flowers and vegetables. Also a member of the WI she entered the annual produce show and won prizes and cups. The other postman in the village was Bill Smale who covered the Ashbury area. Eventually the local postmen and women

*Postal workers receiving awards in recognition of their services after the postal deliveries in Northlew were taken over by the mail vans from Okehampton.* Left to right: *Enid Baker (postmistress), Doris Spry (postwoman), Fred Baker, Bill Spry, official from Okehampton Post Office, Bill Smale (postman), Archie Crocker (Okehampton Post Office), Jim Ware (postman) with Rachel Ware in background. Others who have worked delivering post are Korah Luxton, Horace Sanders, Archie King and Henry Andrew.*

were phased out, and a mail van travelled up from Okehampton to carry out the deliveries. In 2002 the postman is Tony Jones. While on his post round, Tony also keeps an eye on some of the older residents in the district, notifying the 'village' if there is a problem or illness. Tony's happy disposition and cheerful remarks bring a smile to Northlew residents each morning.

In 2002, Richard Westlake is a dental technician and carries out his business from Goosen Farm. Mr Westlake is well known around the district and many clients travel long distances to Northlew for dental repairs and services.

The following are tradesmen working in the district at the time of writing:

M.J. Bater & Sons of Crowden. John Bater began as a wheelwright, thatcher and also did building work and Maurice Bater began the funeral side of the business. Today Richard and his brother Colin continue with the building and undertaking business. Julian Gratton of the Arcade is an established painter and decorator and also undertakes small building jobs and tiling. Andrew Algar of Harpers Hill is a small builder and decorator with many customers in the area.

Simon Squires of Milltown Lane is a sought-after carpenter. He also undertakes decorating and small building jobs. Julian Wilkins of Kimberlands is a highly skilled fitter of luxury kitchens. Julian can supply various styles of kitchens from his catalogues and is well known for his quality of work and kitchen fitting skills. Jim Jevons of Crowden Road will undertake most building jobs, from constructing a porch to small repairs.

Jeanette Lawrence of Station Road and Joanne Maynard of Crowden are mobile hairdressers. They each have a regular client list and are kept very busy. Maggies Curls is a small hairdressing salon established at the bottom of Harpers Hill. The salon is run by Margaret Curry who, before starting her own business, worked in local salons.

Tonya Dufty's dressmaking skills extend to beautiful wedding and bridesmaids dresses. Tonya also has a refurbishing service and can work wonders with a second-hand dress, making it into a stunning outfit. In addition to the dresses, she offers a curtain-making service. Felicity Cole of October Cottage is an interior designer and a skilled picture framer working from her studio in Northlew. Felicity also has a stall at Hatherleigh Market.

*Tonya Dufty with wedding and bridesmaids' dresses exhibited at the Art and Craft Exhibition in 1996.*

Philip and Sue Friend of Wadland Barton, trading as Friends Quality Beef and Lamb, are not only busy running their farm but are also suppliers of very good meat. They will provide a single joint for a Sunday roast, or larger amounts for special functions or freezers. The business is built on traditional quality and good service. Sue and her family support the local farmers' market at Okehampton once a month.

Wayne & Co. of Harpers Hill and Ronan & Co. of Station Road are both home-based chartered accountants, each offering an experienced tax and accounting service. George King of Whiddon and John Wray of Fordatown are both qualified electricians who have lived and worked in the district for many years and can deal with all aspects of the electrical trade.

Ronald Carter, trading under the name of Traditional Leather, has an established business trading from his workshop at Harpers Hill and Barry Welham of Crowden is also an established leatherworker. Both supply handcrafted luxury articles for the home and overseas market. Mr Carter trained as a leatherworker at Harrods, where he served his apprenticeship, and is now a supplier of goods to the store. Mr Welham produces the red dispatch boxes used by ministers of the crown. Morwena Hortop, also a leatherworker at Harpers Hill, imports shoes which she decorates and sells locally. Becky Godwin-Combes, a talented craftworker, is well known for her colourful mosaic-topped tables and glass engraving. Becky also lectures and gives demonstrations to art and craft groups around the district, and is well known for her children's face-painting at the Church festival and other events in the village.

G. Seccombe of Durdon Farm describes his work as 'creating new gardens'. As an established landscape gardening business he is able to landscape a small part of a garden, or take on a much larger challenge, such as a recent project at Dulverton taking two years to complete.

N.J. Chettle of Eastcott Farm has a very interesting business training sheep dogs. There are also holiday cottages on the premises where one can stay for a few days while training a dog. Tarpaflex is run by Mr and Mrs Simon Page of Eastcombe Farm which successfully imports tarpaulins. Leonard Chapman of Crowden is a self-employed clock repairer and restorer. Mr and Mrs Patton of Queen Street run a successful business supplying conservatories, conservatory furniture and accessories. Marilyn Livingstone and Morgen Witzel run a publishing services business from Honeychurch, working for publishing companies in Bristol, London and New York. Lyn Taylor's well-established newspaper business is run from her conservatory in the Arcade.

*Northlew Parish Church.*

*The stocks.*

*Chapter 4*

# THE CHURCH IN THE COMMUNITY

The Parish Church of Northlew has been at the centre of the community for much of its long history. It has been used for weddings, christenings and other happy occasions, and by those showing their last respects for a friend or relative at funerals. The church has provided a place for quiet prayer and reflection in times of war, illness and victory as well as for personal meditation.

The chief landowner of Northlew in the Domesday Book of 1086 is named as Brictric. It is likely that there was a church at this time but no trace of it exists today. This early church would have been much smaller and constructed of wattle and daub with a thatched roof.

*The church porch showing the coats of arms of the Kelly and Trecarrell families.*

## The Porch

The church is entered through the porch on the south side. The carved roses of the fifteenth–sixteenth-century roof have been restored and the floor has been paved with slates. In medieval times the porch was used for the first part of the rite of baptism and the betrothal in the marriage ceremony. People from the parish would come to the porch to read notices. At the time of writing, the porch is still used for notices although the majority are in connection with the church; the Parish Electoral Roll is also always on display there.

On the left-hand side of the porch the stocks can be seen. The stocks had two purposes, one was to inflict a punishment for certain misdemeanours and the other to make a public example of certain individuals as a deterrent or warning to the community.

## The West Aisle and Body of the Church

As one enters the door into the main part of the church, the first thing that is seen is the font; its position symbolises the entry to christianity through baptism. The font is Norman and was probably removed during Cromwell's time. The rector, the Revd T. England, found the font broken and filled with rubbish in the south-west corner of the church. It was repaired and placed in position in 1870. From the font, looking eastwards towards the altar, is a clear view of the main body of the church, which dates from the fifteenth century. The pillars are hewn out of granite rock and those on the south side are monoliths of complete stone from top to bottom. The rood (meaning cross) screen can be seen spanning the width of the church. The original screen was defaced and broken at the time of the Reformation and the upper half was removed in 1810 by the order of the rural dean. At the beginning of the twentieth century the screen was restored by Herbert Reed of Exeter.

Behind the font at the west end of the church stands the tower which, like the font, is Norman.

*The font.*

*The rood screen today.*

*The barrel roof and bosses.*

The tower is probably built over the site of the ancient church and occupies about the same area. The tower houses six bells, the ringing of which is part of the history of the church. The bells were rung to warn of fire and flood and to call to arms. The curfew bell was a signal to put out lights and fires. The curate was charged to toll a bell, night and morning, to call the people of the parish to the house of God. The Revd Sabine Baring Gould collected many songs, one of which was about the bells of Northlew and was written by the Northlew poet, Devereux Evance. The first verse begins:

*One day in October, neither drunken nor sober*
*O'er Broadbury Down I was wending my way.*
*When I heard of some singing, some dancing and*
*singing*
*I ought to remember that Jubilee Day.*
*'Twas in Ashwater Town, the bells they did sound*
*They rang for a belt and a hat laced with gold.*
*But the men of Northlew rang so steady and true*
*That never was better in Devon I hold.*

On the west wall, to the left of the tower, is a Latin inscription which, when translated, reads as follows:

*This church dedicated to St Thomas of Canterbury, began in the time of the Normans, then by the piety of many generations, renewed, added to and adorned. After being miserably neglected for three hundred years and almost fallen into ruins, an age more zealous for sacred things with much love for God, restored as far as possible to its former state in the year of our Lord 1885.*
*S.A. Herbert – Rector, W.H. Bickle – Warden.*

*The east window behind the altar. It depicts the Epiphany and was the gift of Jacquetta Woollcombe at the end of the eighteenth century.*

Opposite page: *Donations for restoring the church.*

# DONATIONS to the FUND for REPAIRING & RESTORING NORTHLEW CHURCH.

| | £ | s. | d. |
|---|---|---|---|
| The Ven. Archdeacon Woollcombe | 100 | 0 | 0 |
| Miss Woollcombe | 100 | 0 | 0 |
| Mrs. N. Vowler | 30 | 0 | 0 |
| Rev. S. A. Herbert, 1st contribution | 10 | 0 | 0 |
| „ „ 2nd „ | 10 | 0 | 0 |
| „ „ 3rd „ | 10 | 0 | 0 |
| G. W. Medley, Esq., 1st contribution | 10 | 0 | 0 |
| „ „ 2nd „ | 10 | 0 | 0 |
| The Ven. Archdeacon Earle | 5 | 5 | 0 |
| Rev. Lewis Woollcombe | 5 | 0 | 0 |
| W. H. Bickle, Esq. | 5 | 0 | 0 |
| Mr. Mills | 5 | 0 | 0 |
| Mr. Dreadon | 3 | 3 | 0 |
| Rev. S. Andrew | 2 | 2 | 0 |
| Mr. James Breyley | 2 | 0 | 0 |
| Mr. Shellabear | 1 | 0 | 0 |
| Mr. John Friend | 1 | 0 | 0 |
| Money from Executors of late Rector | 23 | 16 | 0 |
| Profit from Parish Tea, August, 1882 | 1 | 6 | 0 |
| Mr. Glass, Millcombe | 1 | 0 | 0 |
| J. Bayley, Esq. | 25 | 0 | 0 |
| R. Bayley, Esq. | 10 | 0 | 0 |
| Mr. Dufty | 5 | 0 | 0 |
| Mrs. Kitson | 5 | 0 | 0 |
| Mr. W. Glass, S. Yeo | 4 | 0 | 0 |
| J. Gould, Esq. | 5 | 0 | 0 |
| G. W. Gould, Esq. | 1 | 0 | 0 |
| Mr. W. Glass, Lew Mill | 3 | 0 | 0 |
| The late W. Kitson, Esq., Torquay | 10 | 0 | 0 |
| Mr. John Harry | 1 | 0 | 0 |
| Mr. W. Wood | 1 | 0 | 0 |
| Mr. Thos. Glass | 1 | 0 | 0 |
| Miss Woolland | 0 | 10 | 0 |
| Messrs. Smale, Heath | 1 | 0 | 0 |
| Mrs. Westlake, Wiggadon | 0 | 10 | 0 |
| Mr. C. Copp | 1 | 0 | 0 |
| Mr. Smale, Scobchester | 1 | 0 | 0 |
| Miss Luxmore | 0 | 10 | 0 |
| W. Harris, Esq., Halwill | 5 | 0 | 0 |
| The Right Hon. Earl Fortescue | 10 | 0 | 0 |
| Mr. Edward Glass | 1 | 0 | 0 |
| Mr. A. Friend | 1 | 0 | 0 |
| Mrs. Dennis | 1 | 0 | 0 |
| The Misses Kitson, through the Rev. H. Barnes | 20 | 0 | 0 |
| Rev. J. L. Francis | 1 | 1 | 0 |
| Rev. G. Woollcombe | 15 | 0 | 0 |
| Rev. T. W. Whale, Dolton | 1 | 0 | 0 |
| J. R. Thursfield, Esq., London | 10 | 0 | 0 |
| C. B. Woollcombe, Esq., Brighton | 5 | 0 | 0 |
| Mr. S. Shobrooke, Cruft | 1 | 0 | 0 |
| Misses Shobrooke | 1 | 0 | 0 |
| A Friend | 0 | 10 | 0 |
| Misses Woollcombe, Clifton | 5 | 0 | 0 |
| Mrs. Manning | 10 | 0 | 0 |
| Col. Arnold | 2 | 2 | 0 |
| Mrs. H. Hill, in memory of Thomas Woollcombe, Esq. | 5 | 0 | 0 |
| Rev. M. Brown, Highampton | 1 | 1 | 0 |
| Sir Massey Lopes, Bart., M.P. | 5 | 0 | 0 |
| H. Moulton Barrett, Esq. | 1 | 0 | 0 |
| John Belfield, Esq. | 3 | 0 | 0 |
| J. Wood, Esq., Uphelmstone | 1 | 0 | 0 |
| Sir John Kennaway, Bart., M.P. | 1 | 1 | 0 |
| J. Symthe Osbourne, Esq. | 1 | 10 | 0 |
| R. Borland, Esq. | 1 | 1 | 0 |
| Rev. C. L. Courtenay | 0 | 10 | 0 |
| Col. White-Thomson | 2 | 0 | 0 |
| Rev. E. Theed | 2 | 2 | 0 |
| Some Friends of the Church | 10 | 0 | 0 |
| Mr. Truman | 2 | 0 | 0 |
| J. Carpenter-Garnier, Esq., M.P. | 5 | 0 | 0 |
| Mrs. Puddicombe | 3 | 3 | 0 |
| Mrs. Cane | 3 | 3 | 0 |
| Mr. S. Shellabear, London | 1 | 1 | 0 |
| Messrs. Dingley, Pearse & Co. | 5 | 0 | 0 |
| Mr. & Mrs. W. Madge | 5 | 0 | 0 |
| Miss Warrington, Torquay | 1 | 0 | 0 |
| Miss Stirling | 2 | 2 | 0 |
| J. M. Andrew, Esq., Plymouth | 1 | 1 | 0 |
| Rev. W. G. Morcom | 0 | 10 | 0 |
| Rev. Thomas A. Bewes, Plymouth | 5 | 0 | 0 |
| Mrs. Thursfield, London | 2 | 2 | 0 |
| Mrs. Ashby, Modbury | 3 | 3 | 0 |
| Miss Woollcombe, Sale of Work | 23 | 3 | 0 |
| J. D. Prickman, Esq., Okehampton | 1 | 1 | 0 |
| W. Burd, Esq. | 1 | 1 | 0 |
| Edwd. B. Savile, Esq. | 2 | 2 | 0 |
| G. V. Burd, Esq. | 1 | 1 | 0 |
| J. F. Vicary, Esq., North Tawton | 1 | 1 | 0 |

| | £ | s. | d. |
|---|---|---|---|
| Rev. R. E. Trefusis | 1 | 0 | 0 |
| Mrs. Reddaway | 1 | 1 | 0 |
| Rev. W. D. Pitman | 1 | 0 | 0 |
| G. Cann, Esq. | 1 | 1 | 0 |
| Rev. W. F. Gray | 0 | 10 | 0 |
| Rev. C. Spackman | 0 | 10 | 0 |
| The Crown through Right Honble. W. E. Gladstone, M.P. | 100 | 0 | 0 |
| Edwd. Blackburn, Esq. | 5 | 0 | 0 |
| Rev. W. D. Anderson | 1 | 1 | 0 |
| Mr. Tom | 0 | 5 | 0 |
| Mr. John Gay, Timber | 5 | 6 | 0 |
| Rev. P. L. D. Acland | 1 | 1 | 0 |
| Rev. I. F. Alleyne | 0 | 10 | 0 |
| Rev. C. Holley | 1 | 1 | 0 |
| W. Hirst, Esq., by W. H. Bickle, Esq. | 1 | 0 | 0 |
| Incorporated Church Building Society Grant | 50 | 0 | 0 |
| The Right Rev. the Lord Bishop of Exeter | 10 | 0 | 0 |
| Miss Tucker | 0 | 5 | 0 |
| Miss E. Cummins | 0 | 5 | 0 |
| Miss E. Shellabear | 0 | 5 | 0 |
| Miss C. Crocker | 0 | 5 | 0 |
| Proceeds of Concert, Aug. 17th, 1883 | 3 | 0 | 0 |
| Mrs. Smith, Belfast | 1 | 0 | 0 |
| Rev. P. Williams, Rewe | 0 | 10 | 0 |
| Rev. R. Chichester | 1 | 1 | 0 |
| Mr. Baker, Northlew | 0 | 10 | 0 |
| Ven. R. H. Cobbold, Ross | 0 | 10 | 0 |
| Rev. Prebendary Kempe | 1 | 0 | 0 |
| G. N. Maule, Esq., Ilfracombe | 0 | 10 | 0 |
| H. G. Moysey, Esq. | 2 | 2 | 0 |
| Rev. W. Thorold | 1 | 1 | 0 |
| Col. Troyte | 1 | 1 | 0 |
| Exeter Architectural Society | 7 | 7 | 0 |
| Sale of Work | 1 | 0 | 0 |
| Sir Henry W. Peek, Bart., M.P. | 5 | 0 | 0 |
| Edward Coode, Esq. | 1 | 0 | 0 |
| Diocesan Church Building Society | 20 | 0 | 0 |
| Miss Hepple, Gateshead | 1 | 0 | 0 |
| Sir J. B. Phear | 1 | 1 | 0 |
| G. H. Herbert, Esq., Newcastle-on-Tyne | 10 | 0 | 0 |
| E. J. Oldham, Esq., Strawbridge | 2 | 0 | 0 |
| Mr. Bray, Okehampton | 0 | 5 | 0 |
| Mrs. S. Hooper, Hatherleigh | 10 | 10 | 0 |
| G. Neumann, Esq. | 0 | 5 | 0 |
| Lieut-Col. Madden | 1 | 1 | 0 |
| Right Hon. Viscount Portman | 5 | 0 | 0 |
| Mrs. Kerslake | 1 | 0 | 0 |
| W. H. Holley, Esq. | 1 | 1 | 0 |
| Proceeds of 2nd Concert | 1 | 10 | 0 |
| Thos. Carew Daniel, Esq. | 1 | 1 | 0 |
| Trehawke Kekewich, Esq. | 1 | 0 | 0 |
| Wm. Barnes, Esq. | 5 | 0 | 0 |
| Miss M. A. Down | 0 | 5 | 0 |
| Mr. G. Martin, Lovelands | 0 | 5 | 0 |
| Mr. W. Shellabear, 2nd contribution | 1 | 1 | 0 |
| Mr. S. Shellabear, 2nd „ | 1 | 1 | 0 |
| Mr. & Mrs. H. Smale „ | 0 | 10 | 0 |
| Vice-Admiral E. V. Charlwood | 1 | 1 | 0 |
| Mr. Roger Palmer, Venn | 1 | 1 | 0 |
| Rev. Robert Baker Carew | 2 | 2 | 0 |
| Maj.-Gen. A. De Lisle | 2 | 2 | 0 |
| Proceeds of Concert, April 18th | 5 | 0 | 0 |
| Thos. Gascoigne, Esq., Fishleigh | 2 | 0 | 0 |
| Mrs. Gard, Exeter | 2 | 0 | 0 |
| Capt. Kelsale, R.N. | 1 | 0 | 0 |
| A. Borel Northlew, Esq. | 21 | 0 | 0 |
| J. H. Veale, Esq., Passaford | 1 | 0 | 0 |
| Mr. Evely, Crowden | 0 | 5 | 0 |
| Herbert Woollcombe, Esq. | 2 | 0 | 0 |
| W. H. Kelland, Esq. | 1 | 1 | 0 |
| A Friend | 0 | 10 | 0 |
| Proceeds of Bazaar, June 19-20 | 109 | 5 | 6 |
| W. G. Woollcombe, Esq., Brighton | 3 | 0 | 0 |
| Rev. W. Symons, Tavistock | 1 | 1 | 0 |
| Lucius K. Reichel, Esq. | 1 | 0 | 0 |
| Mr. Collins Trelawny | 0 | 10 | 0 |
| H. B. Were, Esq. | 0 | 10 | 6 |
| J. Selten Willett, Esq. | 2 | 0 | 0 |
| R. W. Hogg, Esq., S. John's College, Cambridge | 1 | 1 | 0 |
| Rev. G. Buckle | 1 | 1 | 0 |
| Gustavus Gidley, Esq. | 1 | 0 | 0 |
| Arthur B. Hutchings, Esq. | 1 | 0 | 0 |
| A. Burch, Esq., Exeter | 0 | 10 | 6 |
| W. H. Jordan | 0 | 5 | 0 |
| R. C. Moote, Esq. | 0 | 10 | 0 |
| G. H. E. Rundle, Esq. | 1 | 1 | 0 |

The 300 years of neglect referred to in the inscription coincided with a time when the rectors were non-resident, when the Church of England was at a low ebb and when Methodism came with its rousing call to fill the place in people's hearts. The Revd Thomas England, who was appointed rector in 1847, recorded his impressions of the church and said that there was a gallery and singing loft at the west end. The tower was shut off from the rest of the church by wainscotting as the ringers maintained that the tower belonged to them. There was a lofty pulpit and reading desk in the body of the church. The roof was leaking and cattle and sheep grazed in the churchyard. It was certainly a picture of neglect, which met the Revd T. England in 1847, and it was through his efforts and those of his successor, the Revd S.A. Herbert, that a measure of glory and dignity was restored.

On the west wall to the right of the tower, is fastened the Table of Continuity, which records that Richard de Boleville was instituted as rector on 20 May 1258, and that he succeeded one named Henry, with surname missing.

*The window in the north aisle shows the resurrection and bears the inscription, 'To the glory of God and in memory of John and Mary Phare and Ann Joanna their eldest daughter, the beloved wife of Michael Caine.'*

From the west wall is a door leading to the vestry. The vestry is where the vestments, the vessels for the Holy Communion service and registers are kept and where the clergy and choir robe. The vestry was added at the time of the Revd John Worthington and dedicated in 1907.

## The North Aisle

In the north aisle is the barrel roof, one of the features of the church; it is the work of craftsmen of the fifteenth and sixteenth centuries. The carved lintels over the windows belong to that period. Angels with opened wings stand on either side and the bosses are revelations of beauty and glory. In the north aisle is the rood stairway which leads to the rood loft; these also date from the fifteenth and sixteenth centuries. The feet of men who climbed them, to read the story of the Crucifixion, to preach the cross or to sing the passion music, have worn the steps. The five pew ends at the head of the north aisle are modern work. They show the village cross, the winged dragon and the initials of St George.

At the eastern end of the north aisle is Rutleigh Chapel. The chapel houses the original memorial to those men of the village who died in the two world wars. The arms of the Kelly family can be seen on the pillar beside this chapel. Mid-week

*The First World War Memorial inside the church.*

Holy Communion is still celebrated in this chapel at the time of writing.

## The South Aisle

At the eastern end of the south aisle was the Holway Chapel, all traces of its former use have now gone and it houses the organ. The organ bears the name Henry Willis, a famous organ builder, and it is one of the smallest and earliest Willis organs. It was brought to Northlew in 1889. Other examples of Willis organs are in St Paul's Cathedral, London, and in Exeter Cathedral. The organs are renowned for their longevity, reliability and tonal quality. Northlew is fortunate to own one of them.

Leading into the church by the organ is the priest's door. In medieval times only the rector would use it. At one time there was a scratch dial on the outside, this was a semi-circle which had the times of the services around it. When the priest entered through the door he would put a stick or gnomon in a hole in the middle of the circle. The people would know by looking at the dial whether the priest was in church and the time of the service. The dial has been worn away and no trace of it remains.

In the south aisle one of the pew ends bears the date 1537. The carved seat ends in the church tell

*The Willis organ.*

the story of the Cross and Passion. The powers of evil are symbolised by the griffin and the dragon. The carvings also tell of the martyr, St Thomas of Canterbury, and some of the seats are carved with symbols connected with him.

As people leave the south door to enter the churchyard, the granite War Memorial is directly opposite.

*Pew end showing the date 1537.*

## The Churchyard

The churchyard is consecrated ground, God's acre (ager-field). The first extension of the churchyard was added and consecrated by the bishop in 1909, and a second extension was added during the incumbency of the Revd G. Clarke 1952–58. Fanny Smale gave the land for this extension. A wooden bench is situated at the entry of the second extension area dedicated to Fred Baker. He was, for many years, churchwarden and organist and during his life made an outstanding contribution to both church and community. On Easter Sunday 2000 a second bench was dedicated in memory of Richard Robinson. The two benches provide an opportunity for people to sit in peace and to ponder. Northlew churchyard is maintained by a small band of volunteers and is one of the best-kept churchyards in the county.

*Northlew churchyard.*

## The Clock

The clock, made by John Smith & Son of Derby, was given in memory of the Diamond Jubilee of Queen Victoria and erected on 22 June 1897. The inscription on the dial face reads, 'Peresunt et imputantur', and may be translated as, 'They pass away, seconds, minutes, hours, and days, and are reckoned in The Account.' The inscription on the clock reads, 'The Gift, to the Glory of God, and in commemoration of The Sixtieth Anniversary of The Reign of Queen Victoria, this clock was erected, 22 June 1897. A Thank Offering.'

## The Lych-gate

The word lych is old English, and means a body, dead body or a corpus. The lych gate is the roofed gateway at the entrance to the churchyard where the body is laid until the procession is formed and the priest begins the sentences. The lych-gate dates from the fifteenth or sixteenth century.

## New Vicarage

The new vicarage was built in the grounds of the former rectory in 1981 for the use of the incumbent. Mr Henry Luxton of Northlew built it in three-quarters of an acre.

## Okehampton Team Ministry

On 7 July 1994, under the Pastoral Measure of 1983, Northlew parish joined with Okehampton, Inwardleigh, Bratton Clovelly, Germansweek, Bridestowe and Sourton to form the Okehampton Team Ministry. The Revd Russell Chamberlain was appointed the first Team Rector and the Revd Ray Voden as Team Vicar.

## The Patron Saint

### *St Thomas of Canterbury (Thomas Becket)*

*The banner of St Thomas of Canterbury.*

The Patron Saint of Northlew is St Thomas of Canterbury who was martyred on 29 December 1170. His body was translated from the crypt to the shrine of Canterbury Cathedral on 7 July 1220. The church festival is the Festival of the Translation. The festival was called the 'Revel', which is a Middle English word, meaning 'making merry'. The festival was held on 7 July and the children were given a day off school. In 1848 when the church was still in a period of great neglect the festival service was deserted but in the streets and Square were booths, shows, a travelling theatre, sports, wrestling and noisy festivity. Men, women, boys and girls danced in the road before the Honeychurch Arms. The public houses were kept open night and day throughout the week and there was much drunkenness. After this it seems

*The lych-gate.*

*Ashbury Church, 1908.*

*The floral dance at the church festival, 1920.*

*The church festival, 1959–60, in the Old Rectory garden. Mrs Wood at the piano.*

that the festival died out until 1873 when the Revd Thomas England held the festival service in the church followed by tea, games and sport in the rectory grounds. This pattern of celebration is fairly closely followed today except that now the festival is held on the Saturday closest to 7 July each year.

## Northlew and Ashbury United in 1876

The parishes of Northlew and Ashbury were united by order in Council on 24 March 1876. Previously Ashbury had been a separate parish with its own vicar appointed at first by the Prior

*The church festival tea, 1994.*

*The Parish Church of Ashbury.*

and Convent of Launceston. From 1566 the church was under the patronage of the Sovereign.

## St Mary's Church of Ashbury

A church has stood at Ashbury since the thirteenth century, perhaps earlier. The list of rectors dates from Robert de Ellewille in 1274. In 1416, the church is named on Exeter Cathedral Roll as Santa Marie de Ayschbyry; the Patron Saint of Ashbury is the Blessed Virgin Mary. The old church was restored around the 1700s by the then landowner, John Woollcombe, MP for Plymouth, Deputy Lieutenant and High Sheriff of Devon. The date over the porch was 1701. In the great storm of the eighteenth century the church was struck by a thunderbolt and one of the pinnacles crashed down to the ground. In 1871 the whole church, except the tower, was pulled down and rebuilt on its old foundation. It was planned by the Venerable Henry Woollcombe, Archdeacon of Barnstaple, to whose memory the reredos was given. Behind the reredos is canopy work showing representations of the Crucifixion and figures of saints in niches. The font is in Caen stone. The carved pulpit is in memory of Charles Bellefield Woollcombe, who died in 1901. The lectern and altar are of carved oak. Unfortunately the Parish Registers, which were kept in the manor house, were charred beyond all recognition when Ashbury House was destroyed by fire on 18 August 1877.

On 1 June 1981 Ashbury Church was made redundant. No church services have taken place since. Today the church is the responsibility of the Woollcombe family but the churchyard remains in the care of the incumbent.

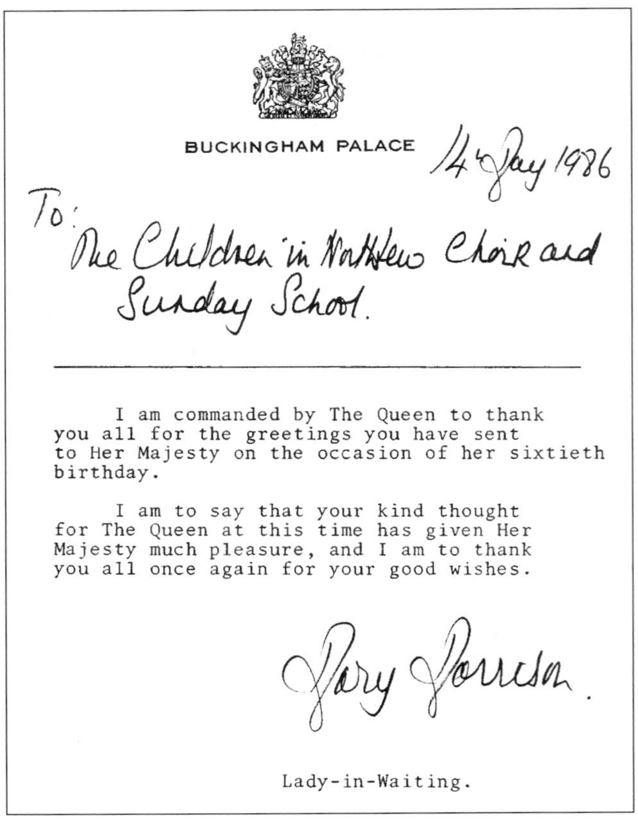

BUCKINGHAM PALACE 14th May 1986

To: The Children in Northlew Choir and Sunday School.

I am commanded by The Queen to thank you all for the greetings you have sent to Her Majesty on the occasion of her sixtieth birthday.

I am to say that your kind thought for The Queen at this time has given Her Majesty much pleasure, and I am to thank you all once again for your good wishes.

Mary Morrison.

Lady-in-Waiting.

*Letter from Buckingham Palace.*

## Sunday School

Northlew Church has always considered the teaching of children in the Christian faith to be of great importance. In 2002, Sunday school is held during the morning service and Margery Rundle and Pat Durston are the teachers. The older children have been involved in the services by reading lessons and doing little plays at special services particularly at Christmas time when they perform Nativity plays. The Sunday school joins in with others in the deanery. The children attend the annual service in July, which is followed by a picnic and games. For three years in the late 1990s Jenny Voden took those between 8 and 11 years for a weekend away at Bernard's Acre at Belstone. They joined children from Hatherleigh and North Tawton for fun and

*Sunday-school outing to Bude. Tom Andrew and John Spry.*

*Sunday-school outing. The Jordan and Eveleigh clans.*

games, worship and assisting with the chores. Sadly, because of 'foot and mouth', the above two events did not take place in 2001.

In the year 2000, Derek Humphreys helped the children make a model to show 'Jesus the living water'. This was shown, along with exhibits by Sunday-school and day-school children throughout the diocese, at Exeter Cathedral. The exhibition, entitled 'Moving the Sun', was held for a week in February.

*Crowden Road showing the original chapel building.*

## Church Room

The Methodists sold the Church Room to the Anglicans in 1910. In 1932 it was converted to a senior department in connection with the school. During the incumbency of the Revd Jack Reason a new floor was laid. In 1996–97 the room was given a face-lift by members of the church. The kitchen was refurbished, curtains made, the hall ceiling lowered, new heaters installed and new tables supplied. Today the room is used for many meetings and social functions. If there is a world disaster, an impromptu coffee evening is arranged and goods and refreshments, supplied by members of the community, soon fill the tables to raise money for the stricken people. The room brings members of the community together in a warm and friendly atmosphere.

## Hebron Methodist Chapel

### *The Beginning – 1811–15*

At the beginning of the nineteenth century Wesleyan preachers established Methodist Societies in Okehampton, Northlew and the surrounding areas. Of these the largest was Northlew; in 1813 it had 15 members, Okehampton had only eight. John Cloke first visited Northlew early in 1812 and his preaching met with an immediate response. Among his first converts were Henry Major and his family, who occupied the house on the west side of the Square which many years later became the manse.

Regular services were established in a private dwelling in the village. The Northlew society continued to grow, and it was decided that a chapel should be built. A site was purchased on the north-west corner of the Square for the sum of five shillings. Henry Major, who was a local builder and carpenter, supplied the materials and built the chapel. Towards the end of September 1815 the building was finished. It was the first chapel in the Okehampton Mission and the first Methodist building in the whole of this part of Devon. The chapel was opened on Tuesday 19 October 1815.

James Thorne
1816–72
b. Sept. 1795
d. Jan 1872
F.W. Bourne
1850–July 30
William O'Bryan
1815–29
b. Feb. 1778
d. Jan 1868
J. Hicks Eynon
1826–88
b. May 1801
d. March 1888
James Way
1826–84
b. Jume 1804
d. August 1884


*The original founders and preachers of the Methodist Chapel, Northlew.*

## The Birth of the Bible Christians – 1815

In August 1815, while the work of building the chapel at Northlew was in progress, a Methodist preacher from Cornwall visited the district. He was the evangelist William O'Bryan, who at the time counted himself a Wesleyan local preacher. William O'Bryan was a very successful preacher, although his methods were not approved by all the Methodist societies. The rebuffs, which he received both in his home circuit and elsewhere, coupled with his obvious successful campaigns in Devon and East Cornwall, were gradually forcing William O'Bryan towards separation from the main Methodist body. Various stewards tried to reconcile William O'Bryan with the main group, but this was not successful. Wherever William O'Bryan preached, people joined the society, he even preached to congregations which refused to leave. So began the denomination which later became the 'Bible Christians'.

## *Whose New Chapel? 1815–20*

William O'Bryan was invited to preach at the opening of the new chapel. The rift between the Wesleyan Methodist Society and O'Bryan caused tension between visitors to the chapel; the Northlew society, however, were not aware of the problem. The society was torn between two loyalties. Who, indeed, was right? Although the exact date is not known, the Bible Christians and the Wesleyan group separated during 1817. The Wesleyans continued to use the chapel, and the Bible Christians held meetings in a barn. Henry Major, one of the founders of the Wesleyan movement, was now excluded from the chapel he had provided. Consequently, he sent in his bill requesting prompt payment. Unable to pay, the alternative was for the building to be transferred to the Christians, debts and all, thus becoming the first Bible Christian chapel. By 1819 the Bible Christian Society worshipped in the chapel and the Wesleyans in private dwellings until they built their own chapel in 1860.

*The Church Room. Originally the Wesleyan Chapel, also used as a Sunday school and later as the school canteen run by Lizzie Wooldridge.*

## *Northlew Circuit 1831–80*

For several years the only chapel was that at Northlew itself. By 1844 there were nine in the circuit, all of which were quite small. Modest though these buildings were their erection represented a considerable act of faith. The one built in 1815 was now considered too small and was refurbished and extended in 1858. The Wesleyans, who acquired a site and erected a chapel in the Square, also shared this enthusiasm. Thus, for many years, Northlew Square could boast the Parish Church in one corner, the Methodist churches in two others and the day school in the fourth.

The Wesleyan Society never grew strong, and at the end of the century could not continue. The chapel was sold in 1910 to the Anglican Church to be converted into a parish hall, and it is still used for this purpose.

There is no record of the beginning of the Sunday school in the Northlew area but it is known that by 1841 it was well established.

*The old Methodist Sunday School.*

## *Further Expansion 1880–1910*

The period between 1880 and 1910 was one of prosperity for churches. Church restoration was fashionable, as was service attendance. The chapel in Northlew was again refurbished in 1889. A piece of land was purchased in Crowden Road and the schoolroom was built. The memorial stone was laid on Easter Monday 1893 and tea was supplied for all the children. By 1880 the candles had been replaced by oil lamps. Up to this time the singing had been largely unaccompanied; soon after 1880 the harmonium (American organ) arrived. These organs became a status symbol for chapels. The American organ was not the only import from the New World. In 1889 the new Bible Christian hymn book was published. The book came into use in Northlew during April 1890.

In 1904 a small field was purchased next to the schoolroom for a graveyard and this was extended by the purchase of a further piece of land in 1914.

## *The End and the Beginning – Forward into the Twentieth Century*

*Hebron Methodist Chapel.*

*Reopening after repairs to Northlew Chapel in 1952. Organist Harold Saunders, Revd Jennings.*
Right to left: *Auntie, Mrs Gratton, little girl unknown, Mr Winnacott, the Revd Clarke – rector of the Parish Church, Mr Saunders, Harold Saunders, George Gratton – Mayor of Okehampton, Mr Brooking, Ern Maurice Bater, George Friend, Ern Shobbrook, Dick Gratton, ?, two ladies unknown.*

During the last decade of the nineteenth century and the first of the twentieth, the Northlew chapel reached the point of greatest prosperity. Large families of ten or a dozen children ensured that there was no shortage of people to fill the chapel or Sunday school. Also it was still fashionable to attend worship.

Methodist union took place in 1907, bringing new ideas and customs. The First World War marked the beginning of the decline in church attendance which continued in the period between, and after, the Second World War.

The union of the churches and the formation of a combined circuit with Okehampton heralded a new era. For the churches it was a serious period of adjustment. The following years were to see social and economic changes greater than any that the nineteenth century had seen. At Northlew the story began with dissention and the splitting of Methodism into rival camps; it has ended with agreement and amalgamation.

## *The Bible Christian and Wesleyan Manse*

### *The Bible Christian Manse*

Records cannot be found of the residence of the Bible Christian ministers in the early period, except that the postal address was c/o Mr H. Major, Northlew. This does not mean that the ministers actually resided with the Majors. It is more likely that they found lodgings with various families in the village, and it is also likely that later, when the ministers were married men, several different houses were rented for shorter or longer periods.

In 1875 the minister was living in a house at the church end of the Arcade. This house had previously been the residence of the curate in charge of the Northlew Parish Church before the building of the Rectory. The Bible Christians never bought this property, which had been divided into two at some stage and was always rented. There is a record of problems with repairs which the landlord was not willing to undertake. As a result, in 1886, the decision was made to purchase a terrace of three cottages in Crowden Lane, together with an adjoining field for £200. It was not stated anywhere what the properties would be used for, whether to convert one or more into a manse, or to build a new house on the adjacent land. The cottages were never used, and after five years it was decided that they had become a white elephant. The cottages were disposed of and the adjoining land was eventually used for a schoolroom and a burial-ground.

*Dedication of the chapel organ, 1970.*

In 1903 the house, which had once belonged to the Major family, became vacant and was purchased for use as a manse, it remained in use until the new manse was erected in 1965. Also, a cottage adjacent to the Bible Christian Chapel was purchased but this was soon sold again.

### *The Wesleyan Manse*

The manse for the Wesleyan Chapel was Church House on the north side of the Square. The house was a manse some time between 1860 and 1910, after which the chapel was sold to become the Church Hall.

### *The Societies in the Circuit*

| | |
|---|---|
| Emmanuel Chapel | Chilla |
| Bethlehem Chapel | Madworthy |
| Bethesda Chapel | Highhampton |
| Providence Chapel | Widdon |
| Zion Chapel | Eworthy |
| Bethany Chapel | Waytown |
| Gilgal Chapel | Bratton Clovelly |
| Providence Chapel | Bratton Clovelly |
| Salem Chapel | Boasley |
| Zion Chapel | Bridestowe |
| Mount Calvary Chapel | Okehampton |

For many years members of the church and chapel have supported each other in a variety of ways both social and spiritual. The people have demonstrated their love for God, each other and the wider community by supporting various fêtes, festivals and special services. During the school summer holidays members of the two churches hold a holiday club for the children of the village. As well as supporting each other at important and special services, since the year 2000 the two congregations have joined together for evening worship once a month.

*Methodist Male Voice Choir quartet. Gordon Saunders, Harold Saunders, Bill Spry, Bill Smale.*

*Graves of the Major family, Northlew churchyard.*

## *The Vestry*

The Vestry was a parochial body which included the incumbent and people of both sexes who were rated for the relief of the poor in respect of the parish, whether resident in the parish or not. It originally had both civil and ecclesiastical functions. The officers of the Vestry were the chairman, the churchwardens, the overseers, the waywardens, the assessors and the guardian. The incumbent acted as chairman. There were two churchwardens, one of whom was appointed by the rector and the other by the parish. The number of overseers varied from year to year; in 1825 there were four and in 1849 there were ten. The number of waywardens also varied. In 1847, there were two and in 1857 there were three for the east side of the parish and three for the west side as well as a foreman on the roads. There were two assessors and one guardian.

The meetings were held at four-weekly intervals so that there were 13 in a year. The meetings were held in the church or one of the public houses. After the school was opened in 1867 meetings were held there.

The Vestry had various duties to fulfil. The churchwardens' duty was to keep the church in repair and the churchyard in order. They were responsible for paying various salaries such as those of the choir and church cleaner. They maintained the church school and took care of the baptism, wedding, confirmation and burial registers. The overseers were responsible for the poor and aged. They made monthly payments to the poor and provided food, clothes, bedding and furniture when required. They found nurses for the sick, supplied surgical appliances and paid for the vaccination of the poor children. They also paid doctors' fees and funeral expenses and kept the poorhouse in repair. They boarded out children and put them into domestic service and met the charges of apprentices.

*Laurie Middlewick, the village policeman, and his wife Mary and sons Raymond and David. Photograph taken in 1931 in the policeman's garden, Milltown Lane.*

The waywardens were the surveyors of the highways and were responsible for obtaining material for the roads and the maintenance of the roads and bridges. They made sure the walls and hedges were kept in good repair. They set the standard of wages; in 1858 a labourer was paid 1s.4d. a day and an old man 10d. daily. The assessors were responsible for assessing the rateable value of the parish. This included the church, the poor and the road rates. They took legal proceedings for the recovery of rates. They were the officers of the law and appointed the constables. In 1854 six able and suitably qualified men were appointed to serve as constables for a year. In 1860, under new law, one constable was sufficient. The assessors also prepared the lists of those to act as jurors and those who were eligible to vote. They administered the Census and dealt with vagrancy. The guardian represented the parish on the Board of Guardians in the Okehampton Union of Parishes after the Poor Act of 1834. The officials of the Vestry drew up forms of agreement between different parties. Below is an example of such an agreement:

> *Farmers with children boarded out. 1835. John Glass hath agreed to keep Mary Hill for the ensuing year, and find her meat, drink, washing and lodging and the parish to find her clothing at the sum of 6d. per week. John Glass.*

The Vestry was deprived of practically all its civil functions by statute many years ago. Current ecclesiastical law provides for the Vestry meeting to take place annually before 30 April. Two weeks notice has to be given for this meeting and details of it have to be pinned on the church door. This meeting can be attended by anyone in the parish with the incumbent as chairman. If there is no incumbent then the rural dean acts as chairman. The agenda consists of the election of two churchwardens, a report by the incumbent on the life of the church and notice is given of the Archdeacon's Visitation. The Church Annual General Meeting usually follows the Vestry meeting and only those on the church electoral roll are eligible to vote.

The churchwardens are still responsible for the maintenance and good order of the church and the care of the communion vessels. They are often appointed joint trustees with the incumbent for certain legacies.

## *The Parish Council*

The Parish Council took over many civil functions around the 1870s. Here follow some interesting snippets from the minutes of the Parish Council.

*12 May 1897 – It was agreed to join other Parish Councils and send a congratulatory address to Her Most Gracious Majesty Queen Victoria on her Diamond Jubilee.*
*29 June 1900 – A sub-committee was appointed to supervise the restoration of the old village cross.*
*19 June 1906 – The village Square was causing concern – it needed repair. The surveyor was asked, 'To get some stones put on and have them rolled in by the steam roller.'*
*26 March 1908 – The pauper list was considered and T.J. was recommended to receive a weekly rise from 3s. to 3s.6d. a week.*
*10 December 1925 – A site meeting was held 'to shed over' the village pump.*
*17 March 1927 – The County Council was notified that the bridge at the bottom of Harpers Hill was, 'Nothing more than a death trap'.*
*9 October 1936 – A public meeting discusses with West Devon Electric Co., the bringing of street lighting to Northlew.*
*2 May 1946 – Victory celebrations planned.*
*24 May 1948 – A public telephone kiosk was to be erected on the East Side of the Square.*
*24 May 1952 – Feathers were rattled at the meeting when it was reported that the North Devon Water Board had replaced the lead village pump with an inferior iron one. A letter was shot off demanding an explanation. In 1962 the Water Board sold the pump to the parish for 1s.*
*With the arrival of mains water in 1953 a twenty-two year campaign for public conveniences in the village was begun. After endless hassle the conveniences were opened on 6 May 1975.*

*Henry Andrew* (on left), *Councillor for Northlew and vice-chairman for 23 years on Okehampton Rural District Council before it became West Devon Borough Council.*

The duties of the Parish Council have changed over the years as much of its authority is now in the hands of the Government, the County Council and the Borough Council. Today there are nine Parish Councillors who are elected for four years. The meetings are held monthly and anybody in the parish is eligible to attend. The councillors closely liaise with West Devon Borough Council and are consulted over local planning issues. The Borough Council levy a part of the Council Tax on their behalf. The Parish Council's duties include the administration of the playing field and the co-ordination of special events. They are the first point of contact for any parishioner. Today each member of the Council has to declare any assets, except financial, he or she has. The erosion of the authority of the Vestry and Parish Council indicates how local government today has become centralised and is less personal to the villagers.

# Register of Electors, 1933.

*(In force 15th October, 1933, to 14th October, 1934.)*

## SOUTH MOLTON PARLIAMENTARY DIVISION
of the
**County of Devon,**

## POLLING DISTRICT OF
# NORTHLEW (UU).

## PARISH OF
# NORTHLEW.

FORM OF REGISTER.

The Register contains the names in alphabetical order of all persons entitled to vote as parliamentary and as local government electors.

The Index letters in columns 2 (*a*) headed "Parliamentary" or 2 (*b*) headed "Local Govt." of the Register (see first page), show the nature of the qualification of an elector as follows:—

| *Men.* | *Women.* |
|---|---|
| R=Residence qualification. | Rw=Residence qualification. |
| B=Business premises qualification. | Bw=Business premises qualification. |
| O=Occupation qualification. | Ow=Occupation qualification. |
| H=Qualification through wife's occupation. | Dw=Qualification through husband's occupation. |

NM=Naval or Military voter.

The entry of the appropriate Index letter or letters against a name in the column 2 (*a*) headed "Parliamentary" indicates that the elector is a parliamentary elector, and the entry of the appropriate letter or letters against a name in the column 2 (*b*) headed "Local Govt." indicates that the elector is a local government elector (for headings see first page of Register). Where no Index letter is entered in one or other of those columns against a name, the elector is not entitled to the franchise to which the column relates.

***Note.***—† Persons against whose names the mark † is placed are not entitled to vote in respect of that entry at Elections of County Councillors.

‡ Persons against whose names the mark ‡ is placed are not entitled to vote in respect of that entry at Elections of Rural District Councillors

§ Persons against whose names the mark § is placed are not entitled to vote in respect of that entry in the case of a Borough, Metropolitan Borough *or* Urban District at Elections for Borough *or* District Councillors as the case may be and in the case of a Parish at Elections for Parish Councillors *or* at Parish Meetings.

* Persons against whose names the mark * is placed will vote at another polling place at Parliamentary Elections.

*a* Persons against whose names the letter *a* is placed are absent voters.

*Jurors.*—Persons who are qualified to serve as such are indicated by the letters printed after their names, thus:—

**J**=Juror. **SJ**=Special Juror.

Dated this Fifteenth day of October, 1933.

BRIAN S. MILLER, *Registration Officer.*

Printed for the Registration Officer of the County by Wm. Pollard & Co. Ltd., Exeter.

S 3 11 56

*Chapter 5*

# NORTHLEW & ASHBURY PAROCHIAL SCHOOL

## *Northlew and Ashbury Parochial School*

The earliest schools in the parish were the dame schools. These were kept by Mrs Morse at Bolland, Mrs Rich at the top of Harpers Hill and another by Miss Vanstone in Crowden Lane. Miss Vanstone later became a teacher at the school.

The middle part of the old poorhouse in the village was used as a schoolroom following the Dame schools. The building was a primitive structure with a staircase outside and five rooms. These were let at sixpence, fourpence and twopence a week, depending on size. The accommodation was very poor. This building, known as the Church House, was leased to Mr J. Bickle in 1705. One master, Mr Tom Hitchings, had lost his right hand in a threshing machine. However, he wrote with his left and used his wooden stump for discipline!

There is reference to 'two mixed schools' in 1856 and in *Billing's Directory* 1857 it says 'There are National schools for boys and girls, partly supported by J.M. Woollcombe Esq. The number of boys is 70 and girls 40.'

In 1863 the overseers applied to the Poor Law Board for permission to sell the poorhouse at auction. In 1864 the Vestry passed the resolution that 'The Parish House' be sold and kept in repair by the purchaser for parish and school purposes. Miss Jacquetta H. Woollcombe bought it in 1865. It was demolished and the new school was built by Baters. It opened in January 1867. Mr Mills was appointed master and Miss Vanstone infant mistress. The school managers were benefactors and local people led by the rector. It was not unusual

*The school, as rebuilt by Miss Woollcombe, in 1867.*

*Schoolmaster Mr Baldry and Marjorie.*

for their wives and daughters to help with the school in a variety of ways. The Revd Thomas England was rector when the school opened and Miss England, his daughter, used to take a class. Miss Woollcombe herself would come in to give singing lessons.

Miss Woollcombe and her brother, Archdeacon Woollcombe, supported the school financially, although there is reference to a Government grant in 1873. He died in 1885 and she in 1888. After her death the school was equipped with new desks, a gallery and apparatus. Mrs George Woollcombe of Morth Grange inherited the property. She lent £200 for the purchase of some additional land and the building of new offices. In 1903 she conveyed the site and buildings to the trust of the National Society for the Promotion of Education in the Principles of the Church of England.

In 1920 the managers bought the schoolmaster's house for £245, at that time the middle one of

*The school as remodelled in 1927/8.*

the three in Fern Terrace. The school buildings were remodelled in 1927. In 1931 the Church Room across the Square was converted into a senior department for cookery, joinery, handicrafts and lantern work. In 1935 land known as 'Church Park' adjoining the school was bought for a total of £384. The opening of this field was a grand occasion held on 6 May 1935, the Silver Jubilee of King George V. Admiral L.C.S. Woollcombe presided and there were church bells, a flag, a band, singing and speeches. The scholars each received a medal. Admiral Woollcombe opened the new gates using a silver key given by Mr and Mrs Newman. The King's tree was named and finally the benediction was given. The tree still stands in the grounds where a set of sturdy wooden play equipment has recently been erected.

The school continued to offer a varied education matched to the expectation of the times. The life of the school remained consistent until 1937 when there was an attempt to remove senior pupils and send them to Hatherleigh. From 1945 the older pupils travelled to Okehampton for their secondary education.

The school was declared Voluntary Controlled in 1984 and the church still plays an important part in the life of the school. Since 1945 it has functioned as a 5–11 primary school and currently has 42 pupils. Many of the village traditions continue but there are no longer holidays for the hunt meet, the church festivals or chapel anniversaries! The curriculum has changed beyond recognition with the introduction of the National Curriculum, literacy and numeracy initiatives, the use of computers and video cameras. The school log-books show that inspection reports always reveal cycles of improvement and decline. However, 2002 finds the school in good heart as this report of the latest inspection demonstrates.

From the *Okehampton Times* May 2001:

*Above average standards and good quality teaching are two of the aspects of Northlew and Ashbury Primary School which have been praised in an OFSTED report. The school was described as having made significant improvements since it was last inspected in January 1997. Inspectors concluded that overall the standards were above average and the majority of the pupils achieved well in relation to their prior attainment.*

*The quality of teaching was good and teachers provided a high level of care, they said. Headteacher Nicola Lampe was absolutely delighted with such a positive report and particularly the rating of 100% satisfactory or better for the teaching. This is a rare accolade from OFSTED.*

### *List of Headteachers*

| | |
|---|---|
| Mr John Mills | 1867–86 |
| Mr W. Heard | 1886–90 |
| Mr Webber | 1890–94 |
| Mr F.G. Turville | 1894–95 |
| Mr A.H. Venton | 1895–1900 |
| Mr Baldry | 1900–15 |
| Mr Newman | 1915–39 |
| Mr Davies | 1939–42 |
| Mr Hamlin | 1942–44 |
| Mr Lane | 1944–45 |
| Mr Gerry | 1945–47 (Acting) |
| Mr Gerry | 1947–59 |
| Mr Forward | 1959–64 |
| Mr J.E.N. Molesworth | 1964–68 |
| Mr E. Thorn | 1968–87 |
| Mrs S. Jones | 1988–92 |
| Mr P. Southcott | 1990 (Acting, summer term) |
| Mrs C. Pitt | 1992 (Acting, summer term) |
| Mrs S. Kingston | 1992–96 |
| Mr T. West | 1996 (Acting) |
| Mrs J. Matthews | 1996–98 |
| Mrs N. Lampe | 1998–2000 (Acting) |
| Mrs N. Lampe | 2000 |

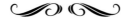

# Extracts taken from original documents

## *1867 The First Week*
### 21 January

*The Northlew Parochial School opened this morning. Admitted 26 scholars in the morning and 2 in the afternoon. The number seeking for admittance would have been greater had not the weather been so very severe and rough. The books and other apparatus not having arrived I questioned the children on several subjects, to find out extent of their knowledge. In the afternoon Miss Vanstone, who is to be the sewing mistress, and also the teacher of the little children, lent me some school books, so with oral teaching I think I can carry on the school until the new apparatus and books arrive.*

*The School Fees vary in the amount and time of payment. First Class Farmers pay 10 shillings per quarter in advance for their children, unless they have three at the school when the third is admitted on 6 shillings per quarter...*

*Second Class or Small Farmers or Tradesmen pay 6 shillings per quarter for their children... Labourers children pay 2d. a week, when there is a second child it is admitted for 1d. a week and so with a third or fourth.*

### 22 January

*Admitted 10 children. Divided the school as far as possible into three classes. Gave the first class a grammar lesson.*

### 24 January

*Miss England visited the school and took a part of the third class in reading. I gave the 1st and 2nd classes a lesson on Geography, Miss England having sent the school a map of the World, a map of England and a map of the Travels of St. Paul.*

### 26 January

*The books and apparatus arrived today. The following were obtained from The Society for Promoting Christian Knowledge. 24 Bibles, 50 Church Catechisms, 24 Common Prayer Books, 18 Histories of England, 12 English Grammars, 24 Scriptural lessons, 97 Reading Books Standard I to V. The following books and apparatus were obtained from the National Society. 1 Black Board with 2 easels, 1 Binn's Register of Enrolment and Withdrawal, 3 Class Registers... 1 Sunday School Register, 30 Clay Ink Wells, several dozen slates 4d. per dozen, 6 dozen plain ruled Copy Books... 1 Box of Pens, 1 Gross of Pen Holders, 1 Box of Slate Pencils, Half Gross of Slate Pencil Holders, 1 Box of Prepared Chalk.*

## *1868*
### 30 September Punishment

*Had to punish several this morning for not being able to say their Home Lessons which for the last few days have been badly said. Cautioned the whole school with regard to this matter and also with regard to the arrival of many of them after Prayers in the mornings, thus disturbing the School Work.*

### 6 May Employment

*The Honourable Edward B. Portman, Assistant Commissioner, visited the school this morning for the purpose of obtaining information relative to the Employment of Children, Young Persons and Women in Agriculture for which a Royal Commission was issued in 1867.*

### 14 December Sums

*The Venerable Archdeacon Woollcombe and Mr England visited the school this morning. Standard V had a lesson in the four simple rules (Avoirdupois Weight). Standard VI one on Multiplication by three figures.*

## *1870*
### 3 March

*Holiday owing to Ploughing Match taking place.*

### 12 March

*School broke up at 11.15 this morning – it being a meet of the Hounds in the village.*

### 6 September

*Being Hatherleigh Fair day several of the children were absent. Work proceeded as usual.*

31 pupils in the late 1800s.

Right: *Perhaps the earliest school group photograph taken before Mr Baldry arrived, when Mr Venton was schoolmaster.*

Higher class in about 1910.

*School play, c.1910.*

Above: *Maypole dancers, church festival, 1920.*

Above left: *Maypole dancers, rectory grounds, 1910.*

Left: *A group photograph taken early in Mr Newman's time at the school.* Left to right, back row: *Char. Medland, Cyril Voaden, John Maynard;* fourth row: *Lillian Friend, Vera Pascoe, Hilda Heggadon, ?;* third row: *?, Dorothy Pascoe, Ethel May, Lottie Styles, Mary Heggadon, Edie Rees;* second row: *?, Laurie Horne, ?, Phyllis Rees, Emily May, Esther Leach, Lillian Sanders, W. Adams, Frank Eastcott, Louis Medland;* front row: *?, ?.*

## 1876
### 15 July Inspection Report

*This school has passed a creditable examination in the subjects of the Standards and in Grammar and Geography. Needlework is good. There are tendencies among the children to talk during their work and to look over the slates of others, which the master ought to use every effort to repress. The means of ventilation must be brought more under the control of the teacher. The classroom ought to be provided with a gallery for the Infants.*

## 1886
### Samples of work for week beginning 3 November

*Taught children "The Echo Round". Standard IV taught Compound Multiplication by factors.*
*Read story to Standards VI and VII for reproduction on slates.*
*Scripture time this week devoted to Church Catechism.*
*Song taught "A Happy Band".*
*Standard IV Compound Multiplication by 3 & 4 figures.*

## 1890
### 14 July Summary H.M.I. Report

*The school has suffered in the early part of the year from changes in the staff and in latter part from illness. The consequence is that I am unable to report much improvement. I think, however, there is good promise. The lower part of the school is in a creditable state of efficiency; the third standard however is exceptionally bad. Reading is a point that needs much attention. I have, under the circumstances, again classed the school as good… The infants' class is in excellent order and very well taught.*

### 15 December Impetigo and Itch

*The Christmas Holidays commenced. The reason for breaking up so early is that Impetigo is very prevalent amongst the children and there are numerous cases of "Itch".*

## 1891
### 11 March Snow

*A great snowstorm commenced on Monday afternoon (the 9th) and continued the whole of yesterday when the school was not opened. Today many of the roads are impassable, consequently only 25 children attended this morning and 29 this afternoon.*

## 1895
### 13 November Drunk!

*The Caretaker was not present and no fires were lighted or even laid. Sent for the woman who came at 8.55 partly intoxicated and evidently recovering from an overnight's debauch. She was quite useless so I sent her home and set a lad to light the fires. I shall bring the woman's conduct before the Committee…*

### 14 November

*I called at Caretaker's house. She was in a fearful condition, face broken, eyes black etc. had been run over while lying in the road in a drunken condition. She is quite unable to perform her duties.*

## 1897
### 23 July Accident

*William Tapp, a boy in the 5th Standard, was charging an alarm gun in the game covers at Lambert last Tuesday (20th) when the weapon exploded in his face. His eyes are injured and his face simply riddled with gunpowder. I saw him today and he will be unable to attend for some time.*

## 1901
### Report on the Mixed School

*The school is conducted with zeal and fairly well taught but the work should reach a higher standard in intelligence and knowledge. The Time Table is not well drawn up and the literary side of the scholars' education does not receive adequate attention. The children, too, are timid, and respond but feebly when orally questioned, otherwise the order is satisfactory.*

## 1911
### 14 September  Report from H.M.I.

*The discipline and general behaviour are very good. Both teachers and children are in earnest, the methods of instruction are good and the work of the children is intelligent and accurate. The value of the teaching in Arithmetic would be increased if more attention were paid to short methods of calculation. Drawing deserves special mention. With a little more attention to foreshortening and light and shade some excellent work will be done. In the Infants class the methods of instruction are good, the children are bright and happy, and the general progress is quite satisfactory.*

## 1915
### 21 June  Outbreak of Measles

*Only 52 present this morning. Measles seem to be spreading.*

### 23 June

*After sending 6 children home this morning it left only 26 (29%). Dr. Young called and closed the school till 12th July.*

### 12 July

*The M.H.O. has ordered the school to be closed for another fortnight. Measles still very prevalent.*

### 26 July

*School reopened this morning.*

## 1916
### 7 May  War Support and Normal Life

*The children brought to me the sum of eleven shillings and eight pence for the sick and wounded.*

### 24 May

*Empire Day. Children brought me 16 shillings for the Overseas Club. Tobacco for the soldiers.*

## 1918
### 15 March  Dig For Victory

*A piece of land for a school garden was acquired and 14 boys detailed to work it under the timetable heading "Handwork".*

### 7 May

*Seed potatoes for school garden arrived last evening. The boys will devote the last hour each afternoon this week, weather permitting, to planting them.*

### 25 October

*5 of the upper boys spent one and a half hours lifting potatoes.*

### 7 June  Off To War

*I, Percy Harry Newman, relinquish my duties temporarily, in this school this afternoon having been called up to join the colours.*

## 1921
### 21 April  School Holidays

*Mr Dufty proposed and Mr Pellow seconded that the suggestion of Mr Newman be accepted:*
*½ day for club, 1 day for chapel anniversary, ½ day for chapel Garden Party, 1 day for Church Festival, Whit break, 4 weeks in August.*

## 1927
### Diocesan Report

*There is an atmosphere of quiet reverence and deep sincerity about the religious teaching in this excellent Church School. The work has been most thoroughly and carefully done and the spiritual welfare of the children is well looked after. In all three groups there is a happy atmosphere. The children show keen interest and are closely attentive. They were well*

*School group, 1926.* Left to right, back row: *Percy Bater, Dick Branch, Percy Curtis, Eric Moyse, Tom Adams, Jack Rees;* third row: *Sid Newcombe, Beat Davey, Margaret Hortop, Hilda Brooking, Fran Lake, Nell Andrew, May Squires, Les Gratton;* second row: *Frank Curtis, Eleanor Davey, May Lake, Dot Squires, Florrie Curtis, Kath Curtis, Isalene Davey, Viola Lake, Queenie Brooking;* front: *Clar Andrew, Lew Gratton, Archie King, Maurice Squires, Stan Newcombe, Ron Moyse, Percy Adams.*

*School group, 1928/9.*

*School group, 1930s.*

*Early 1930s.* Left to right, back row: *Raymond Hicks, Priscilla Fry, ?, Barbara Hucker, Cecil Brooking;* third row: *Claude Smale, Bill Elliott, Cecil Saunders, Audrey Worden, Joan Squires, ?, Pete Wood, Redvers Moyse, Ben Dufty;* second row: *Vera Brooking, Lillain Moyse, Dorothy Worden, ?, Ruby Leach, Joyce Wichett, Hilary Adams, ?;* front: *?, ?, Tom Andrew, Ernie Hicks, ?, Don Hucker, Charles Hicks.*

*School group, 1936.*

*School group in 1938 with Miss Hortop.* Left to right, back row: *Alec Luxton, Vera Brooking, Elsie Lake, Beryl Adams, Vera Leach, Doreen Evely, Lilian Bater, Stanley Madge;* centre: *Bill Penberthy, ? Harris, Olive Hicks, Violet Voaden, Gladys Friend, Mary May, John Spry;* front: *Tom Andrew, ? Harris, Bob Born, Leslie Curtis, Frank Frost.*

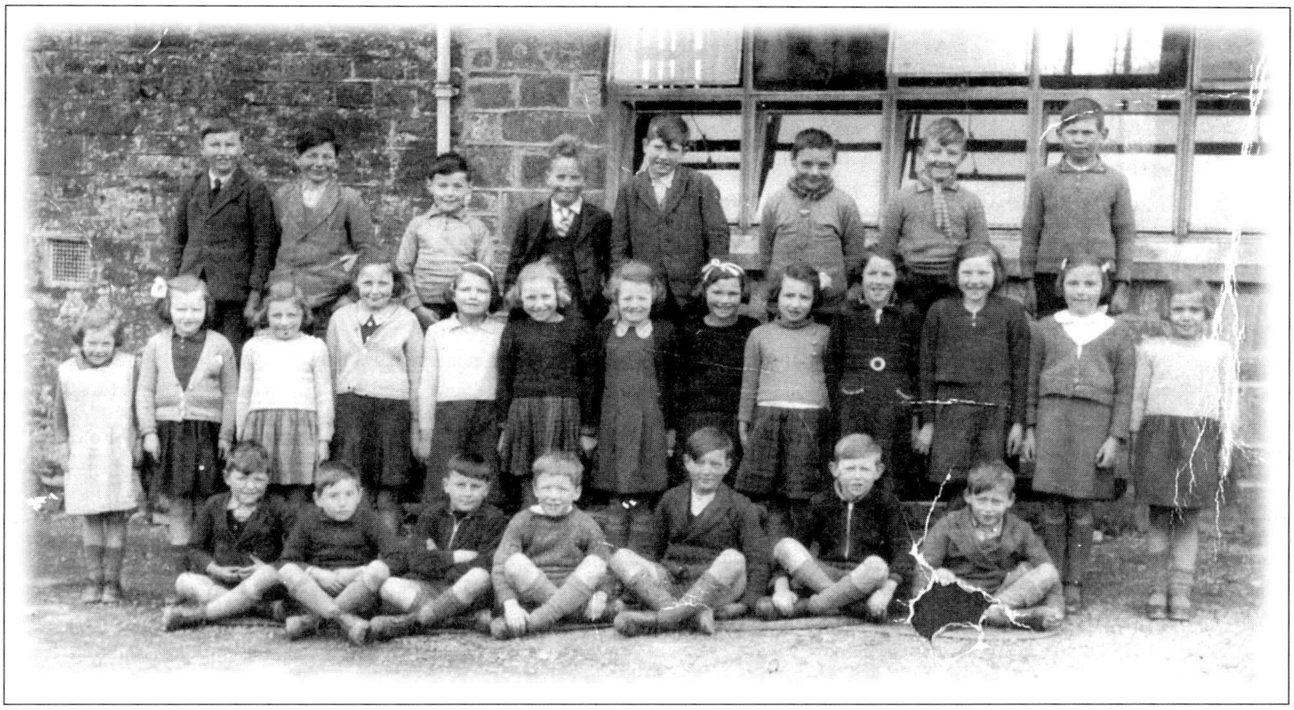

*School photograph, 1940.* Left to right, back row: *Fred Evely, Charlie Gay, Frank Frost, Dick Wickett, Francis Webber, Leslie Curtis, Bill Pemberthy, Alex Luxton;* centre: *Joan Harris, Doreen Evely, Faith ?, Valerie Vorden, Sal Dufty, Beryl Adams, Lilian Bater, Vera Brooking, Vera Leach, Elsie Lake, Hilary Adams, Lillian Moyse, Olive Hicks;* front: *Leonard Worden, Colin Squires, Tom Andrews, Bob Born, Leonard ?, John Spry, ? Harris.*

Left: *School group, 1938.*

***Mr Gerry and Mrs Effie Wood sit in the middle outside the school.***

*informed as to details and they have a sound background of general religious knowledge. The answers were readily and intelligently given and there was a general level of efficiency, which can only be the result of steady and systematic teaching. The general attitude of the children was most pleasing.*

### 1930
### 30 March Use of the Church Room

*The Government and County Inspectors visited the Church Room to see if it would be possible to convert it into a Senior Department.*

### 8 April Recommendations

*The Inspectors strongly urged the Managers to…*
*Clear glass to be inserted into windows.*
*Two wood hoppers to be fitted into the existing framework.*
*Bars to be fitted across. Tops to be made to swing.*
*Benches, platform, curtain rods to be removed.*
*Pantry to be built.*
*Ceiling to be whitewashed, and walls repaired.*

### 1931
### September Conversion

*The Church Room was converted into a Senior Department for cookery, joinery, handcraft, and lantern work. The work was carried out at a cost of £193.*

### 1934
### 18 July Report from Mr. Simmons H.M.I.

*The favourable estimate made in the last report still represents the condition of the school. There has been no change of staff: all three teachers work hard, and take a keen interest in the welfare of the children. A very friendly and homely spirit is a distinctive feature of the school.*
*An important development is to be noted. A practical room, quite close to the school, has been suitably equipped, and is now in full use. Here the boys receive instruction in woodwork and handwork… and the girls in domestic subjects… Regular instruction in gardening, mainly in vegetable culture, has been given to the elder boys… A small plot of ground… is tended by the girls, and has been laid out with grass, flowerbeds and a rockery.*

### 1936
### 26 March Bee Keeping

*Commander Dane gave a talk to the scholars on February 19th in the Church Room about bee keeping. The scholars have formed a bee-keeping club affiliated to the Devon Association of Beekeepers. The hives are being made in the Handicraft Department. The girls are making the veils and the bees will be kept in the school garden.*

### 1937

*A proposal to remove senior scholars to Hatherleigh was bitterly fought by the Managers who produced a pamphlet listing the following:*
*The Advantages of the Village School.*
*A garden for the boys and a flower garden for the girls.*
*A wireless set and gramophone. The BBC instructions are received.*
*A lantern with silver screen and darkened room.*
*A microscope for nature study.*
*A Glaxo baby for mothercraft.*
*A Bee Club. The girls made the veils and the boys the hives.*
*Cookery classes once a week.*
*A canteen twice a week.*
*A playing field for exercise, organised games, and athletic sports.*

*We are building a hall in the playing field for use in wet weather, for games and reading, for physical drill and folk dancing, for a gymnasium with ropes and rings and ladders, and for boxing.*
*We are organising evening, recreational and social work.*
*We are starting an Old Boys' Club.*

*A resolution was passed 'That the Northlew Managers are unanimously opposed to the suggestions of the Committee, and refuse to "agree" to the removal of the senior children to Hatherleigh or elsewhere.'*

### 1946
### Extracts from the report of K.G. Gerry, Acting Headmaster

*The school has completed a year free from the upheavals caused by changes of staff... There is evidence that some of the backwardness brought about by overcrowding during the war years and by other war time conditions has been partially remedied.*
*Thirteen children reached the age of 14 years during the year. Of the four boys, three took up agricultural work, while the fourth is learning boot repairing. Of the eight girls, seven took up domestic work or work connected with their parents' farms and one became a shop assistant. Three junior boys... are proceeding to Okehampton Grammar School.*

### 1947

*Miss Hortop resigned after 17 years, replaced by Mrs Hucker for the Infants.*
*Mr. Gerry appointed Headmaster after 2 years as a supply teacher. His wife became kitchen helper at £1.2s.6d. a week. The cook earned £2.5s.9d. a week.*

### 1950s

*The first day Libby Adams, née Newcombe, went to Northlew School she was sent in a taxi, driven by Mrs Mary Worden, from her home at Horrathorne farm. She was very upset as she did not know she would have to stay all day, so was allowed to play with a doll. Gerald Maynard used to share the taxi from Gorhuish.*

### 1952
### 6 February Death of the King

*Special prayers were said and the school stood in silence as a token of respect for our King George VI, who passed away during last night.*

### 15 February Memorial Service

*A Memorial Service consisting of hymns, prayers, scripture reading and two minutes silence on the occasion of the funeral of King George VI has been held today at 1.50pm. The whole school joined in.*

### 1953
### 29 March Coronation

*The school is closed for one week from today to commemorate the coronation of Her Majesty Queen Elizabeth II. During the present term a great deal of time has been given to making preparations and helping the children to understand something of the importance of the occasion... Coronation Day is on 2 June when there will be a United Service, Sports, Tea, Presentation of Souvenir Mugs, Social and Bonfire.*

### 1962
### 26 September Mystery Illness

*After only one child being absent yesterday 17 children were absent today with sickness, which had come over night. I reported the matter to the County Medical Department who took details and said they would inform the local M.O.H. As children who had not taken school dinner were among those sick they did not think the sickness was caused by a food-born germ.*

*School group, 1946/7.*

Below: *May Day celebrations.* Left to right, back row: *Colin Bater, Wendy Bisley, Raymond Gay, Peter Tapp, Reggie Friend, Reggie Voaden, Grace Adams, Gerald Dennis, Frankie Voaden, Geoffrey Setter, Eileen Parker, Jenny Adams, Jean Parker, Selina Crocker, Pat Bisley, Colin Hutchings;* front: *Attendants and Queen, Shirley Bater, Gloria Gay, Ann Mounter.*

***Six photographs taken in the school playground:***

Girls only from left to right, including, background: *Doreen Sanders, Marge Kneebone, Ann Mounter, Cynthia Curtis, Jean Parker, Jennifer Adams, Grace Adams.*

Front row: *Barry Ware, Gerald Dennis, Edward Voaden, Reggie Voaden, Colin Hutchings.*

Left to right, back row: *Maureen Parker, Jennifer Adams, ?, Pearl Bailey, Peter Tapp, Colin Britton;* front: *Gwen Sanders, ?, Reg Jordan, Ernie Curtis, ?, Reggie Friend, Tom Maynard.*

*Jennifer Adams, Jean Parker, Cynthia Curtis, Ann Mounter, Marjorie Kneebone.*

Back row: *Mary Sanders, Ann Mounter, Marjorie Kneebone, ?, ?;* front: *Cynthia Curtis, Selina Crocker, Doreen Sanders, Mary Voaden, Grace Adams.*

*Pearl Bailey, Marjorie Kneebone, Eileen Parker, Ann Mounter, Maureen Parker.*

*Effie Wood with her class.*

Left to right, back row: *Tom Maynard, Winston Martin, Barry Ware, Peter Tapp;* front: *Jennifer Adams, Reggie Friend, Pat Bisley.*

*Ken Gerry with his class.*

Left to right, back row: *Ronnie Mounter, Charles Baker, ?, ?; centre: Gloria Gay, ?, Brenda Curtis, Rachel Ware, ?, Brian Hutchings;* front: *Rosalind Britton, Betty Born, Ken Gerry, Avril Neno, May Dufty.*

Left to right, back row: *Rodney Spry, Ernie Curtis, Tony Squire;* front: *Sylvia Dennis, Margaret Worden, Shirley Bater.*

*School group in 1954 with teachers standing at either end.*

*Maypole dancers, 1959. Libby Adams, née Newcombe, remembers having a new dress every year for the maypole dance. One year she had much coveted new blue shoes to match but they were unfortunately too small and her feet were blistered by the end of the festival, so the shoes had to be passed on to someone else. She, Margaret and Marion Newton spent ages practising for the maypole.*

*Schoolchildren, 1970.* Left to right, back row: *Carol Hunt, Tracy Guscott, Priscilla Friend, Jane Durston, Helen Williamson, Gillian Westcott, Andrew Hutton, Pat Vick;* centre: *Colin Yelland, Paul Adams, Steven Bowden, Janet Hunt, Katherine ?, Peter Short, Roger Wannacott, Peter Bone;* front: *Julian Gratton, Ian Luxton, Nigel Dufty, Nigel Isaac, Gary Baker, Clifford Jordan, Kevin Davey. Julian Gratton particularly remembers when he and several others had the slipper for misbehaving and when Ian Luxton and Clive Voaden played hookey and hid under the bridge in Trump Lane; it was ages before they were found.*

*School group, 1973.* Left to right, back row: *Janice Elliot, ?, Mary Thorn, Christine Hunt, David Eveleigh, John Durston, Kay Adams, Mr Thorn;* centre: *Stephen Alford, Keith Williamson, Alan May, Ian Dixon, David May, Amanda Baker, Anthony Brooking;* front: *Gary Voaden, Christopher Hunt, Sheila Davey, David Westcott, ? Turner, Stewart Adams, Peter Isaac.*

**1964**
**16 October Election**

*The school closed today, whilst the buildings were used as a Polling Station for the Parliamentary General Election. (The Labour Party were returned to power – much to the regret of the majority of the inhabitants of Northlew.)*

**1970**
**6 July**

*Mr Thorne stated that a Bush record player had now been provided by the County Education Department and was proving very useful. Negotiations for the use of the Victory Hall for physical education were still taking place but it was found necessary for the floor to be treated before it could be safely used for this purpose. Julian Gratton recalls the two climbing frames with ropes in the hall. They had to be put away after every session.*

**1973**
**1 August**

*Regarding the old school bell due to be taken down for safety reasons. It was felt that it should be kept for sentimental reasons in a suitable place. The swimming pool (new) was almost ready for use thanks to great help received especially from Mr D. Adams and Mr J. Jordan. There had been a small swimming pool in a courtyard and the new plastic raised pool with a wooden surround was built in the field.*

**1975**
**8 July**

*The school has done exceptionally well in these sports. 1st in the Inter Schools Rounders Tournament and shared first place in the Inter Schools Sports. At the present time there are 75 children on roll. 17 are leaving at the end of term to attend Okehampton Comprehensive School. 8 new children will be admitted next term, making a total of 66.*

**1981**
**23 November**

*The popularity of the new snack bar could be judged by the fact that the number of children bringing packed lunches has fallen to 3 or 4 from 16 to 18. The price of the meal had been reduced by 5p to 45p but the cost of production still had to be 18p per head.*

**1984**
**12 July Number on roll 27**

*Mrs Vick has recently introduced softball tennis and a kit, which includes racquets, balls and a free standing net should be delivered soon. This new attempt to foster the playing of tennis is being sponsored by the Lawn Tennis Association. The kit is being financed from an anonymous donation of £100 received some months ago.*

*I have received a letter from the Exeter Diocesan Education Committee informing me that the Instrument of Government for Voluntary Controlled Schools should come into force on 1st October 1984.*

# Bibliography

## Deeds and Documents

### The school


| | |
|---|---|
| *1705 9 July* | *M. J. Bickle lease of the Church House* |
| *1865 9 August* | *The guardian M.J. Smale* |
| *1865 26 August* | *Mr J. Smale to Mr J. Major* |
| *1865 4 September* | *Mr J. Major to Miss J.H. Woollcombe* |
| *1867 16 January* | *Mr J. Smale to Miss J.H. Woollcombe* |
| *1888 26 November* | *Mr J.D. Woollcombe to Mrs E.R. Woollcombe* |
| *1892 4 October* | *Mr J. Smale to Mrs E.R. Woollcombe* |
| *1903 10 June* | *Mrs E.R. Woollcombe to the Archdeacon of Totnes* |
| | *Archdeacon of Totnes to Diocesan Trust* |

### *The master's house*

| | |
|---|---|
| *1879 25 October* | *J. Wood to J. Blatchford* |
| *1882 21 January* | *J. Blatchford to Miss J. Woolland* |
| *1908 25 March* | *Miss J. Woolland to G. Blatchford* |
| *1902 10 May* | *G.K. Blatchford to Diocesan Trust* |

### *The playing field*

| | |
|---|---|
| *1962* | *Conveyed to the Diocesan Trust* |

| | |
|---|---|
| *School log books* | *Registers* |
| *1867–1901* | *1886–1930s* |
| *1901–65* | |

*Notes of meetings of the school managers*
*1903–44*
*1845–1984*

Billing's Directory *1857*
Post Office Directory *1856*
Kelly's Directory *1873, 1923*
*Pamphlet produced in 1937 to answer proposal to remove senior scholars.*

*School football teams, 1973/4. There was an annual game of football between the boys who lived in the village and the 'outsiders'. Lots of football was played in the playground and the ball regularly went over the wall into Mrs Shobbrook's garden. She would often put her garden fork through it before throwing it back.*

*Hay harvesting in 1920 at Overlake Farm.*

*Chapter 6*

# THE PEOPLE OF THE LAND

## *Introduction*

Farming has always been the principal source of employment for the people of Northlew. In the past a farmer's family were fully involved with the daily running of the farm and worked together in supporting the farmer. Prior to the Second World War there had been little change in farming for 100 years, life moved at a much slower pace and the cycle of nature, as well as the weather, dictated events. Farmers were forced to contend with wind, rain and a heavy clay soil with the threat of poverty and sickness hanging over them.

There was once interdependence between neighbours; now the farmer mostly works alone. In the past men were busy from dawn until dusk and returned to the farmhouse only for meals. The farmer relied heavily on his farm-hand and often servants lived in, helping in the house as well as outside.

Until the 1950s milking was performed by hand, morning and evening. The milk was kept in churns and taken to the end of the farm driveway to be collected each day. Most families kept a 'house cow' to provide milk, butter, cream and cheese for the farm. The apples grown on the land were made into cider and the farmers brewed their own ale.

The farmer's wife worked as hard as anyone on the farm. She was busy all day long – cleaning, cooking and milking, scalding cream and butter making, feeding calves and poultry, pig killing, pickling pork and plucking birds, especially at Christmas time. She kept geese, cockerels and hens; turkeys did not become popular until the late 1950s. Poultry wandered about the farmyard and were only penned at night to protect them from foxes. As well as all this, the farmer's wife was expected to do the mending and washing!

After the Second World War some of the larger farms turned to dairying, attracted by the regular monthly income provided by the Milk Marketing Board. Black-and-white Friesians became a very popular breed and took the place of the old Devon cattle. Herds were improved by breeding from bulls with a good record for butterfat and milk production. The use of AI (artificial insemination) improved the herds still further. With the arrival of the tractor (the blue Fordson and the little grey 'Fergie') life certainly became easier.

There has been a recent downturn in farming fortunes resulting in an increased pressure to be resourceful, which has in turn led to the diversification of many farms. A Farmers' Market has opened in Okehampton where methods appear to have come full circle. Farmers are having to travel and sell directly to the public, just as they did many years ago.

## *Northlew Farms*

### *Goosen*

During the reign of King Henry VI in 1464 one Sibell Bradston held free one tenor in Goosen (at that time spelt Gosseton) for 3s.4d. Claude Smale remembers the many visits he paid to Goosen to visit Jan and Norah Evely who lived there in the 1930s with their son Bill, a man of little communication who was their contact with the outside world. Jan and Norah lived in the past, their door had not opened in years and it was festooned with the tops of pilchard tins, nailed over holes. Jan had his well-worn place by the open fire where he would talk with great animation recalling tales which, if lacking in fact, he certainly made up for with imagination. He wore an enormous striped shirt with Dorset buttons and his cap remained permanently on his head, except when he manoeuvred it to wipe his face or scratch. Jan and Norah died within days of each other. The property was sold to Denny Adams who retained the land and sold Lower Goosen with six acres of land to Kay and Richard Westlake in 1985. Higher Goosen was demolished in the late 1980s.

### *Kimber*

Mentioned in 1086 in the Domesday Book, Kimber was held from the honour of Plympton by the heir of Robert de Brock. The first part of the name is Old English, and means 'warrior' or 'soldier'. Overkymber is recorded in 1464, when 'Free tenants' were held by Sibell Bradston: '1 toft, 1 tenement with appurtenances. 19s. and heriot. The same Sibell holds free 1 messuage in Eastkymbere, 13s.'

The name of Overlake Farm has changed twice in living memory. Known as Middle and Overlake Farm in the early 1900s, it was first changed to Higher East Kimber and finally re-named Overlake Farm in 1980. Even more unusually, two Kimber farms are now known as Lower East Kimber.

*Four generations of the Adams family at Overlake Farm. Henry, John, Jack and Hilary.*

*The Adams family at Kimber Farm.* Left to right, back row: *Grace Adams, William Heggadon, Michael Adams, Jack Adams, Dennis Adams;* front: *Lilian Heggadon, Marian Adams, Florence Adams, Hilary Adams.*

Dennis and Jean Adams are the fourth generation of Adamses to live at Overlake, others being father Jack, grandfather John and great-grandfather Henry.

*Dennis and Michael Adams outside the original Overlake Farm which was burnt down.*

Overlake Farm at Kimber was the childhood home of Hilary Isaac and her younger siblings Dennis, Grace, Michael and Marion. They lived with their parents in the farmhouse which had been built for their grandparents in 1914, replacing the original cob-and-thatched homestead which had been destroyed by fire. A newspaper report of the incident records:

*Middle and Overlake Farm in the occupation of Mr John Adams, has been destroyed by fire. The fire originated in a loft adjoining the house, and containing about 200 bundles of straw, appeared to be due to a defective chimney. The house was very old and thatched. A brisk wind fanned the flames. The fire was discovered by a farm-hand working in the fields near by. The dwelling-house was totally destroyed, also the adjacent outbuildings. Some of the furniture was saved. Okehampton Fire Brigade was sent for, but could not obtain horses.*

*Jack and Dennis Adams carrying a milk churn.*

Jack Adams remembered sleeping in the granary and anxiously anticipating completion of his new home. Dennis Adams recalls:

*Watching my mother bake bread and cakes in the bread oven – she lit the fire, waited for the wood to change colour, raked out the ashes and then the oven was hot enough for baking. I also remember my father taking poultry and milk to Crediton to sell in his brother's shop.*

Hilary Isaac fondly recollects Sunday visits to her maternal grandparents who lived nearby at Lower East Kimber Farm:

*I remember walking up and down all day leading a horse which was working the elevator at hay-making time. Hay was picked up on a sweep and the corn put in stooks to dry before being taken to the rick. It was my job to feed the chickens. My parents had a servant living in called Ethel Madge and some of the workmen also lived in. There always seemed to be lots of people around and large meals being prepared. There was a cider press at my grandparents' house and I remember breaking off straw to drink the cider.*

*Ada Heggadon and her daughter Florence feeding turkeys.*

*Lower East Kimber Farm.*

At the time of writing Lower East Kimber (1) is being farmed by Michael Adams.

Also in 2002, Edward and Stella Hore live at Kimberley (formerly two cottages called Brittans Hay) in the hamlet of farms which make up Kimber. They keep horses and were the instigators of the Northlew Horse Show which has been held every August since the early 1980s.

East Kimber employed a labourer in 1851 to assist Thomas Phare, his wife Jane and their four children to farm 100 acres. John and Selina Glass lived there in 1881 and were followed by Thomas Lake, Roy Britton, George Fox and the Samways.

Thomas Lake had nine children; the youngest, Arnold, remembers his father talking about a thunder bolt hitting the farm: 'It came down the chimney, knocked father off his settle and killed the dog which was sleeping by the fireside. A large crater was left in the garden.' At the time of writing East Kimber is farmed by Maurice Davey.

Slatequarry Farm was built to accommodate the quarry foreman. The name has been changed and it is known as Lower East Kimber (2). The two farms, East Kimber and Lower East Kimber (2) are, in 2002, run as a single unit by George and Maurice Davey. In 1939 a Mr and Mrs Mills lived there and were followed by the Pasco and Atkins families. Mr and Mrs Mills are remembered for taking in three evacuee children during the war, two boys and a girl (Clem, Peggy and Alex Early from London) whose parents didn't want them to be split up.

*Heggadons at Lower East Kimber.*

Seth and Edith Davey came to Higher West Kimber from Woolfardisworthy in 1934 with their three children Eunice, George and Lewis. Lewis continued to live at the farm and is still there at the time of writing.

A previous occupant of the farm, John Bickle (yeoman farmer of 200 acres and devout Bible Christian), married Catherine, the daughter of John and Catherine Watkins of Northlew Manor, in 1823. John Bickle died in 1858 after 40 years of married life. The family then moved to Lower West Kimber and for the next 20 years Catherine lived 'a pious life as a widow enduring deafness, blindness and much suffering besides.'

Lower West Kimber was the home, during the First World War, of William Smallacombe (rabbit trapper). Smallacombe remembered the German prisoners of war being detained at Ashbury Court – they could be heard singing in the evenings. He also remembered his blind grandfather who, when he lived at Whiddon, walked to Kimber by counting the gateways.

A driver called Stanley Newcombe served with the 8th Army in Italy during the Second World War. He lived at Lower West Kimber and joined as a territorial at the outbreak of the conflict. The farm has recently been renovated and in 2002 is the home of Steven and Marie Hill. West Kimber Farm is the home of Tracey and Mark Annette.

## *Loveland Farm*

Loveland Farm is mentioned in church records as early as 1613 and again in 1679 when the acreage was noted as 'about thirty acres'. Various Luxtons lived there for 50 years from 1789.

*Doll and Phillip with Dobbin in 1955.*

Pip Wilson and his parents moved to Loveland Farm in 1954. They bought the farm from a baker named Hockridge who had lived there for 18 months. Korah and Amy Luxton had occupied the farm for the 12 years prior to Hockridge. Originally Pip and his wife Eileen worked a mixed farm but this slowly changed to a dairy enterprise. Pip recalls a frightening incident in the late 1950s when a Meteor jet aircraft came over the farm, out of control. One of the two-man crew bailed out but was unfortunately killed when his parachute failed to open. The remaining airman survived after regaining control of the plane and flying it back to RAF Chivenor. Eileen, who was very popular and much involved in village affairs, died just before Christmas 2001.

## *Norley Farm*

Norley Farm was mentioned in 1663 when it was then called 'Norleighford'. Originally two farms, Norley East was pulled down. Palmers Norley dates back to the seventeenth century. William Gay lived there in 1889 and was allowed to graze his ten bullocks on Hollow Moor. A century or so ago the property was occupied by the Gloyn, Sanders and May families. William May handed the house over to his daughter Emily who lived there with her husband Arthur Bater for many years. Ted and Pat Durston bought the house in 1963 and sold it to Ray Hudson in 1995.

*Thatching at Palmers Norley.*

*Susan and Jane Durston with Bess, 1969.*

### *Worth – East and West*

Several properties make up 'Worth'. East Worth Farmhouse was renovated in the late 1990s and a silver spoon was found in the thatch. This was a customary tradition carried out by superstitious occupants in an effort to ward off witches. Albert George Dennis remembered watching West Worth burn down in the early 1900s. The barn was converted into a house by George Dennis in 1949 and, at the time of writing, is occupied by Steve Thorne and his family. East Worth (once the home of the Bater family) has been the home of Brenda Curtis all her life. She remembers the reed comber arriving with the thresher when the house was due to be thatched with their own wheat reed. Lower Worth, once the home of the Evely family, was situated further down the field, a modern dwelling replaced it in the mid 1990s and in 2002 it is occupied by the Housley family.

Nearby Seccombe Farm was burnt down in the early 1950s.

### *Blackworthy Farm*

Blackworthy Farm, a Domesday settlement, originally had five dwellings. The present thirteenth-century farmhouse is a medieval hall house with smoke-blackened rafters. Part of the manor of Northlew in the seventeenth century, it remained so until 1947.

*East Worth.*

In 1880 the Toms moved in and stayed for half a century. In 1949, Mr and Mrs Bateman sold Blackworthy to Dr Jim McInnes and his wife Betty from Cardiff. The Scottish doctor was soon in demand as a locum in the neighbourhood and was very popular. After Jim died in 1978, Betty continued to live on the farm, driving her familiar 'Mini' to many village activities until the age of 86. Members of the McInnes family still farm at Blackworthy at the time of writing.

### *Crowden Farm*

Andy Brooking is the fourth generation of his family to farm at Crowden Farm ('Crows Hill'). Together with his wife Priscilla and two children,

***The Brooking family outside Crowden Farm, early 1900s.***

he occupies one half of the fourteenth-century farmhouse whilst his parents Cecil and Peggy reside in the other half.

Crowden is now a 110-acre mixed farm, much enlarged from the 37 acres it encompassed in 1851. William Brooking, who had recently returned from diamond mining in South Africa, bought the farm in 1897. He raised eight children there with his wife Amy. Before the Second World War Mabel Brooking and her mother made weekly trips by pony and trap to Okehampton Market in order to sell ducks, cream, eggs and butter.

Crowden Quarry provided stone to build Northlew School and also the wall surrounding Highampton Methodist Graveyard.

### *Greendown Farm*

Greendown Farm is mentioned in the 1346 Feudal Aids as Grendon Green Hill. Greendown has the same later holders as Kimber and was probably part of it. The farmhouse, built in 1859, replaced an earlier one which is thought to have burnt down. A stone dated 1592 built into the present house is believed to have been moved from the earlier dwelling.

*Greendown Farm, 1947. John Spry, Johnny King, Jack Spry and Emanuel Spry.*

In 1919 Emanuel Spry moved from Inwardleigh to rent Greendown Farm with its 140 acres for £30 per year. He was well served by Johnny King who, over 54 years, worked for three generations of the Spry family. Riding to work on his pony 'Blackberry' he was also a rabbit trapper and cared for the rectory garden. At Devon County Show in 1964, Johnny was awarded the show's principal award for long service; his employers said that 'he could turn his hand to anything'.

Korah Luxton returned from the First World War and worked at Greendown for many years. He was kept busy caring for seven or eight horses which worked the farm until 1946.

*What a beast! Korah Luxton, Johnny King and Emanuel Spry at Greendown Farm.*

Emanuel Spry died in 1956 and was succeeded by his son Jack who died in 1967, the farm then passing to John and Lilian. In 1995 the property was sold to Paul and Victoria Griffiths who moved from Hertfordshire with their two sons.

### *Whiddon*

The name Whiddon means 'Wheat Hill' and has been spelt in various ways. Two farms are called Lower Whiddon. Lower Whiddon (1) was the home of the Bickle family in 1818. The house was always open to visiting clergymen. James Bartlett, who travelled in the Circuit in 1842, described lodging under their hospitable roof and the lovely society at Whiddon at that time. The Evangelist James Thorne recalls his 40-year friendship with John Bickle, the eldest son of the family. John later married Catherine Watkins of Northlew Manor and moved to Higher West Kimber Farm.

In 1839 John and Catherine Bickle gave the land on which Whiddon Chapel was built and it was opened on Christmas Day in that year. John and Catherine's eldest son John, together with his wife Hariet, farmed at Lower Whiddon. In 1886, while the chapel was being renovated, they lent one of their barns in order that services could continue.

The farm was occupied by the Bater family from 1902 until 1921. Shortly after their arrival the house was destroyed by a fire which is thought to have started when the oak lintel above the fireplace caught alight. The adjoining stables were also affected and it was necessary to cut the horses free.

The Smallacombe family moved there in 1921. George, who lived until he was 93 years old, was blind but he would walk from Whiddon to Kimber by counting the gateways. His son William George Voaden Smallacombe succeeded him, followed by his grandsons William, Fred, George and Stanley. Celia and John Sturgeon live at Lower Whiddon in 2002.

Across the lane was Home Farm occupied in 1881 by Alexander Breyley, his wife Elizabeth and two children, Karen and Alexander. Alexander took over the farm from his father but remained unmarried. The building is now derelict.

In 1851 Lower Whiddon (2) was farmed by Emanuel and Jane Spry and they had 319 acres (the same amount as was farmed by James and Ann Jodan who lived there in 1881).

The Luxton family moved to Whiddon in 1902. Korah Paige Luxton and his wife Susannah died in their 80s and their son Korah and grandson Edward continued to farm at Higher Whiddon. Edward recalled the day when they moved with all their furniture on a horse-drawn cart. He and his wife Lucy had six children. Sadly one was stillborn and two, Austin and Gwendoline, died before they were a year old. Their two sons, Harold and Walter Luxton, gave the land for a car park to be built at Whiddon Chapel when Higher Whiddon Farm was sold on the death of their brother Charles. Whiddon Chapel was demolished in 1998.

*Kenneth Smallacombe, Henry Luxton, Walter Luxton, Harold Luxton. Last service at Whiddon Chapel.*

## Durdon Cross Farm

Durdon Cross Farm was once two cottages. One was occupied in 1851 by Henry and Alice Woodman and three children, while in the other cottage lived John Andrews, a thatcher, with his son, also John. Alfred Worden (rabbit trapper) lived there during the 1920s. He would buy the trapping rights from local farmers, set the traps in the hedges and revisit frequently to find out if he had been lucky. Any unfortunate rabbits would be gutted, braced into pairs and put in crates of 24. Then with horse and jingle Alfred would take them to Ashbury Station to catch a train to the London markets. His reward for all this was 8d. (3p) per rabbit. Alfred's son Keith later took over. At the time of writing Durdon Cross is farmed by Trixie and Viv Hannaford.

*Charles May of Heath Farm.*

## Durdon Farm

Charlie Smale, whose family had been tenants at Durdon Farm from the 1830s, purchased the property in the early 1960s. Always farmed traditionally, it now enjoys organic status and has been owned by Geoffrey and Jo Seccombe since 1989. Formerly known as Derrydon (Dairydown?) the cob-and-thatch house and barns date back to the 1660s. In the 1920s Durdon was occupied by Mrs Smale and her sons Lewis, Ernie and Tom. There were two daughters (Amy and Lydia) who were always referred to as 'the maids'. Lewis and his sisters bought the farm for £1,300 in 1934.

In 1991 mesolithic and neolithic flint microliths and arrowheads were found in newly-ploughed land (verified by Exeter Museum).

## Heath Farm

Heath (Heathe) Farm dates back to 1616. Originally comprising three rooms and a through passage, the lower end was a shippon in the nineteenth century. Heath had mullion windows, large rooms, oak beams and a curved stone staircase.

In 1927 Charles May and his brother Fred rented Heath from the Ashbury estate. They farmed together until 1931 when both got married and Fred left Northlew. Charles and his wife Lillian brought up their two children, Mary and John, at the farm. Charles May had been captured in the First World War in Gallipoli. He went on to live until 1994, by which time he was 96 years old. A keen outdoor type, he was seen walking the lanes until six months before his death, waving one of his two sticks in a cheery gesture to anyone he met along his way.

John and Margaret May raised their three sons David, Allen and Brian at Heath and still farm there in 2002.

### *Millcombe Down*

Millcombe Down was once part of the Ashbury estate and the deeds prior to 1863 were destroyed when Ashbury House burnt down. The spelling has changed several times; the earliest record is from 1464: 'Johanna Sher, diverse parcels of land which were lately held of Richard Sher 1 Melcombdon.' In 1827 George Weeks, yeoman, bequeathed Millcombe Down to his daughter.

Until fire struck in the 1940s the house (thought to date from the seventeenth century) and two adjoining cottages were thatched. After that the house was slated and the cottages destroyed. One of Millcombe Down's more colourful occupants was Thomas Glass who paid £505 for the property. A superstitious man, he wore a twitchet or withy bean around his neck, day and night, to protect himself against the evil power of witches. He died on 26 May 1890 leaving the farm in trust for his son upon reaching the age of 21. To his wife Ann (who was 25 years his junior) he left only £20 – 'if she accepted the terms of his will.' Presumably, if she didn't, she got nothing and had to leave!

In 1920 Jack, Alf, Beatrice and Florence Gratton retired from Scobchester and resided at Millcombe Down for 26 years. It was from here that Alfie Crapp operated his milk round in the 1950s. John and Janet Chapman bought the property from Dr Frank Williamson in 1993.

### *Lambert*

Records of subsidy rolls (various taxpayers' lists from the 1200s until 1689) reveal that in 1333 Lambert was called Lamford, meaning the lamb's ford.

An account of the fire at Lambert in 1912 describes a catalogue of disasters which began with calling the Fire Brigade. The firemen were summoned by the ringing of a large bell affixed to St James' Tower in Okehampton. So great was the captain's enthusiasm that, after a few moments' ringing, the bell parted company with its supports and went flying. After further efforts to contact his men the engine started out with only the captain and one member of the regular Brigade on board. The remainder were volunteers, and the enthusiastic captain departed with his somewhat 'scratch crew'. On arrival at Lambert the only water supply was found to be a small stream about a quarter of a mile away. Willing helpers assisted the Brigade to bring a supply to the fire. By this time the flames had got a firm hold on the main building, and the firemen turned their attention to the stables and outbuildings. The furniture was removed from the house in time. After nearly four hours' hard work the house was practically burnt to the ground.

Lambert was rebuilt by the Woollcombes and used as a shooting lodge. During the war a plane crashed there; tragically all the crew were killed.

Mr and Mrs Croysdale rented Lambert from the Smales of Durdon Farm from the late 1920s until after the Second World War. Lt Col John Croysdale, the tenant's son, who at the time of writing is aged 92, recalls:

*After the war Lewis Smale, who had inherited Lambert, offered it to my father, complete with land, for £2,500. Unfortunately, my father was unable to take up the offer. Father could have stayed on as a sitting tenant, but left and went to live with friends.*

### *Eastcott*

Eastcott (Estcote), mentioned in Domesday in 1086, was probably the home of Jordan de Estkote. Lower Eastcott was the home of Mr Bert Jordan who was killed whilst riding his pedal cycle in the early 1940s, when he collided with a policeman from Hatherleigh. His son John married Stella Friend of Wadland Barton, Ashbury. Higher Eastcott, a thatched Devon farmhouse, is now owned by Nicholas and Gillian Chettle who run a dog-training centre and let three self-catering cottages.

### *South Yeo*

South Yeo, meaning 'South of the Water', lies south of the River Lew. It is mentioned in 1464 when Henry Wadland held a tenement in 'Southyeo'. For most of the 1900s West South Yeo was the home of the Duftys. At the time of writing Ben Dufty still lives nearby and is employed as a spear-maker for the thatcher. East South Yeo was, for many years, the home of the Blatchford family.

### *Milltown Farm*

Domesday records in 1086 identify a Walter Nicholl as having paid rent of 2s. by suit of court and heriot. Milltown Farm is a typical Devon

*Lower Eastcott. Sophie Smale and her son Horace.*

*The roundhouse at West South Yeo.*

longhouse which originally had a cobbled floor. There was a saw-mill at Milltown whilst further down the valley at Lew Mill there was a corn-mill. In 1851, Thomas Friend and his wife Mary were listed as living at Milltown with their 11 children. Their second son John married Harriet Short and became innkeeper and butcher at the Honeychurch Arms, Northlew.

Heber Squire bought the property for £1,800 together with adjoining Blonaford Farm for

*Aerial view of Milltown Farm, 27 February 1996.*

£500 from the Ashbury estate in 1918. A Mrs Wooldridge lived at Blonaford and was frequently seen going up to the village in her pony and trap. Sam Squire and his family were the last occupants of Blonaford before it fell down. The roundhouse still remains.

When they went to live at Milltown, Rhoda and Heber had three children called May, Dorothy and Maurice (who was two years old). As well as helping on the farm, Rhoda used to make butter and cream to sell.

Maurice and Phyllis Squire moved from Lower Southcombe with their son Tony in 1947 and remained at Milltown until their retirement in 1968. Tony and his wife Ruth run the farm at the time of writing; they have two sons and a daughter.

### Gorhuish

Gorhuish appears variously as Gohewis (1086 Domesday), Gorehiwiss (Book of Fees 1242), Gorhywys (1285) and Gorhiwishe (1378), meaning 'dirty ground or estate'.

Between 1914 and 1923 Higher Gorhuish (Wood Tenement), now called Wood St David, was the home of Walcott Medland and his wife, who was an invalid after falling in the fire.

Fred and Florrie Smale moved to Higher Gorhuish in 1924 and lived there with their children Phyllis, Edna, Francis, Vera, John and Ernie. Tragically their lives were changed when the youngest baby, Charlie, was born. Septicaemia set in and their mother never recovered; she died aged 40. Phyllis, still only 13 years old, took on the role of mother to the family and was helped by Lily Wooldridge.

Phyllis (Squires) recalls walking every weekday from Gorhuish to Northlew School. The journey to Sunday School was made a little easier by Mrs May of Rocky Cottage who made yeast buns to give to the children on their way home.

Palmers Gorhuish, a cottage which was situated near the present milking parlour, burnt down.

*Aerial view of* (left) *Howards Gorhuish and* (right) *Wood St David, 1974.*

*Hilda and Fred Rowe with Frank Ware on a tractor at Higher Gorhuish Farm.*

*Mark Rundle at Higher Gorhuish Farm.*

Another cottage, Palor, was sited on the lane opposite Prators. Frank and Hilda Rowe moved there in 1934. Hilda was a regular at Okehampton Market where she sold her produce. Her nephew, Fred Rundle, and his family continue to farm there today. Wood St David has been modernised and in 2002 is the home of Chris and Val Mathews and their daughter, Heather.

Howards Gorhuish was occupied by members of the Smale family for many years until William Worden returned from the First World War and lived there with his wife Ada and their three children William, May and Henry. Ada left after the death of her husband in 1974 and went on to celebrate her 100th birthday. The seventeenth-century house still retains many of its original features and has been extended into what was animal housing. The owners at the time of writing are Paul and Heather Richards.

Lower Gorhuish was, until recently, a guest-house run by Ellen Bryan and her late husband, John. Their son Peter and his wife Angela operate Bryan Haulage from the premises at the time of writing, residing nearby in their bungalow 'Woodlands'.

John Lovell who lived at Lower Gorhuish between 1914 and 1930 shot himself in an unfortunate accident when handling his gun. The Hawkins family farmed there during the war, housing evacuee children and Land Army girls.

### *Horrathorne*

In 1249 Horrathorne was known as Harrathorn, 'The Boundary of Thorn'. It was about 300 yards from the parish boundary. Earliest records of Horrathorne date from 1108 when it was owned by the De Clares. It is thought that the original house may have fallen down at the end of the fourteenth century and a new house erected in the 1600s. It is a typical longhouse with an original external stone spiral staircase.

***Stan Newcombe.***

The Kimber family lived at Horrathorne for around 50 years until Percy Adams bought the property. Phyllis Squires has happy memories of visiting Hariet Adams (Percy's mother) every Christmas. A brother, Fred, was born blind but he could play the piano accordion. Stan and Phyllis Newcome bought the farm and lived there for 18 years with their daughters Libby and Margaret before retiring to Okehampton. In 2002 Horrathorne is farmed by Peggy and Edward who have plans to diversify into the tourist industry.

### *Cruft*

At one time Higher and Lower Cruft were all one farm. A Bible Christian chapel was built at Lower Cruft in 1850 by Jonas Squire. It served the area until 1892 when a fire at the farmhouse made it necessary for the chapel to be used as a dwelling. The farmhouse was eventually rebuilt but the chapel never opened again.

*Adrian Dennis harvesting at Lower Cruft Farm.*

Once part of the Ashbury estate, Lower Cruft was sold in 1934, again to the Squire family who farmed there until the mid 1950s. 'Blackie' and Lilian Voaden lived there until 1959 when the property was sold to George and Irene Dennis who farmed until handing over to their son Adrian.

A seventeenth-century cottage built beside what used to be a cart track, Higher Cruft was once a single-storey house. Interestingly it has its own schoolroom which was built in the late 1800s. The Shobbrook brothers lived at Higher Cruft but sold up in 1919 when they decided to go their separate ways. The farm reverted to the Squire family until 1955 when the Guscott family arrived. The house now has six acres and is used for equestrian purposes by the Russells.

Ivan and Christine Guscott moved to the cottage now known as Cruft Gate Farm. Croft Bungalow, built in 1913, is, at the time of writing, being worked as a mixed farm by the third generation of the same family. James 'Reggie' Vincent bought the farm from the Shobbrook brothers in 1919 and it is now being farmed by his granddaughter Pat Hutton and her husband Philip.

### *Waterhouse Farm*

Clive Voaden bought Waterhouse Farm in 1991 and over the following two years modernised it. The barn opposite was converted into living accommodation and is now the home of Bunt and Sheila Voaden.

Clive's great-grandparents Stephen and Frances Voaden lived at Waterhouse. Not of the same religious persuasion, on a Sunday evening they would walk up Harper's Hill together and then go their separate ways. Stephen was a devout Methodist whilst Francis, who was a member of Northlew Church Choir, sometimes sang in Exeter Cathedral.

Dating back to 1330 Waterhouse Farm was once the home of Alice dete Watere from whom the name is derived.

### *Shorts Farm*

Shorts Farm is now part of the 'Stewardship Agreement Scheme'. Since moving from Dolton in 1991, Douglas and Elizabeth Dwyer have kept horses and geese on their 18 acres. Home to the endangered marbled white butterfly, the land has been organically farmed since 1995. George Jordan and his wife Mary lived at the property for 30 years from the 1920s and made their living from scrap-metal dealing and refuse collecting with a horse and cart.

### *Scobchester Farm*

Scobchester Farm was mentioned in Domesday and 'held in the honour of Plympton'. Escob seems to be an unrecorded personal name. 'Chester' indicates a fort but no trace of a fort has been found in the area. The spelling of

*Scobchester Farm, Edward Addison with two aunts.*

*Happy event at Southcombe Farm. Bart Parker, Pip Wilson and his daughter Katherine a YFC member.*

Scobchester appears in 1500. The present farmhouse was built in 1866. William Maynard Gratton lived there in 1914 and by 1920, Jack, Alfie, Beatrice and Florence Gratton were living at Scobchester prior to their retirement at Millcombe Down. The farm was sold by the Ashbury estate in 1935 and subsequently rented to various tenants (Blight, Beasey, Penfolds and Small).

In 1950 Edward and Mary Addison, together with their children, Tom, Mary, Josephine and Edward, farmed there until the property was sold to Robert and Ruth Colbear and their four children. Josephine and Edward still live at Scobchester in a bungalow which was built in the paddock.

## *Village Farms*

Churchgate Farm almost became derelict a few years ago but it has since been sympathetically restored by Ted Durston. It is now as it was in 1810. The house, with its cob walls and thatch, stands to the left of the lych-gate. It has a through passage and previously had a stone staircase and mullioned windows. In the early 1930s John and Polly Friend farmed Churchgate and operated their milk round from a box fixed onto an old pram frame.

James 'Reggie' and Blanche Vincent left Croft Farm in 1934 and went to live at Churchgate. There was always a brisk sale at Christmas when people came to buy their poultry for the festivities. Milk was bottled daily and taken across the Square to the school in readiness for the eleven o'clock break.

Cyril and Freda Voaden lived at Bolland Farm for 70 years until their deaths in 1970. It was here that they brought up their six children – Stephen, Richard, Frank, William (Bunt) and twins Mary and Edward. Frank Voaden and his wife Maureen continued the hard work and are now in partnership with their son Gary. Records of the farm date from 1581 when it was known as 'Boueland' (a curved piece of land). The original house burnt down. At the time of writing, Gary and his family occupy the stone farmhouse which was built in the early 1900s.

A Victorian farmhouse, Eastacombe Farm was built in 1862 by William Smale, replacing the previous dwelling. The name means 'east of the valley'. Eastacombe was occupied by William Smale at the time of the Census in 1881 and it continued to be occupied by members of the Smale family for many years. In 1962 Henry and Mary Dennis bought the farm. At the time of writing, the land is farmed by their daughter Shirley and her husband Tim. The farmhouse was sold in 1991.

Lower Southcombe has been the home of Bart Parker for the past 23 years. Records reveal that it was once spelt 'Southecumb'. In the early 1930s Harry Middleton kept horses there for pulling timber out of the woods at the Ashbury estate.

Fanny Bessie Smale (widow of John Smale) occupied half of the house in the 1940s while her son Tom and his wife Theresa lived in the other half. Fanny lived until she was 83 years old and a year before her death she donated a piece of land to the church, in memory of her husband and son, thereby extending the churchyard.

Phyllis Squires' grandfather, 'Butcher Martin', lived at Higher Southcombe. On a Saturday night it was his custom to give any left-over meat to the needy people of the village. During the winter of 1963 a helicopter landed in a field at Higher Southcombe to airlift Ruth Packer to hospital; she was about to have a baby.

*View of the cross and Church Gate Farm taken 1909.*

# The Wadland Murder

**An extract from a poem written by Jonas Squire of Cruft, born 1799, died 1878.**

*Good people all I pray give ear*
*To these few lines I write.*
*'Tis of a horrid deed was done*
*Happened on Monday night.*

*The nineteenth of March as you shall hear,*
*Eighteen hundred and twenty seven,*
*In Ashbury Parish on Wadland Down*
*There this fatal blow was given.*

*It's of a little boy we find*
*About thirteen years of age*
*And a young woman Aunt to him,*
*Both left this earthly stage.*

*'Twas by a cruel murderer's hand*
*The blood of both was spilt,*
*Who now before the Judge must stand*
*To answer for his guilt.*

*Before the murder he had done*
*He was of good report.*
*He seldom to the alehouse went*
*And gambling did resent.*

*He was in his temper meek*
*And lived a modest life*
*Before the passions of his love*
*Broke out in endless strife.*

*He loved a female to that degree*
*And he had no return,*
*So in his breast the fire of lust*
*At last began to burn.*

*Only by love at first it was*
*The awful work begun,*
*But when he found 'twas all in vain*
*He then the murder done*

*On this young woman, Sarah Glass,*
*About twenty eight years old.*
*She lived a very pious life*
*As I have often been told.*

*In health and strength from home she went*
*And thought so to return,*
*But in their road death laid a snare*
*And in it they did spurn.*

*After this murder he had done*
*Back to a furze brake he went*
*And there he lay two nights and days*
*With sorrows to lament.*

*The third day went he unto a linhay*
*And in the loft he lay*
*And then he saw as you may know*
*The corpses carried away*

*Of those whom just he slain.*
*'Twas with a butcher's knife.*
*Hard was their lot he cut their throat*
*And took away their life.*

*That day to Ashbury he was brought,*
*Committed then he was*
*Unto the gaol of Exeter.*
*'Twas at the Lent Assize*

*There to be tried for the Crime*
*Against him there was laid*
*For murder of a little boy,*
*Likewise a lovely maid.*

*Down on his bended knees did fall*
*And to his Maker pray*
*To pardon what he'd done amiss*
*And did his wrath away.*

*The witness examined was*
*And guilty he was found*
*Of that murder against him laid*
*Committed on Wadland Down.*

*The Judge did then pronounce his doom,*
*"You must be hung" he said*
*And Lord have mercy on your soul*
*After that you are dead.*

*On Monday the second of April*
*Was the appointed time*
*He was to meet his awful doom*
*For this his dreadful crime.*

*When on the scaffold he was fixed*
*He took his last farewell*
*Of thousands that were standing by*
*To see him take his fall.*

*"Behold my name is Thomas Friend*
*For murder I confess*
*Hath brought me to this wretched end*
*To die of sad disgrace."*

**The record of Sarah and Edward Glass being 'barbarously murdered' by Thomas Friend in 1827 can be seen on gravestones in the churchyard, Northlew.**

# *Ashbury Farms*

## *Wadland Barton*

Wadland Barton (Wadel-land) is situated in the beautiful valley stretching between the woodland of the Ashbury estate. Jermianus de Wadeland was Rector of Ashbury in 1297. The old house, which was demolished in the 1960s, was Elizabethan in style and was described in 1952 as being an 'E-shaped' manor house. The date, 1685, is inscribed on a stone set into a wall beside the new house.

Legends abound! One story relates to a fatal accident on the hill near the old kennels when a horse bolted causing the cart to tip. It is said to this day that if you scrape your boot along a ridge in the hedge, no more blood will be spilt. Ethel Friend used to say that 'the ash, plum and dog-rose-covered arch in front of the house should never be removed' because it protected the property from witches.

John and Joanna Palmer lived at Wadland Barton in 1851 with their ten children; the youngest two were twins (Harriet and Mary Ann). In 1878 Charles William Friend and his wife Mary brought up their family of one son and three daughters at Wadland Barton. Sadly Mary died, and Charles married Elizabeth Wood who was a teacher at Northlew School. Two cob cottages opposite the house burnt down in the early 1900s so Charles had a house built on the site for his retirement. Their son Richard Chapman Friend married Ethel Petherick and had two children called Stella and Leslie. Leslie and his wife Betty took up the reins at Wadland with their four children. Their youngest son, Philip, is the fourth generation of the family to farm there.

*Ethel Friend holding Charles Jordan outside Wadland Barton, 1947.*

*Mabel and Ada Friend milking at Wadland Barton watched by their father Charles in 1918.*

## *Stoney Farm*

Stoney Farm burnt down one 1 April in the 1850s. The fire was discovered by a servant who had great difficulty convincing people that she was not playing an 'April Fools' joke. The farmhouse was rebuilt in 1860.

The Dufty family have farmed at Stoney since 1897. Bryan Dufty married Ellen Harry from Milltown Farm. Ellen remembered seeing the railway line being constructed to Ashbury in 1865 and proudly boasted of being a passenger on the first train from Ashbury Station. She also recalled debris flying around during the catastrophic fire at Ashbury House on 18 August 1877. Bryan and Ellen's son 'Jack' married Gwendoline Mary and they brought up their four children, Irene, John, Walter and Mary, at Stoney until 1955 when they retired to Hillcrest Bungalow. John, his wife Frances and Walter have now retired to their bungalow 'Stoney View'.

Several accidents involving horses are remembered at Stoney. William Wooldridge once over-

*Wadland Barton. Dartmoor's highest tors, Yes Tor and High Willhays, in the distance.*

*Stoney Farm. Brian and Ellen Dufty, John 'Jack' and Edgar Dufty. Lady unknown, early 1920s.*

*Irene, Walter, John and Mary Dufty.*

*John, Walter and Frances Dufty.*

loaded a cart and caused it to tip, almost strangling the horse. On another occasion Charles Gratton of Bogtown (who worked at Stoney almost all his life) lit a fire to burn the short straw after threshing. The horse tripped and fell into the blaze. John and Frances handed the farm over to their son Bryan and his wife Marian.

### *Hillside Farm*

Some time around 2000BC two burial-grounds were built on East Kimber Common on land now belonging to Hillside Farm. English Heritage record there being 'two bowl barrows' in an area almost opposite the gateway to Stoney Farm. The farmhouse was built in 1905 by the Hortop family. Mrs Hortop worked hard on the farm as well as caring for her six children, Ella, Harry, Sidney, Merlin, Mary and Margaret. Mr Hortop kept the meal stores at Ashbury Station. Mary and Margaret both took up the teaching profession, Mary at Northlew and Margaret at Boasley.

In 1950, Fred Lambert Eveleigh bought the farm and was joined three years later by his son Peter with wife Rosalind. Ros and Peter remember 1978,

*The Hortop family outside Hillside Farm. Mr and Mrs Hortop, Sidney, Ella, Merlin, Harry, Margaret and Mary.*

*David Eveleigh on combine at Hillside Farm.*

*Ashbury Court*

when they lost their electricity supply due to heavy snow making roads impassable. They were eventually rescued by an Army Snowcat which had travelled along the top of the hedge banks. On board was a SWEB linesman, two soldiers, one policeman and a member of the Dartmoor Rescue Group.

At the time of writing, Hillside is farmed by Michael Dufty and his son Simon. Michael and his wife Tonya experienced the horrors of being the first farm in Northlew to be affected by the foot-and-mouth outbreak in March 2001.

### *Ashbury Court*

Eddie and Carol Williamson arrived at Ashbury Court in 1960. They had often noticed the strange collection of buildings which was later to become their home. The roof was asbestos-covered and from the main block sprouted several long inelegant chimneys and a tall three-storey wing. It was formerly the 'Dower House' for the Ashbury estate and stood next to the local railway station. In the 1930s, after passing through several hands, the main three-storey block was reduced to ground-floor level, possibly due to structural defects. The unsightly chimneys have been removed and the roof replaced on the main property. At various times Ashbury Court has been an hotel, the administrative centre for a prisoner-of-war camp (1914–18), briefly a school and, more recently, a working farm.

## *Foot and Mouth*

Milltown Farm was a victim of the foot-and-mouth outbreak on 24 March 2001, Mothering Sunday. All stock had to be slaughtered and were burnt in the field beside Milltown Lane. The fire was lit at 2.45a.m. on Thursday 29 March and burnt for ten days. The farm had to be thoroughly cleaned and disinfected. Four wooden sheds (the hay barn and calf houses) had to be removed and all gates and cubicles had to be scrubbed. Inspections were very strict and scrupulously supervised. It was decided that the milking bale was too rusty, the result being that all milking equipment was removed and buried in the pits which had been dug on the farm. Cleaning began in early April and lasted until 26 September 2001, when visitors were able to come to the farmhouse again.

*Foot-and-mouth notice.*

*The pyre of burning animals could be seen and smelt for miles*

## *Harvesting*

At harvest time, word passed around the village that a reaping was about to take place. Neighbouring farmers sent a couple of men and threshing machines arrived. They would work from farm to farm until all of the corn was harvested. It was a great social occasion with food and large amounts of drink being consumed in the field.

Above: *Winifred Davey at the wheel with George and Maurice Davey, Fred Newcombe and Pip Wilson on the trailer at Lower East Kimber Farm.*

Above left: *Harvesting at Wadland Barton with Richard Friend and his son-in-law, John Jordan.*

Left below: *Stan Vincent and George Muttram making a hay load at Church Gate Farm.*

*Combining corn at Kimber Farm, late 1950s.*

*Harvesting at Stoney Farm 1968. Walter Dufty, Korah Luxton, Jack Bray, Joe Martin, Marian Dufty and Nigel Dufty.*

### *Horses*

Horses provided the power to pull farm implements such as the plough, harrow and roller. Corn was carried by horse and wagon to the three local water-mills, Crowden, Wigdon and Lew Tuckey, where it was ground into flour. Farmers travelled by horseback and kept a horse and cart for work on their farms. It was said that if a farmer ploughed one acre of land using a 9–10 inch furrow he would have walked 11 miles by the time he finished.

*Horse and cart at Overlake Farm.*

*Korah Luxton and Johnny King.*

*Lower Whiddon Farm. The Luxton family.* Left to right, back row: *Bert, William, Edward, Korah;* centre: *Annie, Amy, Mary-Ann, Blanche, Evelyn;* seated on rug: *Ellen Maria and Mabel Alice.*

*Sheep shearing in the 1920s at Lower East Kimber Farm. Pictured are Jack Adams, Henry Adams, Lilian Heggadon, John Heggadon and others.*

*Chapter 7*

# IN TIMES OF WAR

## *'For your Tomorrow, we gave our Today'*

## *Introduction*

'When you go home, tell them of us and say, for your tomorrow, we gave our today.' These words were spoken by Lew Gratton as the sound of the Reveille died away at the dedication of the new War Memorial in the churchyard of St Thomas' Church, Northlew in 1996. Wartime has had a profound effect upon Northlew over the generations.

## *Earlier Times*

From 1689 to 1815 England was at war with Spain and France. During this time there was no conscription. Men were obtained for the Navy and Army by a system of bounties. The following notice was posted in all Devon towns and villages at that time:

> *4 April 1795*
>
> *At a meeting of the INHABITANTS of this town/ village, held this day pursuant to Public Notice, for taking into Consideration the most speedy Means of raising Men for HIS MAJESTY'S NAVY.*
>
> *It was unanimously resolved that the sum of FIFTEEN GUINEAS per Man shall be given to the FIRST* MEN who may offer themselves for that purpose. Applications may be made to the CHURCHWARDENS and OVERSEERS of the Parish aforesaid.*

It is likely that during these Napoleonic Wars, Northlew had to provide just one man but by the First World War, when conscription had begun, the situation was very different.

## *First World War*

Before the outbreak of the First World War, men were able to enlist and choose between the regular Army, Navy or the Territorials. Men could choose to ignore the demands of national defence. All this was changed by the impact of the First World War. Five million men entered the Armed Forces at the time, the majority as volunteers. War brought about huge changes to lifestyles by Government order. Food was limited and its quality changed, freedom of movement was restricted, news was restrained, even streetlights were dimmed, beer watered down and the time on clocks altered. These profound changes had a marked effect on the country but had a deep and long-lasting influence on Northlew itself. It was reported at the time that out of a population of less than 100, the village sent almost all of its able-bodied men to the war. Northlew, in losing one in four of its residents in the First World War, suffered a higher proportion of losses than any other community in Britain. Out of a population of 100, there were 22 men who never came home from foreign fields to their own.

## *Before the First World War*

Before the First World War, young men of the village attended camp with the Territorials, the North Devon Yeomanry.

*A group of 'Northlewites' at Westward Ho!, 1900.*

# *Some of Those Who Went to the 1914–18 War*

*Garfield Gay, lost in action, Belgium 1918. Volunteered to go 'over the top' to hunt a sniper in place of a married man. He was shot dead on the way back.*

*'Jimmy' Elliott* (right) *with R. Smale.*

*Bert Pascoe* (right) *became a Sergeant and after the war acted as Drill Sergeant when ex-soldiers, now members of the local British Legion, paraded for Remembrance Sunday.*

*Charlie Friend in military uniform.*

Below: *Sid Styles (Coldstream Guards) was discharged in 1915 having been machine-gunned in the legs on two occasions. He was awarded the Military Medal and, after the war, received a disablement pension of 11 shillings per week.*

*Will Watkins, Christmas 1916.*

*Maurice Andrew (Coldstream Guards). Achieved the rare distinction of Officer status.*

*Bill Tapp who returned to the village after the war and became a rabbit catcher. He was a regular at the Green Dragon Inn.*

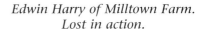

*Edwin Harry of Milltown Farm. Lost in action.*

# *Lest We Forget*

## 1914–18 War

**John Fox Bell**, *lost in action.*

**Frederick William Brooking**, *son of William and Amy Brooking of Crowden, 177th Coy. Machine Gun Corps (Infantry). Died aged 19 yrs, Wednesday, 26 September 1917, Belgium.*

**William Henry Karslake Burridge**, *son of John and Ellen Burridge of Winsford Towers, Beaworthy, husband of Annie Burridge. 1st Battalion Devonshire Regiment. Died aged 26 yrs Sunday, 30 May 1915, Belgium.*

**Charles Crocker**, *lost in action.*

**Charles Dingwall**, *lost in action.*

**James Down**, *1st Battalion, Devonshire Regiment. Died Thursday, 22 April 1915 at Ypres.*

**Garfield Gay**, *lost in action, Belgium, November 1918.*

**Edwin Harry** *of Milltown Farm, lost in action.*

**John Horn**, *son of the late Alexander and Charlotte Horn of Northlew, Beaworthy. 5th Dragoon Guards. Died aged 31 yrs, Tuesday, 26 March 1918, The Somme.*

**Jacob Land**, *son of George and Mary Ann Land of Huntsham, Bampton, husband of Ellen Land. Sergeant, 9th Battalion, Devonshire Regiment. Died, aged 30 yrs, Friday, 26 October 1917, Belgium.*

**Sidney Medland**, *lost in action.*

**William Medland** *(Royal Navy, HMS* Cumberland*), lost in action.*

**George Glass Pellow**, *son of George Pellow of Okehampton, 1st/6th Battalion, Devonshire Regiment. Died aged 28 yrs, Tuesday, 23 October 1917, Basra, Iraq.*

**Christopher Rout**, *lost in action.*

**Charles Saunders**, *2nd Battalion Devonshire Regiment. Died Saturday, 1 July 1916, The Somme.*

**Thomas Saunders**, *son of W.J. Saunders of Houna, Northlew. 34th Battalion, Machine Gun Corps (Infantry). Died aged 20 yrs, Wednesday, 17 April 1918, Belgium.*

**Ernest Philip Shobbrook**, *son of Philip Shobbrook, Crowden Road, Northlew. Royal Navy, HMS* Indefatigable. *Died aged 24 yrs, Wednesday, 31 May 1916.*

**Hugh Leonard Acland-Troyte**, *lost in action.*

**Frederick Whitcher**, *son of Harry and Isabella Whitcher, of The Lodge, Ashbury. 24th (1st. Wessex) Field Ambulance, Royal Army Medical Corps. Died aged 23 yrs, Saturday, 22 May 1915.*

**William Wooldridge**, *8th Battalion, Devonshire Regiment. Died Sunday, 6 May 1917, France.*

**John Morth Woollcombe**, *Major, son of the late Henry Woollcombe. 1st Battalion, Devonshire Regiment. Died aged 30 yrs, Saturday, 3 February 1917, Iraq.*

**William Wallace Yeo**, *son of the late Thomas and Elizabeth Ann Yeo, of Okehampton. Royal Marine Light Infantry. Died aged 24 yrs, Friday, 26 October 1917, Belgium.*

## 1939–45 War

**Lewis W. Curtis**, *son of the late Samuel and Jessie Curtis of Bolland, Northlew. Pilot Officer, Royal Air Force, 149 Squadron, Bomber Command. Died aged 32 yrs, leaving a widow and baby daughter, 4 July 1943, Cologne, Germany.*

**William Kent**, *worked in Ern Adam's Bakery, lost in action.*

**Ronald George Moyse**, *son of James and Rosalind Moyse, Northlew. Corporal, Royal Army Service Corps. Died aged 22 yrs, Monday, 30 August 1943, Moro River, Italy.*

**Ralph William Strong**, *son of Ralph Bower Strong and Minnie Strong of Whiddon Down. Royal Navy. Died aged 21 yrs, Sunday, 9 June 1940.*

Pictured here are: *Sgt Bert Pascoe, R. Brayley* (smoking), *Bill Parkhouse, Edwin Harry, C. Andrew* (seated right).

*Setting off to Yeomanry Camp from the Honeychurch Arms, 1909.* Left to right: *Charlie Friend, Sam Curtis, Fred Smale, Maurice Gloyn.*

# *The Second World War*

*Bill Strong, lost in action on HMS* Glorious, *aircraft carrier, sunk by the German battle cruiser* Scharnhorst.

*Lewis Curtis, RAF Pilot Officer, Bomber Command. Lost in action.*

*Charlie Gratton served at the Western Front in France with the Gloucesters, 1918. When he was sent over the top from his bivvy trench the young man next to him stood up to get his rifle and was blown up. Charlie was wounded but escaped with his life.*

*Will Medland (Royal Navy) served on HMS* Cumberland. *Lost in action.*

The outbreak of the Second World War was announced to people without a radio by Freddie Spencer of Bedfords, Milltown Lane, who rode around the village on his bicycle, crying the news. The mobilisation which followed, saw the call-up of all those aged between 18 and 41:

| | |
|---|---|
| Clarence Andrew | Ralph Littlejohns |
| Dick Andrew | Henry Luxton |
| Frank Curtis | Jack Moore |
| Lewis Curtis | Ronald Moyse |
| Percy Curtis | Stan Newcombe |
| Maurice Curtis | John Parkhouse |
| Sid Curtis | Tony Perry |
| Garfield 'Pop' Gay | Gerald Putt |
| Lew Gratton | Charlie Saunders |
| Harry Hortop | Albert Sutton |
| Bill Jordan | Bill Strong |
| William Kent | Stan Voaden |
| Archie King | Bill Worden |
| Frank Knight | |

(Harry Hortop served in both World Wars and was part of the evacuation of Dunkirk.)

Women also enlisted to serve their country:

Sylvia Dunn, ATS
Pat Freeman, WRNS
Lorna Hookway, WAFS
Lillian Saunders, ATS
Lillian Shobbrook, NAAFI
Dorothy Voaden, WAFS

The threat of an early invasion brought about emergency action to organise resistance. Sandbagged gun positions and roadblocks were erected at the bottom of Harper's Hill beside Dick Gratton's workshop in Crowden Road and at Bolland.

A group of British servicemen was based in a small camp in the Kimber Road behind the new police house, almost opposite Kimber Farm. This Searchlight Battery consisted of two Nissen huts, one for sleeping and one as a mess, a gun position at the entrance to the camp, and the searchlight itself hidden in the valley by the river.

A number of bombs were dropped around Northlew when enemy planes returned home from bombing raids. They fell at Kimber Cross, Rutleigh and Crowden, between Patchacott and Ashbury Station and at the back of Station Road. The Station Road bomb killed a cow and burned stored hay. The Crowden bomb blew in windows along Crowden Road. At Broadbury there was a hush-hush military unit with a complex aerial system. Stories abounded as to its purpose. Presumably it was part of an early radar network.

### 'What my Grandpa told me about Wartime':

*My Grandpa was nine years old when the war started. He lived on a farm which was one mile from the village of Northlew and seven miles from the town of Okehampton in Devon. The first thing he can remember is a lot of soldiers with guns, and tanks around the country lanes. He was issued with a gas mask which he had to take to school every day. The gas mask was in a cardboard box with string to put around his neck.*

*One evening everyone went to the village square. A bus arrived with a load of children and they were called evacuees. There were two lady teachers with them and the children were placed with local families to live with for the next four years; my Grandpa had a boy living on the farm with him. Instead of 70 children going to Northlew School there were now 120. Two big rooms at the Rectory were used as extra classrooms.*

*Ration Books were given to each person and they could have 2 ozs of margarine, 1s.2d. worth of meat, 2 eggs, 1 loaf of bread and 2 ozs of sweets. There was no fruit and he didn't see a banana until 1945 when he was 14 years old. Petrol was rationed to one gallon per week per car and it cost 1s.7d. a gallon (about eight pence!).*

*All the men who were not in the Army joined the Home Guard. They were given guns to defend the country from the Germans. The German aircraft came overhead and dropped bombs. My Grandpa remembers getting out of school, going down a lane and lying in the hedge.*

*As the war went on, the American troops arrived. They were very generous with sweets, candy, chocolate and cigarettes. They came to the bakery in the village every day for lorry-loads of bread. Some of these Americans had dark skin and they were the first black-skinned people Grandpa had ever seen.*

*Every evening they had to put shutters over the windows. There was no street lighting and cars had to have covers over their headlights. A man called the ARP Warden patrolled the village to make sure no lights were showing to the German bombers overhead. The village had a searchlight camp. There were 12 soldiers with a light to shine on the German bombers so the guns could shoot them down. Four or five 'planes crashed around the village. When Plymouth was bombed, people from Northlew went to Broadbury Castle, which is two miles away, and they could see the fires burning in Plymouth over 30 miles away.*

*Farmers were allowed to kill two pigs each year to feed the men working on the farms. They were allowed extra rations for harvesting, thrashing the corn and picking up potatoes. Boys who were 13 or 14 years old were allowed to stay home from school with a work permit to help with the harvest and picking up potatoes. A man called Mr Palk came to Northlew from Plymouth every week to buy eggs, butter, rabbits and any other food the farmers had. He would sometimes bring fish from Plymouth to sell. 12 herrings cost one shilling.*

*Laura Hawkin*

### The Village in Wartime

Most people of active age joined one of the newly-founded volunteer services: the ARP, the Red Cross and First Aid, the Home Guard or the Special Police. No section of the Observer Corps was formed.

Providing blackout for windows called for great ingenuity and, to begin with, the patrolling ARP wardens would diligently rattle doors to point out every chink of light. Road signs were taken down but, before they could be collected, several mischievous children restored them, pointing in the wrong direction, of course. National Registration and the issue of identity cards was organised from the Post Office.

Funding for the initial training of local instructors was provided by Devon County Council Education Department, Northlew being designated an 'Evening Institute' for the purpose. Lectures in First Aid began immediately, given by Dr Woollcombe and Miss Rudland of Highampton.

Two aircraft came down close to Northlew. One, a Spitfire, crashed at Lovelands Farm on a Sunday morning in 1941. The pilot, whose name was Smith, was killed, his body later being laid out in the Chapel Sunday school. Six soldiers, who were billeted with Korah and Amy Luxton at Loveland Farm, were sent to guard the aircraft wreckage until it could be removed for reuse. Tommy Lake, who worked for Jack Adams at Kimber, used his tractor to pull all the aircraft parts to the road where they were collected by a large transporter vehicle. The other aircraft, a Liberator, was piloted by a crew of French Canadians and was seen in flames over Ashbury Church heading towards Homing Down, Inwardleigh. Ten children, who spotted the plane from the school playground, grabbed their bikes and raced over to the crash site where all six crew were found to be dead.

An incendiary bomb landed some time around 1943/44 on the estate of Northlew Manor, igniting a hayrick. Mrs Fison was in the bath at the time and ran out of the house as she was!

### ARP

The county officer in charge of 'B' area ARP was Mr H. Austen of Greystones, Okehampton and Clem and Henry Andrew were the local officers. The required equipment (stirrup pumps for incendiary bombs, sand buckets, etc.) was stored around the village. Harry Wackett, history master at Okehampton Grammar School and a senior ARP officer, issued gas masks from the Victory Hall, these were individually fitted over a period of about one week.

### *Red Cross and First Aid*

Mrs E.C. Smale of Bedford Cottage, having completed and passed several Red Cross courses, was in charge of the First Aid post in the Church Room. She held regular practice sessions throughout the war for her band of qualified volunteers:

Miss Gertie Adams of Kesterfield
Miss Margaret Wickets of South Yeo
Miss Elsie Evely of Crowden
Mrs Mary Worden from the village
Mrs Kathleen Elliott of Harper's Hill
Mrs E.M. Gratton of Bogtown
Katie Gay from the village

Mrs Gwendolyn Croysdale of Lambert was a local correspondent and administrator for the Red Cross and it was through her that fund-raising suggestions were handed down. Throughout the war, Flag Days (house-to-house collections), concerts and 'Socials' were held in the Victory Hall to raise funds for such schemes as Wings for Victory, the Aid to Russia Fund, Comforts for the Devonshire Regiment and the Prisoner-of-War Parcels Fund for which the Women's Institute organised the knitting of scarves and socks.

### *The Home Guard*

The Home Guard attracted the greatest contingent of volunteers. The area Commanding Officer was Major Schofield of the Half Moon pub at Sheepwash. The officer in charge of the Northlew section was Lieut Gregory – Eric Demetrius Gregory MA, the rector of Northlew. He lived as a bachelor with much of the rectory being turned over to storage of equipment for the various Services. Two sergeants were Jimmy Elliott and W.J 'Nipper' Smale. The men were on duty two or three nights a week, sleeping in a hut at Durdon Cross. One duty lasted from 10.00p.m. until 2.00a.m. when two other guards would take over. These men would stay until 6.00a.m. before returning home to their 'day job'. One night, when Lew Gratton was on duty with Revd Gregory, Lew became worried about a ticking sound he could hear. What relief he must have felt when it was discovered to be an alarm clock that the rector had with him!

Joint exercises were sometimes held to test the coordination of the services with the volunteer groups, usually under a code-name. During one such exercise, observation posts and roadblocks, manned by the Home Guard, were set up in order to keep the 'enemy' out of the village. (The enemy were soldiers from Okehampton wearing white crosses on their helmets.) For Norman Born, who later became a corporal in the Home Guard, the temptation for a bit of fun could not be resisted. Being off-duty and coming home from Okehampton by car, he happened upon two of the 'enemy'. After bundling them into the boot of his car, he drove on to the roadblock at the bottom of Harpers Hill. On recognising Norman, the Home Guard waved him through and on into the Square. As soon as Norman parked, the men sprang out of the boot and opened up with 'Bang! Bang!' causing great confusion. It is not known how the exercise referees resolved the situation but there were some disqualifications.

Others who served in the Home Guard were:

| | |
|---|---|
| Percy Adams | Maurice Bater |
| Fred Bater | Cecil Brooking |
| Lew Curtis | Seth Davey |
| Arthur Elliott | Johnny King |
| Korah Luxton | Sid Newcombe |
| Fred Smale | Jack Spry |
| 'Gat' Perry | Bill Glover |
| George Davey | Fred Luxton |
| Bill Smallacombe | Bill Woodridge |
| Fearnley Bater | Wilf Mitchell |
| Reg Vincent | George Jordan |
| Fred Smollett | Jimmy Brayley |
| Fred Moyse | |

### *Police*

The following men were made Special Constables for the duration of the conflict:

| | |
|---|---|
| Jack Adams | Henry Andrew |
| Dick Friend | 'Jazz' Hookway |
| Jim Mills | 'Mannie' Spry |
| PC Bert Setters | Jack Webber |

Late one night PC Setters was on duty at Bogtown when Charlie Friend came through the hedge. Setters, who was reknowned for being aware of most activities in the area, asked Charlie what he had been doing and was given the reply, 'Oh, I've bin over Greendown'. After they had talked of one thing or another, Charlie said that he had to get ready for his post round. Charlie performed many jobs, including killing the occasional pig for a farmer, on the quiet. After watching Charlie walk away, Bert called after him, 'I'm partial to a bit of pig's liver' – even Charlie could not fool the constable.

After the war, and during the Suez crisis, Denny Adams, John Jordan and John Spry became Special Constables.

### *Evacuees*

Quite a number of children, some with parents, and some with teachers, were evacuated to Northlew from Battersea in the south of London. Ronnie, Johnny and Baby Bubb lived with Mrs Smale. When they went back to London, Peter Parrott arrived in Northlew with his mother. They lived in a corrugated-iron house which then became Bater's Yard and later the bungalow at Longview, Crowden. Peter's aunt, Elsie Dawson, came to live with them.

Colin Binnie lived with Rhoda and John Bater at Rose Cottage, Crowden. Aunt Lill also lived with them. Fred and George Brindle lived with Amy and Johnny King in one of the Costeloes houses, Shallowford. Clem, Margaret and Alec Early lived with Mr and Mrs Mills at Lower East Kimber. They stayed on after the war. Three children, surnamed Bevis, lived for a short time at Bedfords, Milltown Lane, with Wilf and Rene Neno. Joyce Copeland lived with Polly Friend at Dingley, Harpers Hill.

Two children, surnamed Bayliss, lived with Mr and Mrs Penworthy in the bungalow on the Hatherleigh road. John Tulley and Edgar Thompson lived with Mr and Mrs Smale at Lower Eastcott. Sylvia Arnold lived with her mother in a cottage on Harpers Hill. Muriel Woolsey and her mother lived at Overlake Farm with Jack and Florrie Adams. Two teachers, one named Miss Price, came and stayed in the rectory where evacuee children had to be taught because of pressure of space in the school. Mrs Mary Hortop was also a teacher at the time.

*Mrs Smale's first evacuees: Ronnie, Johnny and Baby Bubb, all from Battersea. When they went back to London Peter Parrott arrived.*

### *Prisoners of War*

Some prisoners of war were billeted in Northlew and Ashbury whilst others were employed casually. Casual labour usually meant potato picking or helping with the harvest. Six to eight Italian prisoners, together with two guards, can be remembered as having helped with a potato harvest during one morning. Having had enough, they 'spiked' Arnold Lake's tractor fuel tank with sugar, and then spent a very restful afternoon! At other free times, the men would cut willow withies from the hedgerow, weaving them into baskets overnight, and returning the following day to sell them for spare cash. One German POW, Otto Binder, from Hamburg, was billeted for two years at Bolland Farm with the Voaden family. The five boys fondly remember him as a good football player who passed on his many skills.

Mr William 'Willie' Smallacombe, rabbit trapper, of Kimber told how German prisoners of war were kept at Ashbury Court. They could be heard through the window singing during the evening. It is said that one prisoner was shot on the road between Ashbury Court and Loveland Cross.

## The Northlew Secret Service

After the Second World War, the Government introduced early-warning systems throughout the British Isles to warn people of impending nuclear attack. One such system was set up in Northlew.

To begin with, it was put into the police station but after the system was installed the police station closed and the house was sold. Bill and Hilary Isaac were approached to install the equipment at the rear of the village shop. They agreed to manage it and attended various courses to learn how to operate the system. A 'hot-line telephone' was installed and each time this was used a password was requested. Hilary and Bill were issued with a siren to sound in the Square and a set of flares to alert those living on outlying farms and they ran this secret mission for many years. It was no wonder that they had so many telephone calls from the police at night because the security system was being checked. The equipment was eventually declared redundant and removed just a few years before Hilary and Bill retired from the shop.

*Evacuee children with Muriel Woolsey, outside a cottage in Shorts Lane (now demolished), 1941.*

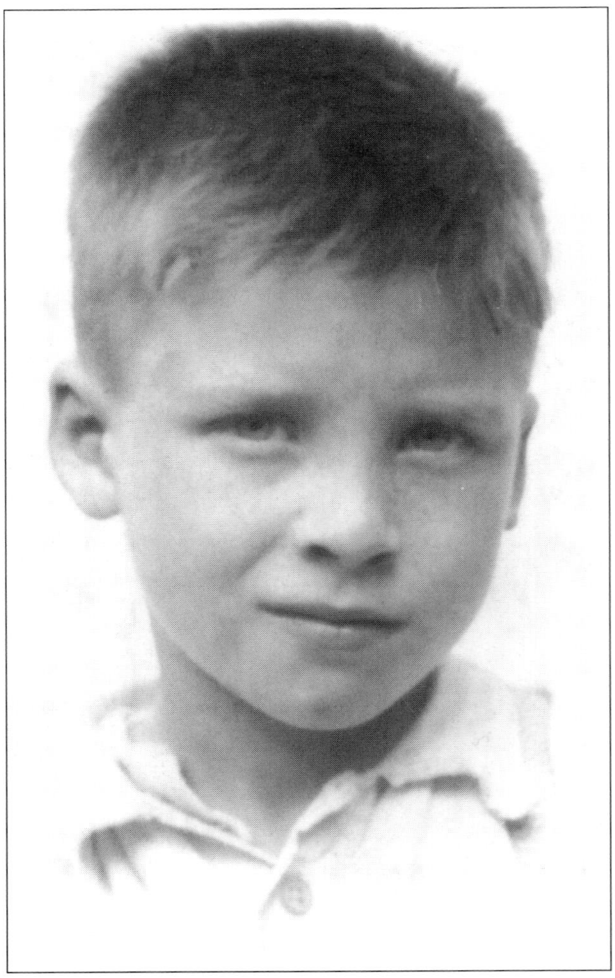

*Clem Early, evacuee, aged 7, 1937.*

# *Memories from Evacuees*

### Muriel Woolsey

*My mother, Cecily Woolsey, myself and my sister Iris, arrived in the Square at Northlew after travelling by taxi from Okehampton. With us were my mother's sister, Winifred Arnold, her children, Sylvia and Eric, and our cousins, Violet Woolsey and Eric Roberts. We were soon divided amongst local families. To begin with we went to Mr and Mrs Hutchins and Mrs Arnold went to Mrs Hortop; Violet and Eric were separated to other families. After a while, my mother rented Well Cottage by the bridge over the River Lew. Further members of my father's family, Kitty and her children Brian and Sheila, soon joined us. They did not stay very long and soon returned to London.*

*My mother and Aunt Win were employed in Ern Adam's local bakehouse. At first the children at school were hostile and expressed the wish that we should return to London. Later we made good friends and Northlew became our home. We then moved to Crowden Road which had running water so there was no more fetching water from the well. We became friendly with Mr and Mrs Ware and Faith Moore. I don't remember ever being short of food as Mr Ware trapped small rabbits for us and we always had plenty of milk and eggs. I remember helping the local farmer's daughter to deliver milk. We knocked on doors for a jug and the milk was measured out of a churn with a ladle.*

*I still remember the number of flowers in the area; hedges covered in primroses and violets and daffodils by the mill. On Sundays we went to Sunday school, both at the church and chapel. I especially recall that on Whit Sunday we wore new clothes and straw bonnets and about this time of year we all stood up and recited texts we had learnt in the Chapel. There were always outings to the sea by Born's Coaches. Once we went to Bude and a group of teenagers got into difficulties in the sea. Luckily, they were rescued but had to stay in the Cottage Hospital at Stratton.*

*My father's parents moved down to Northlew and had a cottage in Station Road. My grandmother worked at the farm across the road owned, I think, by a Mr and Mrs Stevens.*

(Muriel still returns to Northlew today.)

### Clem Early

*If you had asked me where Northlew was, I would not have been able to tell you until 1939. I was then nine years old and the war had just started. Things were starting to become grim for me and for my brother and sister, Peggy and Alec Early. Peggy was eight years old and Alec was six. We were a normal family living in Battersea, London. When the war started we had the choice of staying in London or being evacuated to Devon. My parents decided that we should leave.*

*To this day I can still recall the long train journey from Clapham Junction to Okehampton. On arriving at Okehampton, we all boarded Norman Born's buses that took us to Northlew. When we arrived at the village with 30 other children, we were taken into the church hall and given tea and cakes. It all seemed a bit strange and frightening at that time, wondering if we would be separated, but my brother, sister and I always said that we would stay together at all costs. As things turned out, we were lucky to be sent to a small farm called Slatequarry which was owned by a farmer and his wife, Mr and Mrs Mills. They were good, kind and loving people; the thing being they had no children, so that meant they treated us as their own. All three of us attended Northlew School, walking four miles there and back. I found that all of the local children showed us a lot of kindness and respect, which meant we got on well together. When we left school after the war, Peggy, Alec and myself decided to stay in Devon and not go back to Battersea. The reason being we had nothing to go back to. Our parents had divorced and remarried. Peggy and Alec both found their own way in life and never went back to London. As for myself, I stayed on the farm and worked for Mr Mills until 1953 when I left to join the Army. Mr Mills sold the farm and moved into retirement in the village.*

*Living in Northlew taught me a lot about life, people and self-respect. It was Mr Mills who taught me... things I still find useful to this day; many things about farming, gardening, digging wells and graves, as he was church sexton at the time. He always said to me 'always do a job right and always finish what you started.' He was a man with a lot of sense; men like him are no longer around today. When I look back over the years and the good times that I had when I was a lad, I still find that Northlew is a special place to me. It's my home and I have a very high regard for all of my mates and the people that I knew in that era. What I have written about my time in Northlew is only a small snip of my life in the*

Lewis, Sid and Frank Curtis.

Maurice Curtis.

Below: *Percy Curtis.*

Below: *Jessie Curtis, mother of ten. Five of her eight sons fought in the Second World War.*

*village. I am sorry I cannot write and tell you more of my memories, as there are so many and it would take me the rest of my life to put it on paper. I would like to end by saying I am sure of one thing, I am proud to be a part of Northlew and it will always be my home. I hope one day to have my ashes scattered in Northlew by my daughter.*
(Clem Early, aged 71 years, who also returns to Northlew.)

*'Time is a healer so they say*
*But not for me, I am glad to say*
*The memories I have are here to stay*
*And time will never take them away.'*

## My Own Contribution to the War Effort

*This happened when invasion was expected; a schoolboy's prank that went wrong. I used to cycle every day to Ashbury Station to catch the early train to Okehampton and the Grammar School, passing over Meldon Viaduct on the way. One morning I wrote a note in French which said 'if you want to destroy the bridge meet me at 7.30'. This I signed 'X16', wrapped it around a halfpenny and threw it over Meldon Viaduct. We were always throwing things over the bridge and I forgot all about it. A week or two later I was awakened in the early hours to hear Norman Born shouting up at my parents' bedroom window for my father to raise the Home Guard. My father who was no doubt convinced that German paratroopers were dropping out of the sky at that very moment, threw on his Home Guard uniform, seized his prized Browning automatic rifle and was gone. I had no idea where.*

*The next morning on our way to school I noticed a group of Home Guard manning the sandbagged position at Meldon Viaduct. My father was among them. It later emerged he had no idea why he had been called out, but apparently 'they' were coming! Some weeks later, the whole of the school was called to the main hall and asked to write some words in French. It soon dawned on me that we were writing words similar to my note. What to do? Own up? I presented myself at the headmaster's door. The head listened to my story. 'O Smale, it's you is it? The police will be interested to hear what you have to say.' Detective Inspector Rogers, on hearing my story, gave a sigh. Apparently the note had been suspect from the start, but the risk could not be taken. 'Do you realise that the Army and the Home Guard have been guarding the bridge for three weeks and a Bridge Inspector has examined every part of the bridge?' It was all very humbling and made me feel very foolish and sorry. Going home would be another matter. I confessed to my mother and father, who both listened in astonished silence. There were the usual remonstrations. One thing came out of this; having no great skills at games, the episode ever more ensured my fame amongst my peers.*

Claude Smale

## The Curtis Family – Their Wartime Story

*My great-grandmother, Jessie, was born on 14 October 1876 in the village of Inwardleigh. She married Samuel Curtis at Okehampton Register Office in October 1896, 'because she was young and silly and he was poor'. For a number of years they lived in a cottage close to the river, but because of flooding they moved to Bolland Cottage, Northlew in 1914. They bought it for £50. Samuel kept a cow and calf, a pig, chickens and a record of his daily tasks. Jessie kept house. Over the years they had two daughters and eight sons. When the youngest child was born, Jessie could not decide what to call him. She sent her eldest daughter to register the birth, and choose a name. When she returned, on hearing it was Claude, Jessie shook her head and said she had decided to call him Frank – and Frank he stayed. Samuel died in 1933. Bolland now being too large, Jessie moved to a smaller cottage in the village. When the Second World War broke out, five of her eight sons went away to fight for their country. Jessie would lay awake at night worrying about her sons in turn, where they were and if they were safe.*

*Maurice and Percy had joined the Army; Lewis and Frank the Royal Air Force and Sid the Royal Navy. Lewis did not return home. He was a rear gunner and flew in Stirlings, which suffered heavy losses during the war. He was shot down over Cologne in 1943. It must have been a very long war for Jessie and the pain of losing a son must have been severe. She would have been relieved when the other boys came home. Jessie worked hard for her large family. She not only lost a husband, but eventually outlived three of her children.*

Jill Bennett

# *The Royal British Legion and the New War Memorial*

Garfield 'Pop' Gay, born in the shadow of one World War and a veteran of another, had a dream that inspired Northlew's granite War Memorial. Pop was born in the last days of the First World War, on the very day his Uncle Garfield was killed in Belgium in November 1918. The War Memorial was Pop's dream, literally, as he had a vision of it in his sleep. For almost 80 years the only memorial had been two oak plaques inside the church. In 1996 the community, led by members of the Northlew branch of the British Legion, wanted to build a lasting memorial in the churchyard. Fund-raising events, involving the community, paid for the £3,000 cross in eight months. It was dedicated on Saturday 8 June 1996 at a special tribute.

*Garfield 'Pop' Gay, 1940. Pop's personal wartime experiences led him to campaign for a permanent War Memorial in Northlew.*

The vicar, Revd Ray Voden, introduced the service. A large crowd of Royal British Legion members, relatives of those killed, and members of the public assembled, together with the Northlew Silver Band under bandmaster Percy Adams. The president of the Northlew branch of the Royal British Legion, 'Pop' Gay unveiled the memorial, which was draped in the Union flag. The Venerable John Newhouse, a Second World War chaplain, dedicated the memorial and the chairman of Northlew British Legion, Tom Andrew, read the

*The president of the Northlew branch of the Royal British Legion, Garfield 'Pop' Gay, unveiled the Memorial, draped in the Union flag in June 1996.*

*Dedication of the War Memorial, Saturday, 8 June 1996. Revd Brian Skutt, Methodist minister, the Venerable John Newhouse, the Revd Ray Voden, vicar.*

names of the men to whom the memorial was dedicated. Mr Buchanan played a Pipe Lament, followed by the Last Post by a Northlew Band member. Chairman, Tom Andrew, read 'For the Fallen' which was followed by the silence. As the sound of the Reveille died away, Lew Gratton recited 'When you go home, tell them of us and say: "For your tomorrow we gave our today"'. The Methodist minister, Revd Brian Skutt, offered prayers. Lt Col Guy Lawrence led an act of commitment and Archdeacon Newhouse and Jenny Voden gave readings. The organist was Barry Cappello. The proceedings ended with refreshments in the Victory Hall, provided by ladies of Royal British Legion Committee. Mr J. Dickenson spoke of how the appeal for funds to build the memorial had been launched and of how the target had been reached, thanking those concerned.

Northlew War Memorial stands as a reminder to future generations that peace does not come easily and is a focal point for thoughts and thanks to previous generations.

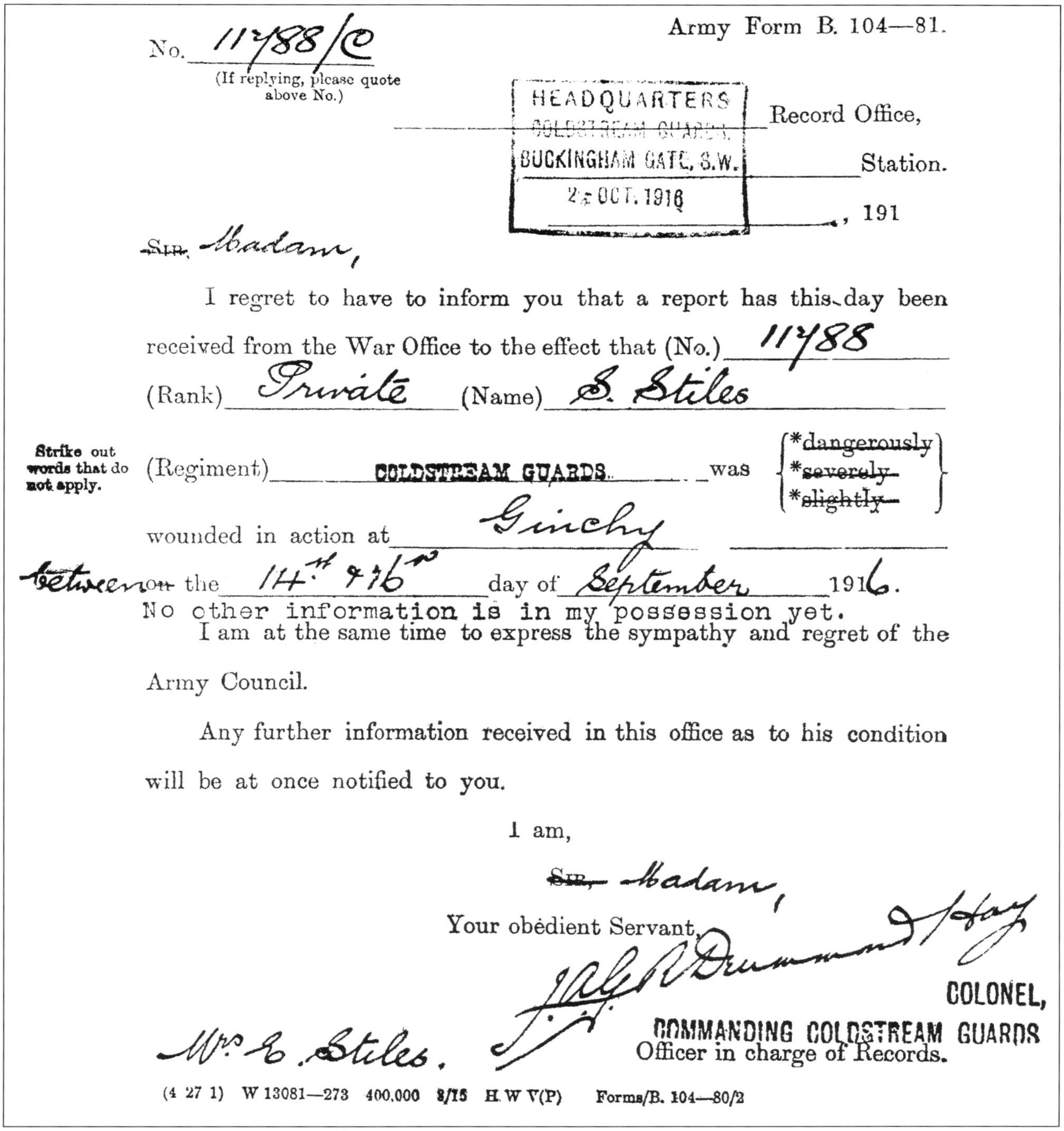

No. 11788/C

(If replying, please quote above No.)

Army Form B. 104—81.

HEADQUARTERS COLDSTREAM GUARDS BUCKINGHAM GATE, S.W. 2? OCT. 1916

Record Office,

Station.

, 191

~~Sir~~ Madam,

I regret to have to inform you that a report has this day been received from the War Office to the effect that (No.) 11788 (Rank) Private (Name) S. Stiles (Regiment) COLDSTREAM GUARDS was *~~dangerously~~ *~~severely~~ *~~slightly~~ wounded in action at Ginchy between ~~on~~ the 14th & 16th day of September 1916.

Strike out words that do not apply.

No other information is in my possession yet.

I am at the same time to express the sympathy and regret of the Army Council.

Any further information received in this office as to his condition will be at once notified to you.

I am,

~~Sir~~ Madam,

Your obedient Servant,

J. A. G. R. Drummond Hay

COLONEL,

COMMANDING COLDSTREAM GUARDS

Officer in charge of Records.

Mrs E. Stiles.

(4 27 1) W 13081—273 400,000 8/15 H.W.V.(P) Forms/B. 104—80/2

*Notification of wounding as sent home to next of kin.*

*The last wagon made by Thomas Andrew, Mid Devon Carriage Works, Northlew, for Mr Smale, Eastacombe Farm.*

*Dog cart.*

Chapter 8

# GETTING AROUND

## Introduction

Horse and cart in Crowden Road.

Before the coming of the railways, Northlew would, like most rural communities, have been entirely self-reliant for transport, probably using teams of horses and wagons. John Betjeman's visit, and subsequent television programme, in 1962 drew comparisons between Northlew and Swindon, the railway town of North Wiltshire. Betjeman pointed out the quiet lanes and causeways radiating from the village square: 'It [Northlew] just stays put in comfortable peace.' The railway, which never came nearer than Ashbury, finally closed in 1966. In Northlew, road transport continues to flourish to the present day.

## Road Transport

In the nineteenth century, the Brooking family provided some of the earliest known transport in the area. Records show that in 1856 William Gay offered a carrier service to Exeter and Plymouth every alternate Wednesday. In 1873 Thomas Brooking ran a horse and covered-van service to the neighbouring markets of Okehampton, Hatherleigh and Holsworthy, as well as providing a local delivery service as far as Exeter and Torquay. In the 1890s Nicholas Brooking took over and continued the business until the 1920s when John Brooking, who was in business as a builder and shopkeeper, carried the business on. John and Kitty Brooking ran their own farm and the shop at the bottom of the Square. At that time, John Brooking abandoned

Henry Andrew inspecting a trailer before sending it out.

Brooking's Stores 1908. John and Kitty Brooking can be seen in the far doorway with Ida Elliott in the nearer.

horse-drawn transport and purchased a reconditioned Thorneycroft lorry from William Rowse of Town Mills, Okehampton. The vehicle, which was green and probably ex-War Department, was used until 1922 when it was fitted with wooden benches, and redeclared as a Hackney Coach. It had a seating capacity of 26 and could be used for both pleasure trips and goods transport.

*The first wagonette for hire in Northlew seen outside the Green Dragon with John Lake in the doorway, 1912/13.*

Long-distance transport would have been difficult prior to the arrival of the railway in Ashbury. John Lake provided the first wagonette for hire from the Green Dragon but before this service, railway passengers made their way to and from Ashbury station either by foot or bicycle.

## The Coming of the Motor Car

*In about 1910, Mr J.R. Wright of Ashbury House owned two cars. One was a large Napier saloon and the other a large, red open-tourer. I cannot remember the maker's name but they were driven by a man named Spicer. The Napier was involved in an accident at Bogtown Corner. Spicer was coming in from Ashbury Station* [at] *about 4.30p.m., when the brakes failed on Bogtown Hill. He could not turn into Ashbury House so drove on into a well opposite Beech House. Later in the day, the car was pulled out by horses and parked where the telephone box is now. As a child, my father took some other children from the village up to Bogtown to see the damaged car. I understand that the car was towed by horses to Ashbury station on the Monday and put on the train to the maker's agent. The red car referred to was sold by Mr Wright to Mr Palmer of the Plume Hotel in Okehampton and for some years used as a taxi.* Fred Baker, 23 April 1993.

*Early motor cars in Northlew.*

Tom Andrew bought the first car owned in Northlew some time around 1914. It too was used as a taxi and was supplied by Messrs J. Glass & Sons of Okehampton. It was a black Model T Ford and the salesman was Mr J.T. Ruby.

*Early motor cars in Northlew.*

Goods now came by rail to Ashbury Station and there was a corresponding outflow of livestock, agricultural products, parcels and rabbits caught by trappers, their hind legs skewered together and packed in hedgerow crates.

### My father, Jim Ware, Rabbit Trapper, by Chris Ware.

*Born in Dolton, Jim came to Northlew with his family in 1922 when he was 19 years old. His parents kept the National Stores, which eventually became Sanders Shop and is now the Tailor's House in the Square. They did not have the shop for very long and Jim's father went to work at Milltown Farm for Heber Squire. Jim was known for his rabbit trapping and would average 40 rabbits a day, seven days a week from 15 September to 15 April. The rabbits were mainly caught by gin-trap since they brought a better price. Jim was an excellent shot in spite of the fact that he had lost an eye as a child after a bout of measles. He would enter into an agreement with a farmer so that for the price of annual rent for the farm, Jim would have sole trapping rights on the land.*

*Jim's day began with a cycle ride to the farm, sometimes as far away as Bowerland, near Sourton,*

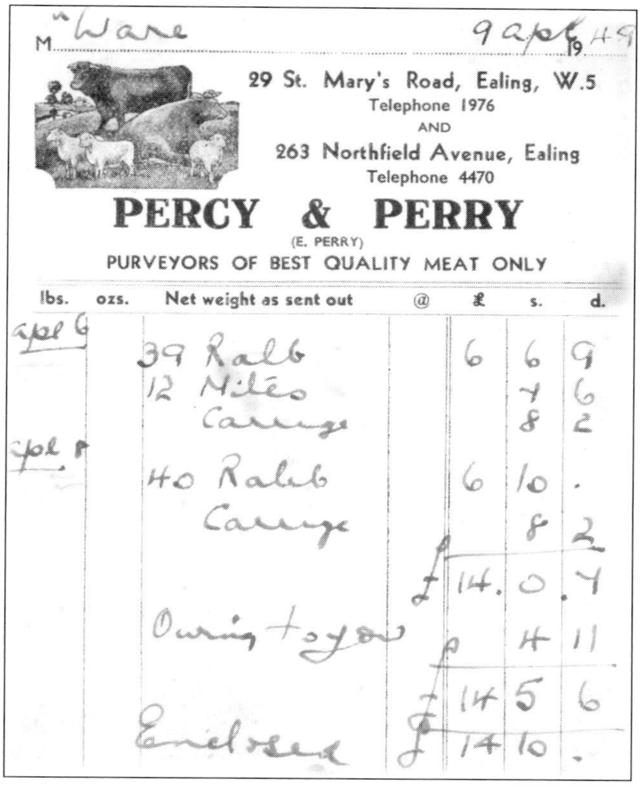

M^r Ware 9 Apl 19 49

29 St. Mary's Road, Ealing, W.5
Telephone 1976
AND
263 Northfield Avenue, Ealing
Telephone 4470

PERCY & PERRY
(E. PERRY)
PURVEYORS OF BEST QUALITY MEAT ONLY

| lbs. | ozs. | Net weight as sent out | @ | £ | s. | d. |
|---|---|---|---|---|---|---|
| Apl 6 | | 39 Ralb | | 6 | 6 | 9 |
| | | 12 Miles | | | 7 | 6 |
| | | Carriage | | | 8 | 2 |
| Apl 8 | | 40 Ralb | | 6 | 10 | . |
| | | Carriage | | | 8 | 2 |
| | | | £ | 14. | 0. | 7 |
| | | Owing to you | £ | | 4 | 11 |
| | | | £ | 14 | 5 | 6 |
| | | Enclosed | £ | 14 | 10 | . |

*Invoice from Percy & Perry of Ealing, London, for rabbits supplied by Jim Ware, 1949.*

*Clem Andrew, with daughter Joyce, beside his 'Regrator' lorry, fitted with seats for passengers, seen outside Church Gate.*

*arriving before daylight to set the traps; as many as 34 dozen. Without a break, Jim would work around the traps, paunching, legging and hanging the catch in various locations ready for Norman Born to collect. Throughout the day, he would move about a third of the traps, sieving them with dry earth to hide them and working until 4.30pm when it went dark. Then, and only then, would he stop for a break and a bite to eat. Tucked under a hedge, he would probably have two pipes of tobacco and a sleep before going for a final round trip of the snares, returning home between 10.00 and 11.00pm.*

*Jim's record catch was 148 rabbits in a single short stretch of hedge at Bowerland. At Mansditch Farm, near Castle Cross he caught 1,100 rabbits the first time over the land and on his second sweep, another 500. Jim could carry 100 rabbits on his pushbike and so heavy laden was it that if it fell over, he could not pick it up. He would take them to Ashbury Station where they were sent to London, arriving in London within 24 hours of being caught. In 1954 with the onset of myxomatosis Jim's trapping career came to an end. He was, however, able to continue fishing, and would go particularly for eels with a length of tailor's thread and wire 'platted' with a bunch of large earthworms. To the amusement of on-looking children he would haul out eels for them to dispatch.*

*Jim was also a gravedigger and would cut the churchyard grass, which he formed into a hayrick ready to sell off as prime hay at the end of the season. It was said he was a real gentleman as long as you did not upset him!*

The West Devon and North Cornwall Farmers depot at the railway station provided a distribution service for farmers. Much of this outgoing produce was sent by the 'regrator' – a little-used term nowadays for a middle-man dealer. Northlew's regrator in the 1920s and early '30s was Clem, brother of Henry and Maurice Andrew, the wheelwrights. Clem purchased what may have been the first lorry in Northlew, which was fitted with makeshift wooden seats and was used by the village for 'wayzgooze' on high days and holidays. It was Norman Born who seized the developing opportunities in road transport. Norman had first come to Northlew from Black Torrington in the 1920s to drive Clem Andrew's lorry, collecting eggs from farms in the area. He took with him a young boy named 'Pop' Gay, who would jump out to open and shut gates. Both of them were to play a great part in the local bus and coach industry. Norman later married Mabel Court, settled in Northlew and, in 1930, decided to start a business running a taxi and hire-car service from the village. Looking around for a suitable vehicle, he found a 20-horsepower Austin in the showrooms of A.C. Turner in Plymouth. The asking price was £25. Without enough money, it seemed that he would have to look elsewhere but Mr Turner, on hearing that Norman could only afford £20, let him have the car for that amount adding that perhaps he (Norman) would buy another car from him at a later date. As Norman's business expanded, that initial act of generosity was remembered and further business followed.

The Austin was taken back to Northlew and Norman would drive local people around the area whenever they needed transport. Car ownership was still a rarity and most folk had to hire a car if they wished to go any distance. Soon Norman obtained a regular income through a contract with

Devon County Council to convey children to and from Northlew School. A single journey was operated to school in the summer, the pupils walking home at the end of the day! During the darker winter months children would be driven both to and from school.

A lorry was the next vehicle purchased by Norman. This was used for coal deliveries as well as for cattle and general haulage. Fitting benches into the open body enabled the vehicle to be used for passengers and, at times, sheep and pigs could be penned at the back with people on the benches in front of them. A short pair of steps was carried to enable passengers to board and alight.

In 1931 Mr L.J. Morris of Morth Grange, Northlew, bought a small 14-seater charabanc believed to be a Model T Ford. With this, on Saturday 19 December 1931, he inaugurated the first bus service between Northlew and Okehampton. Before the opening run, his daughter christened 'The Green Kitten' bus with a glass of Devonshire cider. The return fare from Northlew to Okehampton was 2s.0d.; Durdon Cross, 1s.9d; and Waytown/Lower Gorhuish, 1s.6d. By 1932 the Green Kitten ran three days a week with excursions to Exeter, Bude, Tavistock, Plymouth, Dartmoor, Okehampton and Okehampton hamlets. However, local recollections suggest that Northlew people, particularly Amy Brooking who used to travel regularly to market with eggs and butter, were not fully accustomed to motor vehicles, and felt that Mr Morris drove a little too fast. Indeed Amy approached Norman Born to ask if he would take her to market. The Green Kitten service declined and by 1933 had been discontinued. Norman Born then became the sole operator. Norman was now able to run a regular service, leaving Northlew each Saturday at 10.00a.m. and 2.30p.m., returning from Okehampton at 12 noon and 5.30p.m. It proved very popular and by January 1934 the route was extended to include Crowden. So successful were the services that overloading became a problem and permission was sought to run additional journeys. Purpose-built passenger vehicles were purchased and the first to enter service was a 14-seater Chevrolet, bought for £30. It ran for many years until it was sold to a local farmer.

*Borns Tours outing by charabanc, 1930.* Driver: *Norman Born with passengers inluding Charlie and George Friend, Jimmy Elliott, Henry Andrew, Fred Smale, Archie King, Reg Wood, L. Valance.*

*Outing by charabanc.* Seated beside the driver: *Mr and Mrs Clem Andrew and daughter Joyce.*

*Norman Born's Coaches on an outing.* Drivers: *Charlie Hicks, Bill Jordan and Norman Born.*

## *Pre-War Expansion*

The pre-war period brought many opportunities for expansion, particularly when Alfred Temby of Okehampton decided to sell his business, including three coaches, and the use of the Town Mills premises in Okehampton. Norman could now operate two vehicles on any one day from Fore Street, Okehampton, with 25 destinations varying from Truro to Cheddar. There were also additional contracts for the school buses between Meldon, Fowley Down and Okehampton and a further increase in tours. The use of a canvas cover on coaches was widespread. On fine days it could be rolled back and passengers would enjoy fresh air and sunshine. One former driver on a rainy trip to Paignton glanced in his rear-view mirror to see two passengers holding up umbrellas, and the roof was on!

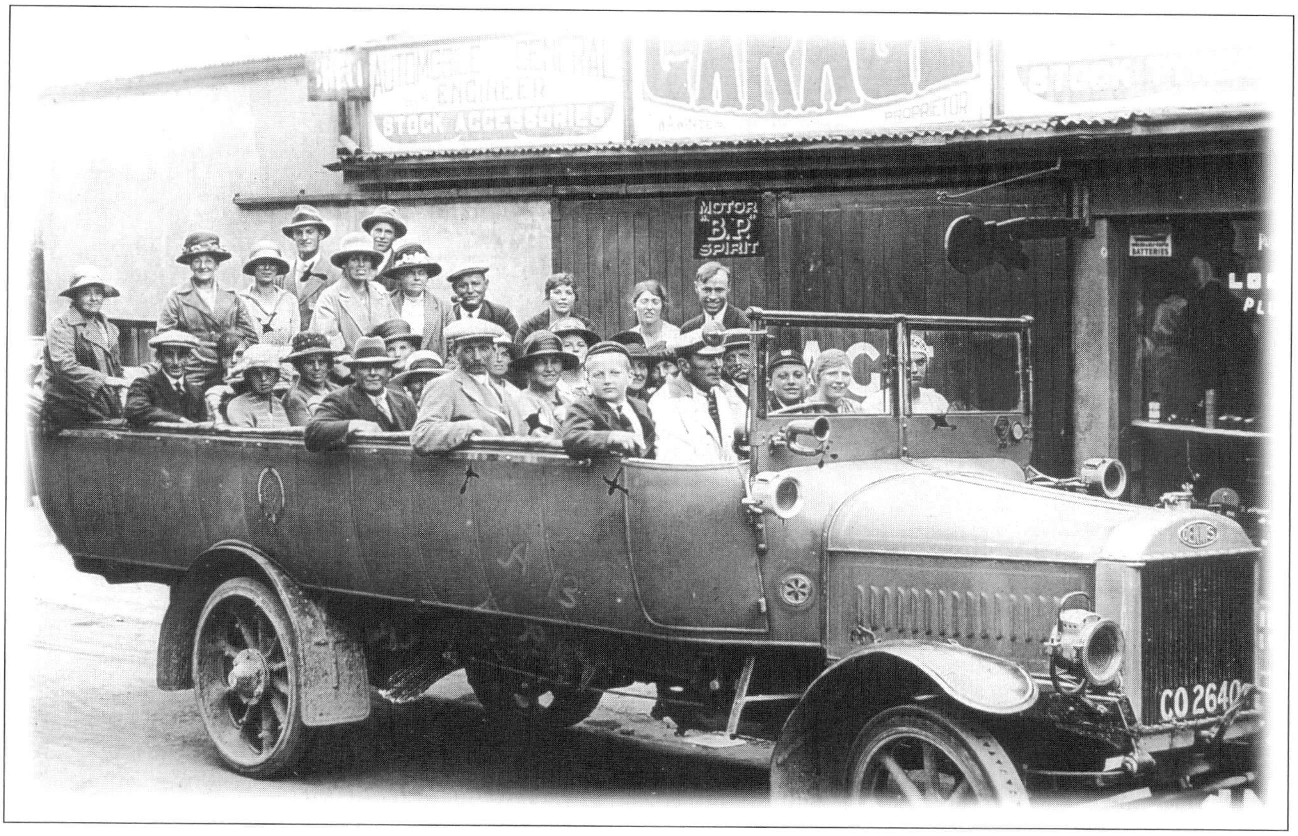


*Outing by charabanc seen here outside the Okehampton Garage.*

During 1939, with the threat of war, the Army began using Dartmoor for training. With soldiers wishing to spend their off-duty hours in Okehampton, late-evening journeys to and from Okehampton Camp began. The service included return journeys if there was a dance in the town. Transporting soldiers back to camp, high on the moor, could be eventful. The bus had a rear roof ladder for luggage, too much of a temptation for those who had spent all their pay. Not having the required sixpence return fare, soldiers would leap onto the ladder as the bus crawled up the steep hills out of Okehampton. A member of staff hiding on the roof would deal out a sharp blow with a ticket rack in order to deter the men from climbing the ladder. The outbreak of war meant that the tours programme and the regular trips had to be suspended. The Plymouth route was reduced to Thursdays only, but since many evacuees had come to the area, trips to the city were very popular. This service was always heavily loaded, even the threat of bombing and the destruction of the main shopping area could not deter travellers. Competition for seats was fierce, so much so that Born's had to put a 32-seater coach on by 1942. This was the first new coach to Northlew and even had its own conductor – Jack Webber, who, in return for collecting fares received a free ride to and from Plymouth.

### Jack Webber: Conductor and Trader, by Pop Gay, Driver

*Jack was a great character who would sit in his area – a double-seat ahead of the entrance, sectioned off... by a length of string. When one day a woman insisted that she wanted to sit in this area, there was quite a to-do. There Jack would sit plucking poultry, feathers flying everywhere, ready to walk miles through Plymouth selling chickens and rabbits. On one occasion, he was still in the market late in the afternoon when fruit was being sold off cheaply. Not wishing to miss a bargain, he bought some strawberries knowing he could make a bob or two on his return to Northlew. The fruit was duly tucked under the seats, supposedly out of harm's way. Unfortunately, a child had a 'little accident' on the return journey, but Jack, undeterred, dried the rather damp strawberries, and, with no one the wiser, they were all sold and enjoyed.*

On one Plymouth trip there were 50 people waiting to climb on board the 20-seat Dennis Ace bus. Pop Gay and Jack Webber were worried, but there was nothing for it but to pack everyone in. The bus took a different route home so as not to attract attention and finally reached Northlew. Pop and Jack wondered what reception they would receive from Mabel Born. However, she was delighted that they had looked after all the passengers.

## *Post-War Years*

Norman now had a fleet of seven coaches, some with upholstered seats! In 1946, the village school was reorganised and the older children transferred to Okehampton Secondary School. Born's Coaches were successful in obtaining the contract for transporting the Northlew students. Keeping the elderly fleet going at this time was no mean feat. On one occasion, Johnny Glover took a party to Exmoor and the coach broke down on Porlock Hill. He left it where it stood and Norman and Pop had to go out in a lorry to tow it back. They took with them a thin towing wire and a new thick rope. The wire was attached to both vehicles and, with Norman at the wheel of the lorry and Pop steering the coach, they set off home. The inevitable happened, seven times in total, and the new rope had to be used. The lorry became grounded on a narrow bridge and had problems negotiating tight bends in Lynmouth but the pair eventually reached Eggesford. Here, Norman, tired out, fell asleep at the wheel and ran into the back of the lorry, knocking out the lights. By Winkleigh, they had almost run out of petrol but they eventually found some in Hatherleigh. They finally arrived in Northlew at 6.00a.m. and immediately started repairing the bus in the dark and rain.

By 1965 the company comprised 14 coaches and a taxi, but due to a decline in passengers Norman sold off part of the business. Norman died on 4 July 1980 leaving a widow and four children. 'Born's Tours' remained a familiar name in the area, being used by his partial successors, Bruce and Parker. Four of his former drivers also ran their own passenger transport business, Pop Gay, Frank Guscott, Charlie Allin and Bill Jordan. Charlie Allin is remembered for carrying a shotgun on the coach. Provided the bus was empty, or carrying very few passengers, he would stop to bag

*Gay's Tours. Pop Gay did work for the Army including involvement in the Queen's Silver Jubilee Tour of the West Country – an honour for a village coach company to be part of the royal entourage to Truro, Falmouth and Wadebridge.*

*Norman Born's 1950 Austin bus, FCO 314, in Okehampton on the market-day service from Northlew. Norman is in the driver's seat chatting to an unidentified man standing on the step. In the background is one of Bill Reddaway's cattle lorries from South Zeal.*

any passing pheasant. Bill Jordan tragically died just as he was about to take over the Station Road premises in Northlew. Norman Born ran the business for more than 40 years; he carried passengers from countryside to town, to school and to the market and shops, for pleasure and leisure. It was Pop Gay who eventually took over the business.

# In More Recent Times

### Carmel Coaches

In 1984, Pop Gay decided to retire and sell the business to Tony Hazell. On hearing of Pop's sale, Tony, together with his wife Pauline and two children, moved to Northlew and took over the business, naming the firm Carmel Coaches, after his children Carolyn and Michael. Carolyn eventually obtained her full PSV licence, national and international qualifications, and Michael, at the age of 18, became qualified to drive. At the time of writing, school contracts for Devon County Council and private hire, together with a range of tours and excursions, are the backbone of the business. Tony's love of older vehicles enabled him to secure the Dartmoor Rover Service using the 1951 Bristol Half Cab and the 1950 Daimler Coach.

John Friend, Barry Shaw and George Ridges maintain the vehicles at the workshops in Station Road, which has been a coach depot since the days of Norman Born. Many of the drivers are women: Juliet Yelland, who has driven for the firm for 12 years; Marilyn Davies, who used to drive London buses; and Pauline and Carolyn Hazell. Judy Turley and Marg Rundle drive regularly part-time and Les Forsdyke has driven for Tony almost since the business began. Dave Jones is a full-time driver and Peter Spry, Bill Ware and Steve Thorne work part-time. There are many other occasional part-time drivers.

*Carmel Coaches' Dartmoor Rover Service. Daimler Coach, 1950, and Bristol half-cab bus, 1951.*

*Carmel coach entering Northlew via Fordatown Bridge with Rockey Cottage in the background.*

The foot-and-mouth outbreak in February 2001 devastated the area and severely affected the business, with three of the regular drivers being subject to movement restriction orders. There were 20 jobs cancelled during the first week and virtually no private hire for the months of March and April 2001. With the local economy dependent upon agriculture, the effects of foot and mouth were felt by all local businesses. At the time of writing, Carmel Coaches continues to be a cheerful and personal service in the local area.

# Rail Transport

Ashbury train station was probably built around 1879 when the branch line to Holsworthy was first opened. In 1881 there were six trains per day and, by 1890, eight trains per day to Holsworthy. The line to Bude was not opened until 1898. Ashbury Station was one of the smallest stations to be found on the West Devon/North Cornwall routes, with a passing loop, tiny goods yard and a few small buildings. It changed very little throughout its existence, even the oil lighting remaining until closure. No footbridge was provided, but the

*Ashbury Station looking towards Okehampton, 1905.*

*Ashbury Station. On the left is the West Devon and North Cornwall Farmers' Depot with Goods Shed behind. In the centre is the original building with the porch, later to become parcels office and waiting room, on the right open up-line waiting room – a miserably cold place which nobody used.*

*West Devon and North Cornwall Farmers' Depot.*

flight of steps on each side of the road bridge allowed passengers to cross between the platforms. The goods shed was small and had a short canopy over the loading points on each side. Signalling was well established when this line was opened, so the 12-lever signal-box formed part of the original fittings. Bill Piper kept the handles brightly polished, never to be touched by bare hands, but always with a piece of cloth. The signal-box also served as a booking-office where tickets could be purchased. By the end of the Second World War, the goods yard had been lengthened to hold 34 wagons, an engine and brake van. Reg Bragg, who lived in the Railway Cottages up the hill, was the stationmaster in the 1930s, '40s and '50s. Bill Piper was his assistant. 'Gat' Perry, who was involved in the unloading of wagons, lived at 'Arcade' in Northlew.

During the 1960s two convicts broke out of Dartmoor Prison and, in their attempt to escape, followed the railway line to Okehampton and then on to Ashbury. It is thought that they entered Wigford Mill and stole jewellery, but it is certain that they broke into the signal-box and the stationmaster's house at Ashbury. Special Constables were called out to assist the local police force in searching farm buildings. Eventually, the two convicts were arrested at a trackside hut between Ashbury Station and Maddaford Moor when smoke from their cooking fire alerted the police.

Gerald Smallacombe and his daughter Geraldine Walter now jointly own Ashbury Station. Geraldine, together with her grandmother, Mrs Olive Smallacombe, live in the converted station house. Alan and Tracy Lear bought the old goods shed and freight yard and are planning to site a railway carriage on the siding. Mrs Olive Smallacombe has lived at Ashbury Station for 64 years having been married to the signalman when the station was last open.

*An early view of Ashbury Station.*

*An early view of passengers waiting for a train to arrive.*

*The stone road bridge at Ashbury Station, 1930s.*

*Train waiting at the down platform, Ashbury Station. The passenger crossing can be seen.*

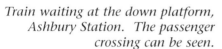

*Ashbury Station signal-box. Reg Bragg, stationmaster, with his assistant, Bill Piper, who kept the 12 signal leavers brightly polished. Bill would occasionally allow children to wait in the warmth of the signal-box after a chilly cycle ride from Northlew.*

***Northlew Friendly Society. The church parade in 1914 followed by lunch, annual meeting and sports. The parade was always held on the last Thursday in May and became known as 'Club Day'.***

Right: *Northlew Friendly Society's annual Club Day, outside the Honeychurch Inn, Harpers Hill. This is at the time when the inn was also a Livery Stable or 'Posting'. Louis Adams (in top hat), known as 'the Dragon'. Jim Shobbrook (in top doorway) lost his legs in the First World War, in the lower doorway is Sam Curtis and Bill Tapp (with bicycle). The young boy with the flag is Percy Andrew, the boy to the right is C. Curtis. The little girl is Vera Pascoe, the boy at back is Reggie Wood, the boy on far right is Will Watkins.*

*Northlew Friendly Society (Men's Social Club) annual parade outside the church. Northlew Band is seen joining the parade, early 1900s.*

Chapter 9

# THE VILLAGE AT PLAY, PAST & PRESENT

## Introduction

In nineteenth-century England, self-respecting workers and small traders built up, as a means of escape from the stigma of the Poor Law and the inquisitions of charity, their own agencies of mutual help. Such organisations as Penny Banks, Co-operative Societies and Friendly Societies grew rapidly. With fewer than one million members in 1815, Friendly Societies totalled four million members by the 1870s. These Societies represented the collective efforts of men to finance their own protection, combining the virtues of thrift and self-help. Many of the present Northlew clubs and societies have arisen as a direct result of the original Friendly Society.

## Northlew and Ashbury Men's Social Club

The Northlew and Ashbury Friendly Society, later to become known as the Northlew and Ashbury Men's Social Club, was founded in 1907 by Herbert Woollcombe. Most parishes in Devon had a Friendly Society at that time into which members paid three shillings per quarter. The benefits of the society were, on production of a doctor's certificate, nine shillings per week 'Bed Pay' or six shillings per week 'Walking Pay'. The Men's Social Club gathered in the cob barn at Elmfield, a property that is, in 2002, occupied by Jed's mother, Mrs Dryden. The walls were painted green and red, there were newspapers, a small library and a three-quarter-sized billiard table.

*Northlew Friendly Society Club Day sports, early 1900s. Man in the middle in suit is Edgar Harry of Madworthy Farm.*

## Club Day

The Social Club held their annual meeting on the last Thursday in May, 'Club Day'. This began with a service in the church, followed by a roll-call of members made by the secretary, William Shobbrook. Members who failed to attend were fined one shilling. The Band would then head a procession to the school where members enjoyed a meal of roast beef and vegetables, followed by plum pudding and beer. This meal was provided by the tenants of either the Green Dragon Inn or the Honeychurch Arms, tenders for which had to be obtained about a month before. After the meal, the president, Herbert Woollcombe, would hold the Annual Meeting. During the afternoon, sports would be held in Stiles Meadow, followed by a public tea. Throughout the day, stalls would be set up in the Village Square. Mr and Mrs Charles Trigger would arrive from Dolton with a horse and covered wagon to sell home-made sweets, sugar sticks and biscuits. In later years, they used a Ford van. Dick Hellier, from Holsworthy, ran another stall and sold knives of every kind, cut-throat razors and reading glasses. As night fell, the Square was lit by oil flares and the day would end with a dance in the school, continuing until about 2.00a.m. Music was provided by Harry Drew from Okehampton with his accordion, who arrived in a wagonette, driven by Cabby Bates from the White Hart, Okehampton.

A further room was added to the Victory Hall in approximately 1924, the Social Club moved into this and a full-sized table was provided. Membership at that time was one shilling per quarter. The Friendly Society, or the Men's Social Club as it was known, closed in 1928.

*Northlew Band outside the newly built Victory Hall, c.1920. Originally there were no funds available with which to purchase uniforms, so members wore their own clothes, the only semblance of uniform being their headgear – bowler hats to begin with, and caps later on.* Left to right, back row: *Walter Sanders, Fred Bater, Henry Friend, Charlie Friend, Reggie Wood, Ern Adams, Merlin Hortop, Sam Brooking, C. Smale;* front: *Cecil Brooking, Ern Smale, Harold Friend, Fred Baker, Sid Stiles, Archie King.*

## Northlew Silver Band

There has been a band in Northlew, with the exception of the war period, for the last 90 years. It was started in 1911 by the members of the Northlew and Ashbury Men's Social Club. The church organist at the time, Tom Craig, knew of some second-hand instruments for sale in Tavistock, and, together with Jack Webber, also an early enthusiast, traced these instruments for purchase. Under Tom Craig's tuition, the members began mastering their instruments. John Palmer of Bratton Clovelly was the first bandmaster. The practices took place in the blacksmith's shop with oil lamps for lighting, and no heating at all during the winter months. Early engagements were at fêtes and carnivals.

The outbreak of the First World War caused the band to cease functioning as its members left to serve their country. It was not until 1920 that it was reformed under a new bandmaster, Reg Wood, son of Tom Wood who owned the tailor's, outfitter's and grocer's shop at London House, Northlew. Reg was a well-trained and highly accomplished musician, he taught piano and, for years, was the church organist. Under his direction the band flourished.

The first uniforms appeared in 1927. John Webber very generously offered to purchase second-hand uniforms, provided the band members would wear them. 16 brand new outfits were bought in 1935 and were worn for the first time when the band played at the village celebrations to mark the Silver Jubilee of King George V and Queen Mary. At this, the band led a procession of schoolchildren dancing the floral dance around the village, returning to the Square for the presentation of medals and celebration beakers.

Below: *The Revd John Worthington, whose photograph hangs in the Men's Club, was a driving force in the band's formation.*

*Northlew Band, an early photograph.* Left to right, back row: *Fred Baker, Charlie Friend, Henry Friend, Sam Brooking, Harold Friend, Tom Smale, Archie King;* middle row: *Percy Andrew, Fred Bater, Reggie Wood, Merlin Hortop, Ern Adams, Walter Sanders;* front: *?, Cecil Brooking.*

*Northlew Band seen in the rectory paddock in their new uniforms. The total cost of the uniforms amounted to £56 or £3.10s.0d. for each suit. With only 16 uniforms available, one wonders how the various sizes and shapes of the bandsmen could be accommodated. The uniforms were still being worn as hand-me-downs in the 1970s.*

*Northlew Band in fancy dress, 1918. With bell, Louis Adams; trombone, Will Hortop; drum, Bill Badcock; trombone, Archie King; trumpet, Will Watkins.*

*Northlew Band, Bonfire Night procession. Torches are carried by Harold Sanders, Charlie Friend, W.J. Smale and 'Gat' Perry. In front is John Jordan, who farmed Ashbury and served as a Special Constable.*

The Second World War depleted the band of its strength once again but reformed in 1946. The bandmaster at the time was Fred Baker. The secretary, Percy Adams, gave tuition to the 20 new members who had joined. Funds being short, and new instruments and music needed, it was decided

*Northlew Band in the Victory Hall.* Left to right, back row: *?, A. Webber, W. Glover, C. Brooking, T. Maynard, E. Pocock, W. Skinner;* centre: *A. White (who tutored the band), H. Sanders, F. Bater, G. Sanders, C. Baker, A. Friend, B. Luxton, W.J. Smale (chairman), P. Adams, ?, W. Jordan, F. Baker, J. Webber;* front: *G. Knight, R. Jordan, G. Maynard.*

*Northlew Silver Band: W.J. Smale, chairman, presenting Ben Luxton with his baton on appointment as bandmaster, 1950s. Great strides were made during the 1950s, beginning with the band becoming a member of the South West Brass Band Association in 1950. Entering the contests sponsored by the Association, they met with early success, coming second at the first attempt under the direction of Mr Ben Luxton of Okehampton.*

*Northlew Silver Band, early 1960s.* Left to right, back row: *Bill Skinner, Percy Adams, Charlie Baker, Audrey Friend, Henry Cole, Cecil Brooking, ?, Fearnley Bater;* centre: *Jack Webber, Tom Maynard, ? Wright, Gerald Maynard, Peter Pocock, Bill Smale, Gordon Sanders, Archie Webber, Colson Isaacs;* front: *Brian Hill, Harold Sanders, Ben Luxton, Fred Baker, Reggie Wood, Fred Adams (visually impaired accordion player), Trevor Hill, Philip Wonnacott.*

in 1948 to hold a Guy Fawkes fancy-dress parade on the Friday nearest to 5 November, culminating with a bonfire in the Square. The band led the torchlight procession, and the bonfire was followed by a dance in the Victory Hall. These celebrations were so popular and successful that they have become the Northlew Carnival and a regular event ever since.

*Northlew Silver Band: South West Brass Bands Association 26th Annual Championships held at Paignton, 1972. The band repeated their initial success on several subsequent occasions, being rewarded with a well-earned first place in the 1969 competition held at Paignton. They are shown here wearing their new ex-Bideford Bands uniforms.* Left to right, back row: *Julie Bissoni, David Gilbert, Helen Spry, Graham Church, Charlie Baker, Christopher Hunt, Claire Millership;* centre: *Fernley Bater, Mrs Church, Graham Alford, Paul Church, Henry Church, George Richards, Shirley Brooking, Francis Church;* front: *Monica Brooking, Maurice Davey, Tom Maynard, Crispin Church, Percy Adams (bandmaster), Cecil Brooking, Roger Gilbert, Bill Jordan.*

Joining the band, like joining the choir, was almost to be expected for village boys. No previous experience was necessary. Lessons took place in the refreshment room of the Victory Hall when youngsters began on cornets or tenor horns. The heavier instruments, such as euphoniums, E-Flats and B-Flats were reserved for older band members such as Archie King and Bill Parkhouse. Band practice was weekly and extra lessons took place at Fred Baker's house for novice players. These beginners would be playing 'third cornet parts'; not the main tune or the 'twiddly bits' assigned to first cornets. It was said that the star first cornet player, Merlin Hortop, always played an octave higher than the score. The novices, however, just supplied the notes in waltzes and marches, always on the same note.

### A First 'Playing Out' by Claude Smale

*Our first 'playing out' was at Bratton Club Day. Our instruments would have to be gleaming so I was made to spend fruitless, and no doubt fractious, hours with the Brasso tin. No uniforms would fit us youngsters, of course, but I had been privileged to wear a band hat. The braid was already tarnished and the inside padded out with the* News Chronicle, *but I felt like a king! We had two easy pieces to play, 'The Highwayman' and 'North Star' – both marches.*

*Northlew Band, here thought to be photographed for the first time, 'playing out' before the days of uniform outside Tom Wood's outfitter's and tailor's shop, c.1911.*

*For our first piece we were told by Fred, I thought, to put up 'North Star'. This I dutifully did and I played my third cornet part faultlessly. 'Next up,' said Fred, 'put up North Star.' Astonished, I protested 'Us've just bin playin' tha'.' Fred looked at me pitifully. 'Aw!' he said. 'All the rest of us've been playing Highwayman!'*

*Northlew Silver Band, 1960s. The band eventually became the Northlew Silver Band when the parish of Ashbury was incorporated. The band claim to be the only 'village' band in Devon.* Left to right, back row: *John Neno, Archie Webber, Bill Glover, Cecil Brooking, Tom Maynard, Peter Pocock, 'Sneezer' Bevan;* centre: *Arthur White (bandmaster, Sidmouth Band), Harold Sanders, Fernley Bater, Gordon Sanders, Charlie Baker, Audrey Friend, Ben Luxton, Bill 'Nipper' Smale, Percy Adams, Gordon Butler, Bill Jordan, Fred Baker, Jack Webber;* front: *Neil Butler, Graham Knight, Reggie Jordan, Gerald Maynard.*

*Northlew Silver Band, December 1999. Three of the four generations of the Brooking family who have played in the band are seen here at the celebration of Cecil's 60 years' service to the band: Simon Brooking, Cecil Brooking, Andy Brooking.*

*Northlew Silver Band Christmas Concert in the Victory Hall, December 2001.* Left to right, back row: *Marilyn Livingstone, Charles Baker, Tracey Spry;* centre: *Len Smith, Pat Carter (secretary), David Gilbert, Cecil Brooking (treasurer), Joanne Maynard, Sharon Dufty, Simon Brooking, Sarah Gilbert, Andy Brooking, Nicola Richards;* front (seated): *Roger Gilbert, Tom Maynard, Maurice Davey (bandmaster), Peter Spry, Ron Carter, George Davey (president).*

In 1971, younger people were encouraged to join, and since that date many children from Northlew and adjoining villages have played in the band. It was the policy to encourage youngsters to join and special tuition and practice evenings were held for them. The bandmaster was Percy Adams, having joined in 1934, and become secretary in 1938 – a position he filled for more than 30 years. He was bandmaster until 1997 when he retired. In 1995, following two years of letter writing, the band was successful in their bid for £12,500 for new instruments from the Sports and Arts Foundation. After Percy's retirement, Maurice Davey became bandmaster and continues at the time of writing. George Davey became president when Gordon Alford sadly passed away. The band hold their practices at the rear of the Victory Hall on a Wednesday evening in their own premises which were acquired 25 years ago. Previously, practices were held in the Church Room. They play at fêtes and carnivals to raise funds, as their greatest expense is music score. After a difficult year due to the outbreak of foot and mouth when all social and village events came to a halt, the band reassembled in the autumn of 2001 to the delight of the village.

*Carnival float 'Jim Blades & Co, Barbers', c.1910. Before Northlew Band's Carnival became a Bonfire Night tradition, the village had a Carnival using horse-drawn vehicles.*

*Carnival Queen Eileen Parker with Marjorie Kneebone and Cynthia Curtis, 1951.*

*Northlew Carnival, Carol Jordan and Wilfred Spry in fancy dress. Spectators include Hilda Rowe and Bill Isaacs, early 1950s.*

*Grace Adams – Carnival Queen, 1952.*

*Carnival Queen May Dufty with Gillian Jordan and Bridget Friend, 1960.*

*Grace Adams crowning Jean Parker as Carnival Queen, 1953.*

*Nurse and ambulance driver are Olive Newton and Jack Webber, 1960s.*

*Connie Banbury and Lilian Spry in fancy dress.*

Left: *Marian Adams, Carnival Queen, with attendants, Marion Squire and Carole Jordan, 1963.*

*Some 28 Carnival Queens with the first, Eileen Wilson (Parker), seen here at the November 2001 Carnival in the Victory Hall.* Left to right, back row: *Eleanor Dryden, Angie Short, Julie Letchford, Kirsty Lindsay, Trish Rundle, Clare Millership, Sharon Cole, Susan Hawker, Joanne Maynard, Natasha West;* centre: *Julie Chick, Bridget Cole, Libby Adams, Julie Andrew, Kay Algar, Tina Adams, Sarah Maynard, Shirley Maynard, Winifred Davey, Caroline Friend, Jo Luxton;* front: *Marian Lester, May Burridge, Phyllis Martin, Jean Adams, Joyce Dunn, Marj Brown, Eileen Wilson.*

*Carnival costumes: Nigel Isaac, Paul Adams, Peter Isaac, Stuart Adams and Sarah Adams, 1970.*

Right below: *Harem Girls in Women's Institute sketch: Hilary Adams, Grace Adams, Marion Gerry.*

*Northlew St John's Ambulance Brigade, 1957.* Left to right, back row: *Henry Andrew, Revd Geiple, Mrs Loram, ?, ?, Mr Maddaford, ?, ?, Miss Mitchell, Revd Parsons, Mrs Smale, group leader;* centre: *Marion Worden, Margaret Newcombe, Marion Adams, Sandra Breyley, Betty Newton, Sandra Millership, Carol Jordan, Brenda Jordan;* front: *Sheila Mounter, Bridget Friend, Elizabeth Newcombe, Anne Elliott, ?, Wendy Voaden, Marion Squire, Gillian Jordan, Pauline Taylor.*

## The Churchwomen's Guild

The Churchwomen's Guild has existed in the village for almost 100 years and in the past attracted a substantial membership of all ages. Meeting on the third Wednesday in the month and traditionally chaired by the incumbent's wife, it was, and still is, part social club and part church working party. Covers for the church kneelers were made by the guild and members have frequently raised money for various church requirements. At present the guild meets together with the Methodist Fellowship and most members of both organisations are aged over 60. Miss Enid Baker, a keen member and organiser for many years, presented a set of red chairs and white and blue pyrex teacups in the Church Room to the guild in the 1950s.

*The Northlew Women's Institute celebrated the 50th anniversary of the formation of the WI Movement in Devon by Mrs J. Jordan presenting a wooden seat to the village on behalf of members. Present were WI members, Parish Councillors, Northlew Silver Band and representatives from village organisations. June 1970.*

## Northlew Women's Institute

The first committee of the Northlew Women's Institute met on 23 February 1922 with nine committee members attending. This group of energetic ladies, led by Rosetta Pinnock, was known as the Northlew Women's Social Club; subscriptions were 2s. per member. The membership increased over the following five years to 48 members in 1927, reducing to 33 members by the time the Second World War was declared. The Women's Institute then suspended their activities, although during the war they assisted with fund-raising and 'Comforts for Troops' events. The group restructured and once again became active. There was a six-month break in 1993 due to lack of support but interest was rekindled and the Northlew Women's Institute is still active in 2002.

Over the active 71 years of Northlew's WI, family names re-occur; foremost being Mrs Adams, but also Mesdames Jordan, Spry, Friend and Curtis. The Adams family spans three generations, the grandmothers of the current vice-president being founder members. The meetings were held in the Victory Hall, where a coal stove had to be lit before any function during the winter months. Each year a 'deserving cause' would be chosen and the ladies would make a special effort so that a donation could be made towards a community project. The following have benefited over the years:

*Presentation at annual Women's Institute Produce Show, early 1950s.* Left to right, back row: *Lilian Spry, Kate Gay, Charlotte Smale;* centre: *Doris Spry, Mrs Friend, Ivy Curtis, Ruth Medland, Mrs Furse, ?, Hilary Adams;* front: *Mrs Vincent, Mrs Jordan, WI Official. During these years the members have organised whist drives, dances, skittle tournaments, produced plays and produce shows for the community as well as improving their artistic skills and home economics by inviting speakers and demonstrators to the monthly meetings.*

*Northlew Women's Institute, 1965.* Left to right, back row: *Miss Shobbrook, Mrs Cleverdon, Mrs Yelland, Mrs Gratton, Mrs L. Spry, Mrs E. Wilson, Mrs J. Adams;* centre: *Mrs Lacey, Mrs D. Spry, Mrs I. Curtis, Mrs D. Hortop, Mrs C. Smale, Mrs S. Jordan, ?;* front: *Mrs J. Spry, Mrs C. Friend, Mrs M. Born, Mrs B. Jordan, Mrs B. Vincent, Mrs F. Adams, Mrs Dunn.*

Exeter Hospice for the Terminally Ill, Royal Devon & Exeter Hospital Baby Unit, Freedom Fields Hospital Ultrasound Machine, the Exeter Orthopaedic Hospital, The Castle Hospital Lift Fund and, recently, The Okehampton Eye Clinic and the 'Green Wellie' Appeal of 2001. In 1965 an invitation was received from Buckingham Palace for a member to attend a Garden Party in May. The lucky lady was Mrs W. Spry. Miss Baker, postmistress, had the privilege of meeting the Prince and Princess of Wales in March 1983.

Over the years the ladies have entered the Okehampton Agricultural Show and the Women's Institute Co-operative Competition. They have been successful with two second places in 1997 and 1999 and a first place in 1998, together with reaching the finals of the Skittles Tournament.

## *The Northlew and Ashbury Victory Hall*

The original founding trustees managed the Victory Hall from its earliest days. On becoming a registered charity in August 1973, a management committee made up of 11 elected members and 12 members representing organisations within the village took over the running of the hall. Currently, Denis Adams is chairman, Ted Hole, vice-chairman, Lyn Taylor, secretary and Janet Millership, treasurer. Becoming a charity gave access to grants to enable extension work to be carried out and gave relief from both taxation and local rates. Repair and maintenance of the building has always been a concern so fund-raising was particularly important. Since the 1920s, fund-raising has been called 'the effort' and the 'Annual Effort' was especially important. Such an effort for Christmas 1929 was a concert, featuring the Delabole Optimists at which Mr T. Wood, Mr T. Andrew and Mr D. Putt showed people to their seats while Mr B. Dufty, Mr H. Andrew and Mr A. King were at the door. Mr B. Dufty promised a basket of apples with Mr Hortop and Mr Friend offering to sell them. Mr Putt provided refreshments for the concert party. The principal fund-raising event in recent years has been the Northlew Horse Show, which raises approximately £1,000 for the fund each year. The horse show reflects a tradition of gymkhanas and sports, which were held in Northlew and Ashbury as part of the 'Welcome Home Fund'.

*The Victory Hall, Northlew, photographed not long after completion, 1921.*

### *Victory Hall Events Over the Years*

#### Concerts and Socials

Concerts generally took the form of a series of arranged musical turns with some comic songs and sketches thrown in. There were concert parties who went round the district but usually the performers were from the village. Typically, the Methodist Male Voice Choir would sing, piano pupils of Reggie Wood would play some pieces and members of the band would perform. There would be sketches or comic songs, usually in exaggerated dialect, making fun of local events and personalities. The school usually contributed with items involving the children. In between there might be games, competitions, spelling bee's or a fancy-dress parade. Vera Perry was a natural stage

*Elaine Peak, Methodist minister's wife, in role 'Nobody likes a fairy when she's old', at the British Legion Christmas Party, December 2001.*

performer and seemed to have a comic part in every sketch. Roddie Rees of Ashbury was a gifted tenor and Ben Dufty of South Yeo invariably contributed as a bass solo. Mr Ellis, then living at Broomfield, was an accomplished violinist.

For any occasion in the Victory Hall there would be refreshments of tea and sandwiches, usually taken during an interval, when people would chat together. A truly social event, which remains unchanged to this day. Recent events include British Legion Christmas Parties, a musical evening held in aid of Methodist Church funds, Harvest Supper and Christmas Lunch in aid of St Thomas' Church funds, band concerts, Parent Teacher Association dances and discos, as well as table-top sales and more.

**Early Film Shows**

Mr Nicholls, a friend of Jack Webber, came from Plymouth with a projector to show films. These were silent and mostly cowboy films, or Charlie Chaplin features. The hall would be filled and, because it was unheated, coats were worn. Hats, however, had to be removed. There were frequent breakdowns; the projector would chatter to a halt and the screen would go blank to loud groans of derision and dismay. There would be quite a wait whilst all was put right. The first 'talkie' seen in the village was provided by a Bourneville Cocoa team. A van arrived during the day; invitations were sent round and the film shown in the evening. With the extra incentive of 'free samples' there was a good turnout.

**'A Northlew Song' sung to the tune of 'Widdecombe Fair' at one of the many Victory Hall Concerts**

*Six men o' Norloo bevore ee now stand*
*Born an' bred een the County o' Debbem*
*An six fairer men een the world you won't find*

*Than Ken Southwick, Ken Gerry, Tom Andrew, Bill Smale,*
*Reggie Wood an' Dr McInnes & all...*

*Us went up t' London one fine summer's day*
*Went there by airplane us did – ees ee fey*
*An' it pitched down in Hyde Park before it got dark, with...*

*Us strapesied inside o' the gert G.P.O.*
*Axed ver a poind o' paint daunt you know*
*But they told us they nivver sold paint Oh, No, No, to*

*So London you zee idden up t' the times*
*Tidden up to' Norloo an' that you will find*
*For over t' Henry Andrews there's paints of all kinds, for...*

*Tom Pearce, Tom Pearce, lend me your grey mare*
*Yers a vew turnips left behind from March fair*
*Us've run out o' petrol but 'er 'll git us there with...*

This song was probably performed in the 1960s.

### Dances

Probably one of the most popular early dance bands, usually a quintet, was 'The Premier Dance Band' from Okehampton. Jimmy Gale, the hairdresser, who played piano, whilst his daughter played the saxophone, was bandleader. She played very well, her leg pumping violently to the beat of her right heel. There was an ambitious drummer and other players came and went from time to time. It was the home-grown Reggie Wood, alone on the piano, who was most favoured by the keen dancers as providing the best dancing tempo. Reggie would play all night if need be, his head cocked to one side to avoid the cigarette he had constantly on the go, surveying the crowd over his glasses and droning the tune under his breath. Another popular dance band was called 'The Elite'. Les Vallance is fondly remembered as having played the trombone, when it is said he would have been 'good for half an hour and then he'd fade out'. He often had to be carried home! Men tended to gather on one side of the hall and women on the other. If there was a certain lack of boldness, this was soon eased by the 'excuse me' dances, when a man could exchange partners by tapping the shoulder of another. The village policeman, invariably, would be hovering outside, his cape on his shoulder. Tom Baker would be at the door taking money and Henry Andrew would be master of ceremonies. An MC was deemed essential for every kind of do, even whist drives, and Henry was always it.

Dances such as 'The Lancers' were regularly featured because they always had been and everybody knew the steps. Likewise, 'The Military Two-Step' was popular. There were always plenty of takers for the quicksteps and waltzes, far fewer for the more tricky foxtrots. Wartime brought out conflicts between the younger and older generations as new dance tunes became popular. The greatest upset, however, came with the arrival of American troops from Halwill. They flooded the dance floor and, in the end, brought along their own noisy jazz band. This took the stage during the interval and, inevitably, took over. The younger people, eager to be up to date, embraced this 'jitterbugging' style, but for many old folk, the world had taken a turn for the worst. A military police jeep usually accompanied the Americans and would join the local policeman outside the hall.

### Youth Club

The Youth Club was started after the Second World War, approximately 1946–48, by the headmaster and his wife, Mr and Mrs Gerry. Club meetings were held in the Victory Hall and, initially, there were about 12 to 16 members. Two of the local boys used to play the piano for dancing and singing. Indoor hockey was played using a soft ball and there was also table tennis and darts. In spring and summer football and netball were played outside. The Youth Club also performed a few short, one-act plays. Occasionally, there would be an evening coach outing. The Youth Club carried on in this way for a few years and then numbers began to dwindle. Miss Baker, the postmistress, with the help of Revd Geiple, started it up again in the Church Room. When Revd Geiple left, the new rector, Revd King, took over with Mrs Pat Durston, Mrs Katie Gay and Col Langdon with help from any mother who could spare the time. The numbers increased to about 30 children, which was too many for the Church Room so the club moved back to the Victory Hall. After a while, the older children became more interested in the local Young Farmers' Club and so the Youth Club ended again.

In 1986 the Methodist Sunday School started a Questers evening run by Brenda Curtis and Winifred Davey for all village children. The ages catered for were nine to eleven year olds, and as there was nothing in the village for younger children, Questers included five to nine year olds for

*Youth Club, in concert, early 1950s. Hilary Adams, Cecily Curtis, Cecil Brooking, Vera Brooking, Henry Luxton, Valerie Worden, Joyce Brooking, Joan Tapp, Richard Bater, Phyllis Brooking, Vera Gay.*

*Youth Club Concert, early 1950s, 'The Old Log Cabin'.*

*Youth Club play* The Thresher, *early 1950s.*

*Youth Club outing to Dartmoor, July 1952.*
Left to right, back row: *?, ?, ?;* centre: *Pip Wilson, Michael Adams, Ruth Medland, Richard Bater, Bill Isaac, Hilary Adams;* front: *?, Miss Wonnacott, Peggy Martin, Phyllis Brooking, Joyce Brooking.*

*Questers Youth Club craft work, 2002.*

the first half of the evening and nine to eleven year olds for the latter part. A while later, a junior craft evening was started on Friday nights. The Questers Youth Club reached their 21st anniversary in 1997 and celebrations were held. At the time of writing, the Questers have been running for more than 25 years. Although it has changed over the years from the original Youth Club, it has proved to be very popular. Mothers still continue to take turns in helping out. The Club has raised considerable amounts for different charities and the building of the Methodist Hall in Northlew.

**Northlew Amateur Football Club**

Bill Mounter was always interested in football but, to watch a game, he had to travel to Black

*Northlew Football Club. First Annual Club dinner in the Victory Hall.* Seated at table, left side: *Bill Voaden, Tom Andrew, Steve Voaden, Ron Arthurs, Colin Martin, Ray Vallance, Derek Packer at end;* right side: *Bill Mounter, Wilf Neno, Stephen Voaden, Pip Wilson, Bill Isaac, Denny Adams, Colin Hutchins. In the background can be seen Dr and Mrs McInnes, Mr and Mrs Vallance, Keith Worden and Reggie Wood.*

*Northlew Football Club, following success on the pitch, began a stage career dressed as the Northlew Majorettes, 1986.* Left to right, back row: *Brian Andrew, Marcus 'Bugsy' Barrett, Roger Voaden, Julian Gratton, Brian Friend, ?,?, Paul Adams;* front: *Allison Snell, ?, ?, Nigel Isaac.*

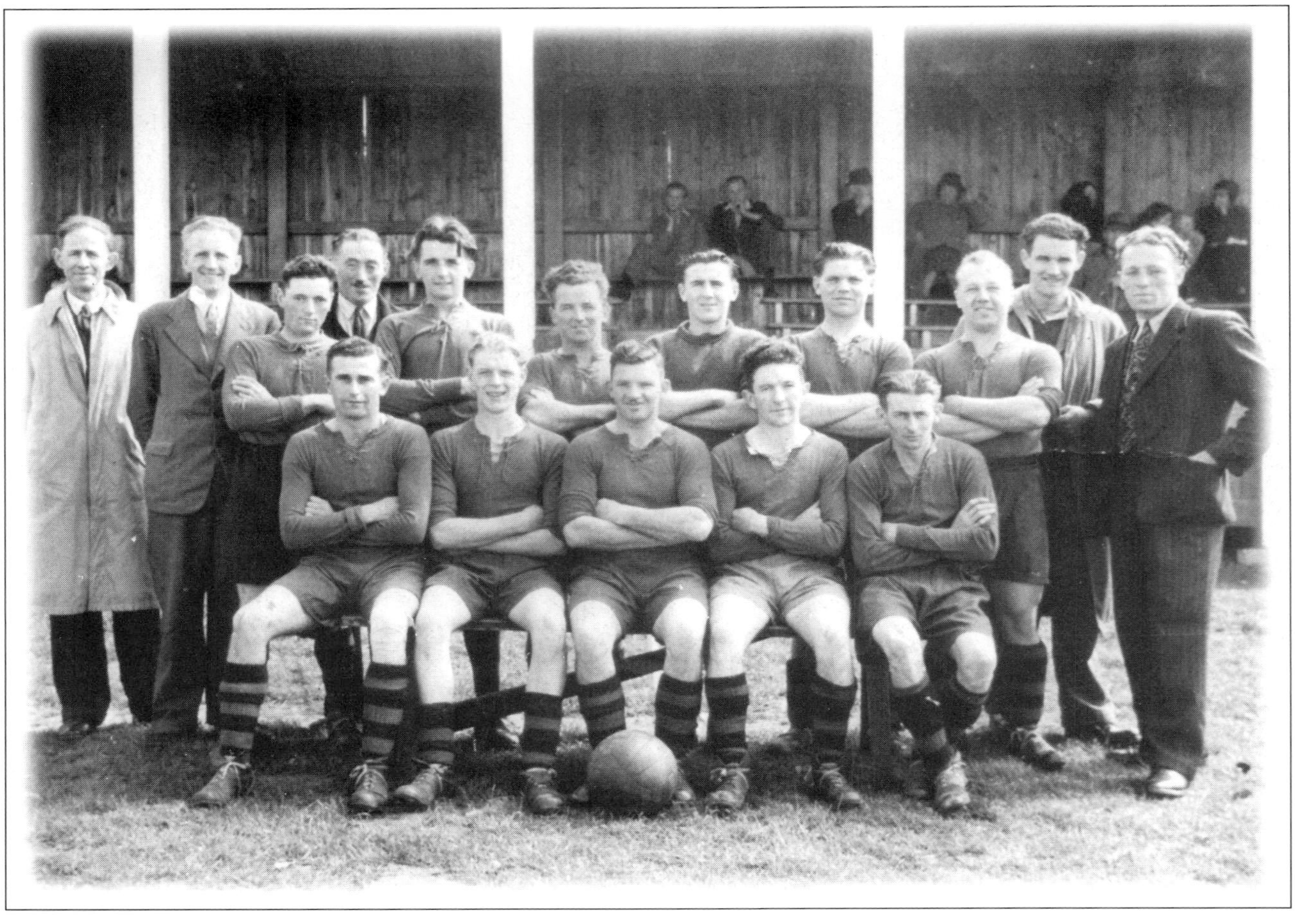

*Northlew Football Club. In spite of playing soldiers from Okehampton Camp to make up a hard, physical team, victory did not always come easily. This team is at the Stratton ground prior to losing 10-0, and after a cup of tea, travelling to Bude to lose 8-0! Otto Binder, a German prisoner of war billeted at Bolland Farm also played for the side.* Left to right, back row (officials): *Bert Hucker, Bill Mounter (chairman), Jim Ware;* back row (team): *Stanley Vincent, Bill Jordan, Wilf Neno, Tom Andrew, Tommy Addison, ?, ?, 'Grunter' (a professional player);* front: *Jock Weeks, Peter Dufty, George Matthias, Dick Andrew, Victor Bailey.*

Torrington. In 1948 he took along Tommy Addison and David Knowles, who played for Black Torrington. Bill Mounter approached the Northlew Men's Club with a view to starting the first Northlew team known as 'The Robins'. In the early years, the team changed in a shed behind a village shop. Hot water was provided from the shop kitchen to fill two tin baths. In 1963, they

*Northlew Football Club pantomime* Reindeers to the Rescue, *1987. Memories of Julian Gratton as Santa Claus and Trevor Breyley under the influence of alcohol as a rather over-friendly reindeer will live for years to come. Also appearing were Nigel Isaac as the fairy and Peter Isaac as the dame.*

*Northlew Football Club pantomime* Babes in the Wood, *1988. Amongst the cast were Marcus Barrett, Nigel and Peter Isaac, Alan May, Allison Snell, Christopher Hards and Julie Brown.*

*Northlew Football Club, 1999/2000 season.* Left to right, back row: *Jason Sandford, Marcus Barrett, Steven Squire, Simon Page, Carl Downes, ?, Neil Arthurs, Gary Ware;* front: *Bevil Smithers, Joe Burrows, Simon Squire, Alan May, Paul Sanders, Phil Greenaway, Matthew Adams.*

moved to changing facilities in what used to be the bakery office. Bill Spry obtained hot water and filled the baths ready for when the players had finished. In 1998, Northlew AFC celebrated their golden anniversary and looked forward to continuing success in the future. Two things can be guaranteed, however, that Northlew will always play with a gritty determination and the wind at East Kimber will always be stronger and colder than anywhere else in Devon.

### The Royal British Legion

The British Legion has been in existence for 80 years, the Northlew branch having been formed in the late 1920s. Charles Gratton, Lew Gratton's father, was one of the original members. Following the closure of the Friendly Society/Men's Club, the British Legion continued the tradition of an annual Sports Day held in Styles Meadow. In more recent years, the Northlew and District Legion have held a Christmas Party in the Victory Hall for older inhabitants. Tom Andrew, chairman of the Legion for many years, and his wife, Vera, have organised these enjoyable parties, which include the Northlew Silver Band and other local musicians, such as the Buchanan family. At Christmas 2001 the Methodist Sunday School provided the musical entertainment. Members organise and collect locally for the annual Poppy Appeal, which in November 2001 raised the outstanding sum of £1,702.60.

### Northlew Skittles

*Northlew Ladies' Skittles 'D' Team, 2002.* Left to right, back row: *Linda Taylor, Hilary Isaac, Janet Millership;* front: *Barbara Nash, Pat Carter, Christine Wayne. The skittles teams have been involved in various charity competitions in order to raise money, particularly for the Devon Air Ambulance and a defibrillator to be carried by the Devon Ambulance Service. The ladies' and men's teams jointly hold an annual dinner and presentation of trophies at the end of each season and also a Dinner and Dance at Penstowe when over 300 skittles players attend.*

*Northlew Ladies' Skittles 'A' Team, 2002.* Left to right, back row: *Pam Friend, Peggy Brooking, Kay Vallance, Monica Davey, Shirley Maynard;* front: *Winifred Davey, Mary Friend, Olive Yelland.*

*Northlew Men's Skittle 'A' Team, 2002.* Left to right, back row: *Tim Parsons, Stanley Friend, Steve Squire, Julian Gratton;* front: *Denny Adams, Norman Vallance, Ernie Curtis, Bart Parker.*

*Northlew Ladies' Skittles 'B' Team, 2002.* Left to right, back row: *Diane Grierson, Dorothy Cole, Sheila Voaden, Jean Curtis;* front: *Ruth Squire, Peggy Voaden, Marcia Taylor.*

*Northlew Men's Skittles 'B' Team, 2002.* Left to right, back row: *Pip Wilson, Cecil Brooking, Andy Brooking, Char Baker;* front: *Brian Dufty, Paul Griffiths.*

*Northlew Ladies' Skittles 'C' Team, 2002.* Left to right, back row: *Sarah Maynard, Rosanna Davey, 'Mellie' Davey;* front: *Sharon Dufty, Jo Maynard, Julie Letchford.*

*Northlew Men's Skittles 'C' Team, 2002.* Left to right, back row: *John Millership, Michael Yelland, Philip Yelland;* front: *John Yelland, Reg Friend, Juliet Yelland.*

*Northlew Men's Skittles 'D' Team, 2002.* Left to right, back row: *Steve Rocket, Nigel Dufty, Steve Thorne, Peter Richards;* front: *Alan May, Kevin Davey, Phillip Worden.*

Northlew Men's Skittles Team began on 11 September 1986 when Michael Coles, Frankie Voaden, Pip Wilson and Tony Squire, together with help from Bill Mounter, set up the club. The Ladies' Skittles Team began in the same year and consisted of two teams. There are currently four men's teams who play in the Victory Hall on Tuesday evenings and four ladies' teams who play Thursdays. Both teams share the skittle board and pins and play from September to April in the Holsworthy and District League, the men in the second division and the ladies in the third. No men are allowed to play in the Ladies' League but ladies are allowed to make up a team in the Men's League! Tony Squire won the Knockout Cup at Holsworthy in the year 2000. The Skittles Teams have been involved in various charity competitions in order to raise money, particularly for the Devon Air Ambulance and a defibrillator to be carried by the Devon Ambulance Service. The Ladies' and Men's Teams jointly hold an Annual Dinner and Presentation of Trophies at the end of the season and also a Dinner and Dance at Penstowe when over 300 skittles players attend.

### The Lambretta Rally

Michael and Rachel Karslake of Kesterfield had a museum of Lambretta scooters for the Lambretta Club during the 1950s/1960s. The museum contained examples of almost every model Lambretta produced. Each year in September the village would be visited by up to 500 riders for a rally. Although slow to start, these rallies continued for almost ten years. There was a marquee at Kesterfield, and the event lasted for three days. On one occasion, it was reported that 84 barrels of beer were consumed at the Green Dragon.

### Coffee 'n' Chat Club

Miriam Greaves, wife of the rector, Alan Greaves, began the Coffee 'n' Chat Club in the mid 1980s. Lillian Gratton took over the running of the group when Miriam and Alan Greaves moved to Sidmouth and, at the time of writing, Marlene Mahoney and Marj Brown run the club. The Coffee 'n' Chat Club meet once a fortnight in the Church Room for a 'coffee and chat'. Each year the club enjoys an annual outing and has visited the Cornish coast, the Dart Valley Railway and Dartmoor, always accompanied by a cream tea. In previous years when membership was greater, the club held a Christmas turkey buffet, followed by bingo, which all members thoroughly enjoyed. The club holds fond memories of past members and Marlene and Marj are determined to honour a promise made to Mrs Greaves to keep the Coffee 'n' Chat Club running.

### The Green Dragon Darts Club

*Northlew Green Dragon Darts Team, 1950s.* Left to right, back row: *Bill Arthurs, Tom Andrew, Bill Isaac, Jack Kigby, Ernie Huxtable, Chris Ware, Bill Voaden, Jim Ware;* seated: *Peter Eveleigh, Percy Brock, Henry Luxton, Bill Mounter, Ken Southwick (landlord).*

*Green Dragon Men's Darts 'A' Team, 2002. Char Jordan (captain), Marcus Barrett, Alan May, Philip Hutton, Vic Jordan, Mike Johns, Mike Adams, Clifford Jordan. Each year the League holds a special charity competition in support of such charities as the British Heart Foundation, CLIC, Royal National Institute for the Blind and Devon Air Ambulance, raising approximately £800 each year. The chosen charity for 2002 was Force, an Exeter-based cancer charity, which involved 40 players in a competition held at the Green Dragon Inn, Northlew, in March 2002.*

Although there may have been many friendly darts matches, it was not until the formation of the Lane Dart League in the late 1950s that inter-village competitions began. It was Captain Lane of Iddesleigh who provided a cup in order to promote a darts league involving local communities. Within a short while, Northlew had joined the league as the Green Dragon Darts Club and continue to this day as one ladies' and two men's teams. In recent years, the club has won the League Fours Competition and, for three years in a row, the Bude Round Table Darts Marathon. The club's highest achievement in the League has been third place. Each year, the club continues the tradition of holding an Annual Christmas Dinner for all members. Every week, September to April, matches are held in the friendly spirit of local rivalry, which was Captain Lane's original intention.

*Green Dragon Men's Darts 'B' Team, 2002.* Left to right, back row: *John Palmer, landlord, James Ware, Steve Shelton, Jeff Solomon, Steve Squire;* front: *Brian Andrew, John Millership, Simon Squire, Philip Yelland, Richard Hutton.*

*Green Dragon Ladies' Darts Team, 2002. Andrea Ware, Traci Yelland, Alison Shelton, Jane Turner, Libby Adams (captain), Linda Taylor. The Ladies' Team was formed in approximately 1986, having won both the League Singles and Pairs Competition in 1997 and in the year 2000 were runners up in the Pairs with Sue Hards winning the Singles Competition.*

**Northlew Mother and Toddler Playgroup**

The playgroup was formed initially as the Mother and Toddler Group on Tuesday, 13 November 1979. It officially became the playgroup on 3 June 1980 when the supervisor was Linda Hammond, chairman, Barbara Hockley, treasurer, Val Spry and secretary, Wendy Parkhouse. The playgroup, formed by the efforts of young mothers in the area in less than two years of fund-raising, achieved registration and began its two-day per week sessions. There were between 15 and 20 children at that time. Initially, toys and equipment were bought through fund-raising with sponsored walks and bazaars. A lottery grant in 1998 enabled the group to purchase new toys. Due to declining numbers of children, the playgroup ended in February/March 2000.

*Northlew Playgroup Christmas Party, December 1981.* Included here are: *Karina Hulls, Geoffrey Griffiths, Joanne Maynard, Louise Curson, Annabel Ratcliffe, Melanie Davey, Caroline Spry, Rachel Wimberley, Leon Parkhouse, Sarah Kent, Sarah Squire, Louise Wimberley, Stephen Cole, and Gillian Spry.*

# Claude Smale's Childhood

### *Haircuts*

*Memories of haircuts loom large, they are the first to come to mind! If you were on a visit to Okehampton, you might get sent to Webb's where the exercise was painless and you did not emerge shorn. More usually, I was despatched to Jack Webber who, when not engaged on his other activities, provided his artistry as a hair-stylist for a tanner (2.5p). A 'styling' by Jack was hardly less painful than a visit to the school dentist, you sat in his doorway, and he hung a rag around your neck and started in with clippers that were a shade on the blunt side. My eyes would water and clippings would stick to my face; probably these were tears of anguish because, on emerging, I would be acutely aware that my shadow showed a sharp circular outline and only boys from the sticks had hair like that.*

## No Mains Water or Electricity

*Our own well was not 'for drinking' so we used the village pump – as did all the cottages around the Square. Despite heavy use, I remember the pump drying up only once, when we had to resort to the one at 'lower pub'. The well in the Square was later dug deeper by Tom (or was it Jim?) Maynard. I remember the schoolchildren chanting 'Ding! Dong! Bell!, Tom is in the well!.' We fetched water in pitchers and buckets, for some reason the pitchers were reserved for drinking water, which was stored under the stairs along with meat and milk. We also fetched water for poor Annie Gowing, our severely arthritic neighbour. When you go to great trouble to get water, you learn to use it sparingly and the same water might be used several times before, finally, for floor washing. With no scullery area, washing-up was done on the end of the back-kitchen table as was our personal washing, an enamel bowl serving all purposes. Glymiel Jelly was used for real grime! Soda crystals were often used instead of washing powder. With no waste disposal, dirty water was tipped on the garden.*

*Annie Gowing with Percy Aubertin, Ruby Avery, Rita and Betty Down, Edie Moore, Grace Aubert and one unidentified person in 1927. Annie retired to the house next door to live with Emily Down after long service with Sir Archibald Heard whom she revered. Her hands were crippled by arthritis and she would mutter constantly under her breath 'Haw-thole rheumatiz' but she would revive when recounting the wonders of Sir Archibald's household.*

*Eva Mary with Lizzie Hales outside Bedford Cottage not long after the purchase. The door to the 'linney' is on the right. Note the cobbles are free of weeds! The wood box is on the left. The water butt stood outside in my time and was always full though there was no guttering to the roof.*

*Mother with Ken and Rosemary Elliott in front of our well in Milltown Lane. The well was filled in and covered in the late 1950s by my father and only a mound remains.*

*Mains water came to the village in 1954.*

*We had a washstand in the big bedroom with a jug-and-basin set but this was reserved for guests. Hot water, heated on the 'Primus' or the 'Beatrice' oil-stove would be carried up in a kettle and the 'slops' brought away by my mother in the enamel slop pail, along with those from the chamber-pots perforce in use until 1954 when mains water arrived and we had an inside toilet. Washing day, always a Monday, involved my father filling two wash baths from our well using a bucket and rope. The 'black kittle' was then unhooked from the 'chimbley crooks' and, with some strain, the boiler hung in its place. Water was then baled into the boiler. On Mondays, the rubbish from father's workshop was burned up and I remember vividly the steam and the stink of the leather parings. The washing was frequently stirred and dipped out while still boiling-hot using the 'poker stick'. One bath was reserved outside for the rinse – always tinted with 'Reckitts Blue'. (Flat irons were heated on the Primus, tested on a spare piece of material, and rubbed with soap while being used.) After the wash, more water was heated in the boiler for our weekly bath, taken in a tin bath in front of the open fire.*

*Oil lamps give poor light and, at dusk, domestic activities more or less came to a standstill. We had an Aladdin lamp, fitted with an incandescent mantle but, if you jolted the table, chances were that the fragile mantle would collapse in black smoke. We went to bed with candles. (Father stored bends of leather under my bed and I lived with the smell of them.) On bake days, you might take a hot brick to bed as well, one warmed in the oven and wrapped in newspaper.*

## Sundays

*On Sunday mornings the black-'stauve' was got going ready for the bake. Sunday roast was done with potatoes round the joint but with water added and always a suet pudding. I do not recall vegetables being on sale; you grew your own and helped out those who could not. Out of season, dried peas were set to soak overnight and served with sugar along with root vegetables. While the oven was hot, there would be a bake-up to last the next few days: pasties galore, cakes and buns (commonly saffron) and various tarts. Once in a while, the clome oven in the wall would be heated with a faggot for bread making. Sunday felt different, it was a special day of rest; my mother wouldn't even touch her needle on a Sunday, we all got into our best clothes (you wouldn't dare be seen in anything else) and I was not allowed out of the lane for play. After dinner, there would be the dreaded Sunday school for which we had to learn the collect of the day and recite the creed and the catechism. Boys sang in the choir for all Sunday services except communion and were paid a penny per service – a bounty put into our hands on Easter Sunday, when we also had newly-washed surplices.*

*The village was sharply divided into those who were Church and those who were Chapel, from family*

*Father in the garden with our dog Rose and me, 1928/9.*

*'Granfer' Smale dolled up as I never ever saw him, for Uncle Alf's wedding, c.1933.*

*habit mostly. After evening service, the two congregations mingled in the Square for a long time talking. If you had not been to service you kept your face out of sight. Afterwards, courting couples and hopeful singles made off for a walk, always towards Ashbury.*

### Ailments

*There was no doctor in the village, most people called either Dr Gwynne of Black Torrington or Dr Woollcombe (later Dr Wright) of Okehampton but Nurse Bray looked after confinements and minor medical matters. For many, my mother was first port of call for first-aid treatment for injury, etc. She also did much of the 'laying out' at deaths.*

*Traditional wisdom still held sway. It was unwise to sit on damp grass or you would get piles, goose-grease on brown paper would prevent a chill (Grannie's idea), a Mrs Dart of Highampton 'pointed' for ringworm. I am not sure what this entailed beyond 'pointing' at the offending lesion but Mrs Heber Squire of Milltown consulted her and the ringworm went away, bee stings were a good thing for rheumatism and I recall Mr Toms, the village policeman and a bee-keeper, arrived with a jam-jar full of bees to 'treat' the hapless Annie Gowing. She endured her treatment as she did her constant rheumatism, but I never heard of any improvement. School healthcare was coming into its own: there was already an optician and Dr Price the MOH would sound the children with his stethoscope, but most dreaded by far was the school dentist. He set up shop in the classroom and we went in to alphabetical order. He had a pedal-powered drill but I do not remember many fillings being done, mostly it was extractions, the poor victims being issued with a cardboard spittoon and sent on their way.*

### Christmas and Boxing Day Rabbiting

*At Northlew School, the last day before the Christmas holiday was marked by the arrival of Father Christmas. He had a white beard and a red suit all right but he came in a Morgan three-wheeler which, strangely, was exactly the same as the one owned by Merlin Hortop, brother of our teacher Mary. Canon Harvey would say prayers and, afterwards, we lined up to receive our little gifts. On Christmas Day there would be early communion followed by choir for morning service with carols but, thereafter, the day was free. For Christmas dinner there was always 'fowl', in those days something of a treat and sometimes won at the local Whist Drive. In the evening, friends would come and the 'ashen-faggot' would be brought out. This was always prepared some time before and left in the 'linney' to dry. It burned in the open fireplace with a fierce hot flame and, for once, the house was warm – instead of huddling over the open fire, now you could not get near it! The faggot was always bound with many 'bames' and, every time one of these cracked, there would be a toast – this was the custom. Drink was usually Mother's home-brew or cider perhaps brought by Sam Northam from Milltown.*

*Alternate years, we visited my grandparents in their small cottage at Black Torrington. Grandfather Jim was a spare man whose arms showed every vein and muscle and his hands were coarsely calloused. Jim worked on the roads as a stonebreaker for Devon County Council. I never saw him without an eye patch; he had lost an eye cracking stones but, of course, saw nothing by way of compensation. Like many others, he wore kneepads, which he somehow contrived out of straw. He even had straw in his boots. When he arrived home from work, he would remove his boots, hang them over the fender, put the straw in the oven of the black range and settle into his Windsor armchair with his feet also in the oven – and sleep. Their front kitchen had a floor of 'lime-ash' but the rear kitchen floor was still beaten earth. I remember now the dank musty odour that pervaded the house, what I now know to have been damp. In those days, beds which had been unused for a time would have to be aired. No doubt my Grannie did all she could to dry things but I remember still the striking chill of the sheets and the difficulty in getting warm. We did not have a wireless but they had one, even at that time it had come out of the Ark. Frequently it would utter no sound except interference and I would be despatched 'downtown' to exchange the accumulator for a charged one or to pour water over the earthing rod which had been driven between the cobbles. Without exception, the men folk would go rabbiting every Boxing Day. It not only provided for the pot but it was a favourite pastime. To make the ferret more eager, it would have been starved of its usual bread and milk. As a young boy, I was never a great fan of the ferret but I was always made to hold the wretched thing while its mouth was tied up. Father again used his five-ply cobbler's thread; one loop behind the ears and one loop around the nose. This was 'coping' the ferret to prevent it killing a rabbit in its hole and remaining underground with it.*

### Customers Calling

*Father's ledgers, up to the 1960s, are most revealing; most people, farmers included, kept a running account which was never actually paid off. People would call, invariably after dark, to pay off something on account. The drill was always the same, 'Can't come een you, ebbem changed me boots' so they would stand in the open doorway for what seemed like hours while those of us inside froze – if we weren't frozen already. I remember the many times my mother and I sat perished; there would be long silences and we'd think 'They're going now' but no, the visitor would be off on some new topic.*

*Mother also had her customers. Having trained as a dressmaker with Westcotts of Okehampton she made outfits for ladies of the parish – mostly for special occasions. When her customers came for fittings, I was despatched to the back kitchen – to freeze. Housework was often set aside while mother treadled her Singer sewing machine to meet a deadline and things were often fraught when she unpicked after some set-back. Most of her customers still wore calico corsets ('stays' they were called) laced together at the back, stiffened with whale-bone or braided steel and linked at the front with very heavy-duty hooks and eyes.*

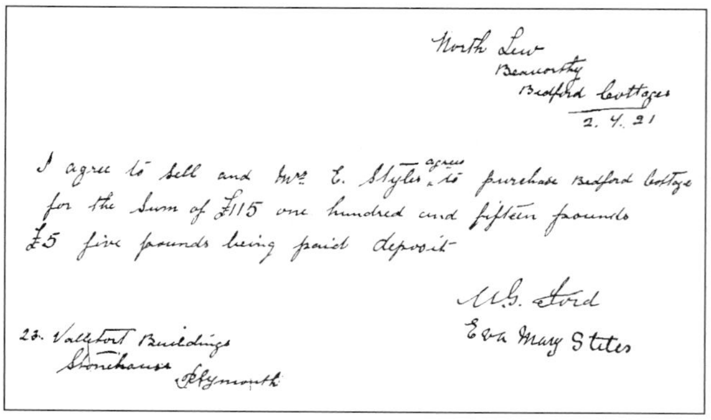

North Lew
Beaworthy
Bedford Cottages
2. 4. 21

I agree to sell and Mrs E. Styles agree to purchase Bedford Cottage for the sum of £115 one hundred and fifteen pounds £5 five pounds being paid deposit

M.G. Ford
Eva Mary Stiles

23. Valletort Buildings
Stonehouse Plymouth

*Eva Mary purchased Bedford Cottage in 1921 for £115, as this bill of sale made with the owner, Mr Ford, bears witness.*

*The Norton side-car outfit which father used for his deliveries – always it seemed on the west side of the village. There were frequent stoppages to replace the silencer which kept blowing off and we always had to return before nightfall because the acetylene lamps would block up. (Carbide for acetylene lamps was sold by Jack Webber and I remember some older boys recounting how you could put some in a bottle with added water and throw it in the river – and run!)*

*The Scant family, Crowden Road, 1910.*

*Edie Bowden who married Harry Middleton and farmed Southcombe. When Harry died, she married her childhood sweetheart Sid Stiles.*

# A Devonshire Cross

Grim, solemn and stern stands Northlew Cross,
Brooding o'er a village fair,
Oblivious to mortals' gain or loss
Only time it deigns to share.

Down the deep Vale of bygone ages
When Temples were trod by Druid Sages,
From earth's foundation was hewn each block
Sculptured from out the eternal rock,
And beneath their depths may secrets lie
Hidden for ever from mortal eye.
The Roman and Dane, Saxon and Gaul
Have risen, have reigned, and vanished all.
No hand may paint that primeval scene
When Briton first trod this village green,
When maidens here danced to Tambourine
And crowned with pride their Gipsy Queen.

Then still and fair were these moorlands wild,
And flowers and streams in forests smiled.
The boar and the wolf did freely roam
These hills and valleys—their native home.
Brave knights in armour to battle rode,
And seeds of empire by valour sowed.
Tradition still tells of legends old,
And lingers one here that oft is told:
A wondrous stag that none could snare
Found here from pursuit his final lair;
So swift of foot and supple of limb
No deer of the plains e'er matched with him.

Who followed his path followed in vain,
No rivals could long such speed maintain,
And good hound and horse that tracked his trail
To capture and slay were doomed to fail.
No rider so bold or hound so fleet
The great antlered stag at bay could meet;
Though chased by many his end to see
They chased for naught for Satan was he:
And this ancient Cross was built to tell
How 'twas here at last in death he fell;
And beneath entombed will folklore say
This devilish stag at rest doth lay.
Fable and fancy the mind may fill,
Yet broods o'er the scene a myst'ry still.
Who was the herald that chiselled and plan'd
Six sides to the wind that blows o'er the land?
What mean those symbols? What their design?
Tomb of a chief or purpose Divine?
Did preacher here preach to listening flock
Ere time was ticked by yon belfry clock;
Ere infant and bride and solemn pageant
Entered within those portals ancient?
There's naught to recall in hist'ry's page
Who plan'd these stones in far-reaching age;
No record to tell of why or when
This granite pile was reared by men.
All is enshrined in mystery deep
While the grey old Cross mute watch shall keep,
Indented and worn by children's feet,
Who still as of old here love to meet;
While wayfarers sit to think and rest,
And watch the great sun o'erflood the west.
They come and they go and pass away
While Northlew Cross it sees but a day,
Yet when this shall rest in the mould'ring past
A cross there is that for ever shall last.

Northlew, Devonshire.

D. A. Roderic Evance, F.R.G.S.

Bessie May at Rock Cottage, Rocky Lane (before the thatched porch was added). Grace Bowden, who acted as housekeeper around the village in the event of sickness, also lived there.

Wedding of Arthur (Jimmy) and Ida Elliott. Jimmy was a keen gardener and competed in flower shows. Their daughter Kate married 'Pop' Gay.

Church Fête, 'gossipin' in the 1960s. Left to right: Ivy Curtis, Lottie Smale, Jack Spry and Dick Friend.

Reuben and Lil Avery with daughters Ruby and Rene. Reuben drove a steamroller and, later, severely broke his leg in a motorcycle crash coming home from work.

# *Village Characters*

Like every village Northlew has its characters. The following people have contributed in their own way to the life of the village.

## *The Old Clerk*

When the Revd T. England was instituted in 1847, the Parish Clerk was William Lobb. One of the Clerk's tasks was to make the responses during church services while the congregation remained silent. The Clerk would also read out the times of the services. On one occasion William Lobb neglected to do so. The rector asked him the reason for this and William replied, 'There was no occasion, for your reverence is always to one time and all the parishioners now well know it.' William Lobb was Clerk for 40 years and he died in 1859.

## *The Village Poet*

The village poet was Devereux Alfred Roderick Evance. After an adventurous life in America he came to Northlew with his sister and lived in the house next door to the chapel. He had a tenor voice and played the violin, concertina and flute. He composed songs and waltzes and wrote poems on the subjects of nature, spring, the Village Cross and war and peace. His sister, Alice Virginia Evance, wrote a poem about her grandfather's clock, called 'The Passing Time'. She died on 19 March 1921, aged 84, after which Devereux lived alone in one room with his treasures and pets. He boiled his water and cooked the little meat he had on a small oil stove, the windows of the house were never opened and soap was almost a luxury. He loved, however, to receive visitors, who would play his compositions, sing to him, listen to his tales and admire his poetry. Devereux died on 10 November 1926 aged 83.

## *The Old Huntsman*

There is a small white tablet in Ashbury Church belfry in memory of Charles Strickland. In the charred remains of the old Registers, which survived a fire in 1877, he is described as a 'Huntsman'. He lived in the old cottage opposite the farm at Wadlands with his wife Elizabeth and became gamekeeper at Ashbury when the hunt was given up. He died on 25 June 1859 aged 61. The tablet records simply, 'A man without reproach, beloved by all.'

## *The Old Poacher*

The old poacher went about the village, lanes and woods wearing a slouch hat, rough shooting jacket

**The Isle of the Ocean,**

A WAR SONG,

BY

D. A. R. EVANCE, F.R.G.S.,

Author of "War and Peace," etc.

PRICE TWOPENCE.

All proceeds will be devoted to the Royal Patriotic War Fund.

S. & A. JAMES, PRINTERS, OKEHAMPTON.

**The Passing Time.**

My Grandfather's clock stands grim and old,
And it ticks—and ticks—away
In the summer heat or winter cold,
Tick-tick by night and by day.

Me and mine—me and mine!
The pendulum swings in rhythmic time,
No matter what to others betide—
They seek for themselves, the world is wide—
Me and mine—me and mine.

Thee and thine—thee and thine!
Tick-tick-tick-tick—on the sands of time.
What can I do for my neighbour this day?
And the stranger too—can I smooth his way?
Thee and thine—thee and thine!

Me and mine—thee and thine,
Pass swiftly on to another clime,
Broken links of a severed chain.
Yet the law of kindness will remain
For thee and thine—for me and mine.

The life here and now is but a drop
In the Ocean of Eternity;
The works of the clock may quickly stop,
But the River of Life flows eternally.

ALICE V. EVANCE.

*Grannie Watkins lived in the west part of her daughter Lil Avery's house at the top of the Square. The house was shared with Reuben, son Will Watkins, granddaughters Rene and Ruby and long-time lodger Jack Blatchford, the village chimney sweep. (Jack carried his brushes and kit around on his bicycle and wore all-black cloths.) Grannie Watkin's room smelled always of toast (made on her open fire) which she seemed to live on. She had a large green parrot in a brass cage which repeated Grannie Watkins by saying 'Aw-my dear soul' – and shared her toast.*

*Gran and Grandad Worden, early 1900. Grandparents of Audrey Vincent.*

*Mrs Ada Worden was born in 1889 and moved to Northlew when she was six. She eventually married William Worden and they farmed at Higher Cruft Farm and later Howard's Farm, Gorhuish. She celebrated her 100th birthday in 1989 and died on 17 December the same year.*

Left: *Bob Born making Mrs Smale 'haysweet'.*

and corduroys. He carried his gun under his arm, his traps in his hand and his ferret in his pocket. He understood the voices of nature and the ways of birds, beasts and fish. He was able to make and throw a fly and knew where the fish were and how best to catch them. The poacher was a sportsman to the marrow and a country gentleman; kind, good-natured and always ready with a cheery word and greeting. He had a good sense of humour and loved a joke and used to say, with a smile upon his lips and a sly look in his eye, that he always caught his Christmas dinner in the Parson's Wood.

### *The Washerwoman*

In the 1930s, Emily Sanders lived in the village at Cross Park and used to walk miles collecting washing which she would deliver once it had been laundered. People used to say to her, 'When you die, I hope you'll leave me your feet!'

## *Ancient Village Customs*

Northlew was an isolated village and, as a result, the people developed their own customs, none of which remain in existence at the time of writing. Mobility, mechanisation and the Welfare State are possible reasons for this. However, there are village traditions which have developed, such as the Carnival and its procession and the Christmas tree in the Square. These traditions, instead of being individual or family focused, bring the community together. The old customs include:

### *Christening and Festival Cakes*

The person who carried the baby to the church, brought with her a christening cake. The cake was small and round, made with currants, saffron and spice. If the baby was a boy, the cake was given to a girl and if the baby was a girl, the cake was given to a boy.

The day before the Festival of St Thomas of Canterbury, 7 July, was called 'bun-baking day'. Large round buns, with spice and currants, were made and placed on sycamore leaves.

### *Lent Crocking*

On Shrove Tuesday the poor men and women would go around to the big houses and farms to crave a pittance. They carried two bags on their shoulders, a white one for flour and the other for barley meal; they were rewarded with a portion of flour or meal, or with a piece of bacon. Sometimes they were given a few coppers.

### *Wassailing*

On Twelfth Night the farmer would go to the orchard with his men and a large pitcher of cider. They would make a circle around one of the trees bearing the most fruit and drink a toast in verse.

### *Yuletide*

At Yuletide, a great ashen faggot was dragged into the kitchen and bound round with beams or bands. It was burnt in the wide open fireplace on Christmas night, with merrymaking and rejoicing. The party gathered round the hearth and watched the blaze. The burning through of each of the beams was a signal to the company for refreshment and slices of cake. Bread and cheese were handed round. Some people sat and gossiped about the good old days, some played cards, some joined in country games and dances.

### *Crying the Neck, Harvesting, Gleaning and Making the Hay Sweet*

In the past, the man who reaped the last sheaf at harvest time, waved it, ran off a little and shouted three times, 'we have un'. The other reapers cried 'What have ye?' and the man replied, 'A neck, a neck'. The neck or little corn-man was then plaited with the ears upward, taken into the farmhouse and hung from a crook in the ceiling over the dining-room table. The old one was taken down and given to the birds.

It was customary for the farmer's wife to step into the field before the reapers and cut the first few handfuls of wheat for the church. These she made into little sheaves and then took them to the altar.

After the field was raked, one of the church bells was rung as a signal to the gleaners. The bell would be rung by one of the men of the village whose name had been posted on the church door. He would ring it at 8a.m. to signal the start of gleaning and again at 6p.m. to end it. The women and children were up early and would wait by the gate until the bell was rung. Each family of gleaners paid the bellringer a fee of twopence or sixpence for his services. A stock or thrave of corn, called the gard sheaf, was left near the gate until the farmer was ready to admit the gleaners.

A young man would kiss his sweetheart through hay which he had twisted into a circle; this was supposed to make the hay sweet.

*This banner, depicting various village scenes, was made by the schoolchildren for display in the Millennium Dome.*

*Chapter 10*

# CONCLUSION

## *A New Millennium*

Talks and meetings had been held all over the country in order to plan ways to celebrate the new millennium. At last the time had come. On Friday 31 December some villagers gathered in the church at 8p.m. for a short, quiet service to ask for God's guidance in the years ahead and to thank Him for all their blessings. Following the service people wandered across the Square for refreshments in the Methodist Hall, where other villagers had already gathered. A number of people stayed for some time, others went to make themselves ready for the dance in the Victory Hall or other celebrations. At 11.45p.m. many villagers gathered in the Square and, as the church clock struck midnight, a great cheer went up and 'Auld Lang Syne' was sung. Afterwards, fireworks in the Old Rectory garden and Ashbury lit up the sky.

The next morning, Saturday, the village was quiet as people slept in after the celebrations. Then, to break the silence at midday, the church bells rang out, joining those throughout the country in welcoming the new millennium and proclaiming 2000 years since Christ's birth. On Sunday evening the church was full for a Songs of Praise service with the Methodists and Northlew Silver Band. Although it was midwinter, people

*A new heating system being installed in the Parish Church in October 1999.*

*The vicar taking a photograph of Percy Adams, one of the oldest residents, opening the History Exhibition on 19 May 2000. Also in the picture is Jenny Voden, who gave Percy a buttonhole.*

*All the children at Northlew School and Playgroup were presented with special millennium books by the vicar.*

*Percy Adams with some of the members of the history group.* Left to right: *Lena Williams, Molly Atkinson and Jenny Voden.*

benefited from the new heating system, which had been installed to mark the millennium.

On the weekend of 19 May an exhibition of photographs, information and objects depicting the history of the village was on display in the Victory Hall. Other attractions for the weekend were beautiful flower displays in the Parish Church and refreshments in the Church Room. As well as local visitors, the exhibition attracted people from all over the county. As a conclusion to the weekend, at 3p.m. on Sunday, a service for the renewal of marriage vows was held in the church. Couples who had been married in Northlew during the last 50 years came to this special service which was led by the vicar. The Revd Hilary Ison gave the sermon, on the joys and troubles of family life. After the service refreshments were enjoyed in the Church Room and Lilian and John Spry cut a special cake as it was their wedding anniversary.

*Children dressed as Victorian schoolchildren for the exhibition.*

*Children enjoying the Victorian classroom at the exhibition.*

*The font decorated with flowers by Frances Dufty.*

*A floral display by Eileen Wilson in the Parish Church.*

The Parish Council arranged games and sports in the Parish Field for all the children on Saturday 24 June. This was great fun and if the noise was any indication of the level of enjoyment, then a great time was had by all. After the games the children enjoyed a tea party in the Square. On Sunday 3 October 1999, the vicar accompanied Eileen and Pip Wilson and Peter and Rosalind Eveleigh to a service at Crediton Parish Church. During the service the representatives of the churches were given a yew tree sapling which came from a tree which was thought to be about 2,000 years old. The tree was lovingly cared for by Peter and before the Church Festival Service on Saturday 8 July 2000 it was planted in the churchyard. Let us hope that the tree, a symbol of everlasting life, thrives like the old ones in the churchyard, so, like them, it will look down on a changing but loving and caring village community.

*Richard Yelland and Samuel Dufty plant the millennium yew tree.* Also in the picture: *Stuart Wilson (curate), Bishop John Richards and Raymond Voden (vicar).*

*The presentation of paperweights, a gift to the children of the parish by the Parish Council.*
Left to right: *Janet Millership (secretary of the Parish Council), the vicar, the Methodist minister, Emily and Abigail Davey, Christopher Humphreys and Thomas Adams; John Grierson of the Parish Council is in the background.*

*Northlew WI with a banner embroidered for the millennium. Embroiderers were Hilary Isaac, Maureen Voaden and Rosalind Eveleigh.*
Left to right: *Ros Eveleigh, Maureen Voaden, Jean Argentiere, Hilary Isaac, Betty Woods, Lilian Spry, Sheila Voaden, Diane Grierson.*

## Conclusion – 2001: A Year of Hardship

John Peak, Methodist minister and agricultural chaplain recalls the effects of foot and mouth on a farming community:

*It is 24 February, Elaine and I have been at Northlew for six months and we love it here. Today is a Saturday and we walk down the winding lane that leads away from our home. On the roadside banks of snowdrops nod in the breeze, primroses are coming out, daffodils are big with bud. A blackbird sings and sings against the pale-blue sky. All is well. ( O Lord God, what a beautiful world you have created.)*

*Later, that evening, I am on my way to Bow, travelling to a Farm Crisis Network meeting. As I arrive I see a disinfected straw barrier across the entrance. The owner keeps goats. 'That's a bit over the top,' I think, as I go into the meeting, 'foot and mouth is 300 miles away from here.' Next morning, Sunday, I wake up and switch on the radio. Foot and mouth is at Highhampton, three miles from my front door. (Lord, this is a nightmare!)*

*We are in March now and things seem to be getting out of hand. We don't venture out of the village on foot. All the farm entrances are barricaded with disinfected straw. The funeral pyres have reached us. I drive up to Castle Cross and can count six burnings clearly visible. Five of my seven churches have closed, and yet if there was ever a time for pastoral care this is it. I sit at home on the end of a telephone and resort to reaching out to my congregations by writing pastoral letters. People are still stunned by the enormity of what has happened. (Lord, where are you in all this?) Elaine and I go into Okehampton. A stench pervades the town. Someone is burning foul, rotten meat on a gigantic barbecue. The streets seem empty. Some women pass us by with scarves covering their mouths and noses. (Lord God, this is surreal!)*

*The worst moment comes on a Sunday in April, at nine o'clock in the morning. I'm getting ready for the 9.30a.m. chapel service at Northlew. The phone rings. I hesitate, not wanting to be interrupted, and then answer it. A woman speaks quietly. (Lord, how did I know she was terrified before she even spoke?) 'What is it?' I ask. 'I've locked myself and the children in the kitchen,' she says. 'My husband is threatening to kill himself. He's gone out with a gun, I've just heard a shot.' I swear my heart stops. The silence hangs for eternity. (Oh Lord God – help! They never taught us about this when we were training... ) The situation gets resolved peacefully, but I'm left wondering if it will be for real next time?*

*As we move into April the crisis deepens. Some good friends send me money. 'You will know who needs it,' they say. Sure enough my next phone call is from a desperate sounding mother, 'I have four children to feed, and not even bread to give them,' she says. This is Dickensian, and I can't get my sceptical head around this one. I check with an acquaintance in the area. 'Do you know Mrs.......?' I ask. 'Yes, I do' she says, 'I was there this morning, and she has no food in the house.' I send £100 which she gets the next morning, but how long will that last her, I wonder? (Lord, I feel so helpless. Did you feel like this when you were among us?)*

*Because I am an agricultural chaplain, I become involved in helping to administer the Green Wellie money, and here I find more hurt. A quiet old gentleman rings me one morning. 'I'm sorry to trouble you,' he says. 'I've never done anything like this before, but now we are desperate.' The story unfolds. He has farmed all his life with his brother and his brother's wife, on a rented farm. They had saved from their meagre profits, always hopeful that they could put away enough to buy a house to retire in. Some years ago they realised that it was hopeless, so they decided to save for a pension instead. Profits dropped to nothing, somehow they survived, but now with foot and mouth they haven't sold anything since the autumn and their pension savings have dwindled away. They have no income, and no savings. 'Now you see, we are too old to go out to work...' He hesitates, 'Do you think the fund can help us in a small way, we can survive on very little?'*
*'How old are you?' I ask.*
*'I'm seventy-five,' he replies.*
*When I put the phone down tears are rolling down my face. (Lord, I haven't cried for years – what is happening to me?)*

*It is August and everyone is exhausted, but at last there is a glimmer of light. It is weeks since the last outbreak and the horror is receding. Too early to say yet that it is over, but we hold our breath and wait. Dartmoor is open and I walk over the moor to Cranmere Pool. All I can see is the waving grass, the contours of the hills, a few black-and-white belted Galloway cattle, the occasional sheep. There are no people. All is quiet and at peace. (Lord, are you telling me something?)*

*Christmas comes like a silent breath. It has been with us always. Ever since childhood this magical season has crept upon me unawares. We gather in the Green Dragon to sing carols. Laughter and chatter ring across the bar. I am there with them. I still have all the questions, and few answers, but somehow I can learn to wait and trust. For this moment I am at peace. Winifred plays the keyboard and we all sing. Our voices rise and drift out into the quiet night. 'O come all ye faithful' we sing, 'Joyful and triumphant, O come, let us adore Him, Christ the Lord.'*

*John Peak, methodist minister and agricultural chaplain.*

*Northlew Billiards Team, Okehampton League, c.1964. John Spry, Phillip Spry, Norman Born, Bill Heathman. In 1924 the Billiards Club, being part of the Men's Social Club, moved into the Victory Hall. There was a three-quarter-sized, and a full-sized, table available. In 1936, another table, which had been used in the 1936 Billiards Championship at Thurston Hall in London, was purchased from Riley's for £80.00. After the Second World War, snooker became more important than billiards at the club. The club won the Okehampton Billiard League in 1964.*

*Northlew Snooker Team in the Men's Club, January 2002. Brian Smallacombe, Frank Voaden, Michael Cole, Brian Hill, John Spry. The teams thrived and enjoyed a great deal of success during the 1980s when there were about 22 members. After extensive fund-raising, toilets were added to the club in the 1950s. John Spry, long an active member, held the position of treasurer for 19 years until the year 2000. Sadly, at the time of writing the club is in decline, no doubt suffering competition from television, computers and videos.*

# BIBLIOGRAPHY & SOURCES


Taylor, A.J.P., *English History 1914–1945*

Grimley, Roger, *Motor Buses of Northlew and Okehampton*

Fraser, Derek, *The Evolution of the British Welfare State*

Cole, G.D.H., *Introduction to Economic History 1750–1950*

Hoskins, W.G., *Devon*

Maynard, J., *Remarkable Incidents in the Life of John Maynard*

Mitchell, V., *Local Railway Transport History*

Parsons, Revd R. Keith, *Souls For Your Hire*

Romaine Hervey, Revd Canon W., *A History of Northlew* (unpublished)

*Western Morning News*

*Okehampton Times*

*Freddie Spencer and Claude Smale with the washing baths which were constantly used for play. Whenever Reg Vincent passed with his cows for milking Mrs Smale would stand guard with the broom and shoo them away to stop them drinking all of the water.*

*Clement Andrew, landlord of the Green Dragon, the proud owner of one of the first cars in Northlew.*

# SUBSCRIBERS

Paul M. Adams, Devon
Thomas J. and Joseph W. Adams, Northlew, Devon
Michael J. Adams
Mr T.J. Andrew, Northlew, Devon
Mr and Mrs J.E. Atkinson, Northlew, Devon
Mr and Mrs M.J. Atkinson, Horsham, West Sussex
Mr J.F. Atkinson, St Hellier, Jersey, Channel Islands
Kathleen J. Aubertin, Torrington, Devon
Susan J. Bolt, North Tawton, Devon
David Born, Huddersfield, Yorkshire
Gillian Bowden, Higher Odham, Highampton, Devon
Marilyn L. Breyley, Churston Ferrers, Brixham, Devon
Rex Bridgwater
Cecil M. Brooking, Crowden, Northlew, Devon
The Brooking Society, UK
Mr and Mrs A. Brooking, Simon and Megan, Northlew, Devon
Marjorie F.O. Brown (née Kneebone), Northlew, Okehampton, Devon
Captain and Mrs A.R. Buchanan, Island of Mull
Hazel Buchanan, Northlew, Devon
Amber Buchanan, Northlew, Devon
May Burridge, Plymouth, Devon
K.J. Burrow, Bucks Cross, Devon
David and Carol Carrier, East Worth
Pat and Ron Carter, Northlew, Devon
Mr Derek and Mrs Elvira Chivers, Northlew, Devon
Mr and Mrs Robert E. Colbear, Northlew, Devon
Michael and Dorothy Cole, Northlew, Devon
B.E. Cole, Greenwell, Yelverton, Devon
Noel J. Wheadon and Amanda Y. Coleshill, Northlew, Devon
Brian and Janet Crittenden, Northlew, Devon
Margaret, Peter, Sarah Currie, Northlew, Devon
Ivy D. Curtis, Northlew, Devon
Brenda Curtis, East Worth, Northlew, Devon
L.N. Davey, Higher West Kimber, Northlew, Devon
Winifred Davey, Northlew, Devon
The Davey family, Higher West Kimber, Northlew, Devon
Nancy Pincombe Docksai, Reston, Virginia, USA
Stacey Dufty, Northlew, Devon
Bryan and Marion Dufty, Stoney Farm, Northlew, Devon
Peter B. Dufty, Plympton, Devon
Laura-Jane Dufty, Northlew, Devon
Simon Dufty, Northlew, Devon
Michael and Tonya Dufty, Northlew, Devon
Samuel N.J. Dufty, Northlew, Devon
B.W.J. Dufty, Northlew, Devon
Joyce Dunn, North Tawton, Devon
Miss J. Durston, Northlew, Devon
Miss S. Durston, Northlew, Devon
Mr and Mrs J. Durston, Northlew, Devon
Mr and Mrs C. Durston, Northlew, Devon
Mr and Mrs S. Durston, Northlew, Devon
Miss A. Durston, Northlew, Devon
Mr and Mrs E. Durston, Northlew, Devon
Roy A.D. Dyer, Broadwoodkelly, Devon
Gillian Ellam (née Born), Filey, Yorkshire
Mrs Betty M. Evans, Okehampton, Devon
Mark D. Eveleigh, Northlew, Devon
Mr and Mrs T.H. Eveleigh, Marnhull, Dorset
Rosalind M. Eveleigh, Ashbury, Northlew, Devon
Katharine J. Eveleigh, Torquay, Devon
Jeff and Hazel Evely, Godfrey Gardens, Bow, Devon

# BORN'S BUS SERVICES.

## TIME AND FARE TABLES.

## NORTHLEW TO OKEHAMPTON.

### Wednesdays and Saturdays.

| | W | S | S | S |
|---|---|---|---|---|
| | a.m. | a.m. | p.m. | p.m. |
| CROWDEN dep. | — | 9-55 | — | — |
| Northlew .. .. | 9-30 | 10- 0 | 2- 0 | 7- 0 |
| Eastacombe Cross .. | 9-32 | 10- 2 | 2- 2 | 7- 2 |
| Durdon Cross .. | 9-35 | 10- 5 | 2- 5 | 7- 5 |
| Oake Cross .. | 9-45 | — | 2-15 | — |
| Waytown .. .. | 9-50 | 10-15 | 2-20 | 7-15 |
| East Down Cross .. | — | 10-20 | 2-25 | — |
| Hill Town Cross .. | — | 10-25 | 2-30 | — |
| OKEHAMPTON arr. | 10- 5 | 10-30 | 2-35 | 7-20 |

| | W | S | S | S |
|---|---|---|---|---|
| | p.m. | p.m. | p.m. | p.m. |
| OKEHAMPTON dep. | 12-10 | 12-30 | 5- 0 | 11- 0 |
| Hill Town Cross .. | — | 12-35 | 5- 5 | — |
| East Down Cross .. | — | 12-40 | 5-10 | — |
| Waytown .. .. | 12-25 | 12-45 | 5-15 | 11-15 |
| Oake Cross .. | 12-30 | — | 5-20 | — |
| Durdon Cross .. | 12-35 | 12-55 | 5-30 | 11-25 |
| Eastacombe Cross .. | 12-38 | 12-58 | 5-33 | 11-28 |
| Northlew .. .. | 12-40 | 1- 0 | 5-35 | 11-30 |
| CROWDEN arr. | — | — | 5-40 | — |

S—Saturdays only. W—Wednesdays only.

### First and Third Saturdays only.

| | a.m. |
|---|---|
| WEST WORTH CROSS dep. | 9-45 |
| Greendown .. .. | 9-50 |
| Crowden .. .. .. | 9-55 |
| Bogtown .. .. .. | 9-55 |
| Northlew .. .. .. | 10- 0 |
| Eastacombe Cross .. .. | 10- 2 |
| Langaton Cross .. .. | 10- 5 |
| Gribbleford .. .. | 10-10 |
| Westacott Cross .. .. | 10-15 |
| Oake Cross .. .. | 10-20 |
| Waytown .. .. .. | 10-25 |
| OKEHAMPTON .. arr. | 10-35 |

| | p.m. |
|---|---|
| OKEHAMPTON .. dep. | 5- 0 |
| Waytown .. .. .. | 5-15 |
| Oake Cross .. .. | 5-20 |
| Westacott Cross .. .. | 5-25 |
| Gribbleford .. .. | 5-30 |
| Langaton .. .. .. | 5-35 |
| Eastacombe Cross .. .. | 5-38 |
| Northlew .. .. .. | 5-40 |
| Bogtown .. .. .. | 5-45 |
| Crowden .. .. .. | 5-45 |
| Greendown .. .. | 5-50 |
| WEST WORTH CROSS arr. | 5-55 |

GREAT MARKETS: Depart OKEHAMPTON 4-0 p.m. Arrive NORTHLEW 4-30 p.m.

A Bus will leave BOGTOWN on OTHER SATURDAYS at 1-55 p.m.

### FARES:

| | Return | Single |
|---|---|---|
| West Worth and Greendown .. | 2/6 | 1/6 |
| Crowden and Northlew .. | 2/3 | 1/6 |
| Bogtown .. .. .. | 2/6 | 1/6 |
| Durdon Cross .. .. | 2/- | 1/3 |
| Westacott Cross .. .. | 1/9 | 1/3 |
| Oake Cross.. .. .. | 1/6 | 1/- |
| Waytown .. .. .. | 1/5 | 10d. |
| East Down Cross .. .. | 1/3 | 9d. |
| Hill Town Cross .. .. | 9d. | 6d. |
| Gribbleford .. .. | 2/- | 1/3 |

Children aged 3 to 14, Half-price.

Gladys and Fred Evely, Bow, Devon
John Feltham, Northlew, Devon
Mr C.K. Fenton-Evans, Northlew, Devon
Mrs Miriam Fielden, Sidmouth, Devon
S.R. Friend, Waytown, Okehampton, Devon
Joyce P. Friend
Kenneth and Cynthia Friend, Burnards House Farm, Holsworthy, Devon
Graham and Susan Friend, Higher Newbridge Cottage, Merton, Devon
P.C. Friend, Wadland Barton, Ashbury, Devon
Garfield Gay
Mrs E.M. Gay, Magpie, Petrockstowe, Devon
Mrs Marian Gerry, East Budleigh, Devon
Julian and Cindy Goacher, Warminster
Revd Martin R. Goord, Herne Bay, Kent
Keith and Brenda Gratton, St Austell, Cornwall
Lew and Lilian Gratton, Northlew, Devon
Les and Gladys Gratton, Okehampton, Devon
Julian Gratton and Linda Taylor, Northlew, Devon
Margaret Haggerty (Wivill-Kimber), Plymouth, Devon
C.B.E. Hales, Plymouth, Devon
Pete and Val Hampson, Ashbury, Devon
Anna K. Handley, Harrogate, North Yorkshire
Mrs Esme Hann, Okehampton, Devon
Trixie Hannaford, Northlew, Devon
Rosemary E. Harmer, Sutton, Cambridgeshire
Mrs Mary Harrison (née Wreford)
Susan Hawker, Langtree, Devon
Howard and Elizabeth Hayter, The Old Mill, Crowden, Northlew, Devon
Miss Morwenna Hortop, Broomfield, Northlew, Devon
Barbara Hucker, Northlew, Devon
Hutton, Croft Farm, Northlew, Devon
William and Hilary Isaac, Northlew, Devon
Mrs Brenda Isaac (née Jordan), Launceston, Cornwall
Mr and Mrs G. Jacobs, Ashbury
Andrew R. Janes, Taunton, Somerset
Robert W. Jefferies, Northlew, Devon
Judy Jones, Shallowford, Northlew, Devon
Charles Jordan
Mrs Shirley Keates (née Bater), Shaftesbury, Dorset
Jennifer A. Kewell, Rustington, Sussex
Mary Lacey, Devonport, Devon (Littlejohns DTR)
Arnold C. Lake, Bratton Clovelly, Devon
G.P. and D. Lawrence, formerly of Northlew
A. Grace Letheren, Hatherleigh, Devon
Laurie Light Esq., Northlew, Devon
Gabriel and Stella Lindsay, Crowden, Devon
Kirstie Lindsay, Crowden, Devon
Marilyn Livingstone, Northlew, Devon
Alec Luxton, Chilsworthy, Holsworthy, Devon
Harold Luxton, Highampton, Beaworthy, Devon
Faith and Henry Luxton, Okehampton, Devon
Walter Luxton, South Petherwin, Launceston, Cornwall
Paul R.P. Madge (Madge Family Historian), South Petherton, Somerset
Marlene A. Mahoney, Northlew, Devon
Veronica Martin, Lower West Heanton, Buckland Filleigh, Beaworthy, Devon
Phyllis Martin, Torquay, Devon
Chris and Val Mathews, Wood St David, Higher Gorhuish, Northlew, Devon
Brian and Jenny May, Higher Street, Hatherleigh, Devon
Gerald Maynard, Bude, Cornwall
Tom and Shirley Maynard, Northlew, Devon
Joanne Maynard, Northlew, Devon
Florrie R. Millership, Broomfield, Northlew, Devon
Janet and John Millership, Northlew, Devon
Les Millership, Melbourne, Australia
Shaun L. Millership, Broomfield, Northlew, Devon
Graham E. Monk, Torquay, Devon
Iris O. Moore, Torrington, Devon
John Moore, Northlew, Devon
Valerie Morris
Bryony E. Newhouse, Oxford
Robert G. Newhouse, Rising Sun, Cornwall
Mrs S. Nimptsch (née Woollcombe), Kensington, London

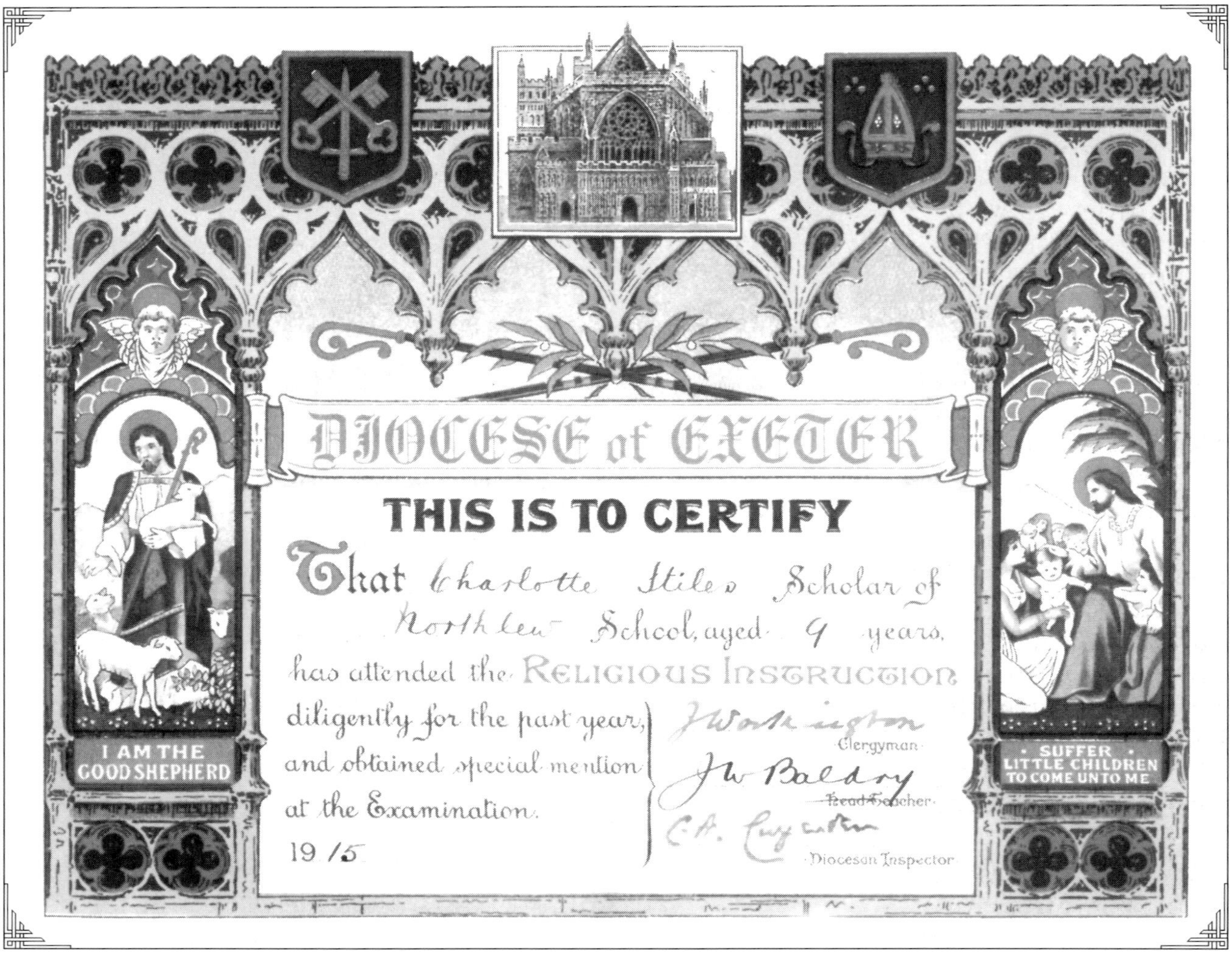
DIOCESE of EXETER
THIS IS TO CERTIFY
That Charlotte Stiles Scholar of
Northlew School, aged 9 years,
has attended the RELIGIOUS INSTRUCTION
diligently for the past year,
and obtained special mention
at the Examination.
1915
Clergyman
J W Baldry
Head Teacher
Diocesan Inspector
I AM THE GOOD SHEPHERD
SUFFER LITTLE CHILDREN TO COME UNTO ME

Betty D. Northam, Okehampton, Devon
Irene F. Northey, Broadwood, Lifton, Devon
Northlew and Ashbury Primary School
Michael and Sally O'Brien, Northlew, Devon
Irene and Ron Oldale, Northlew, Devon
Ms Joanna L. Oughton-Allen, Northlew, Devon
Bob Page, Eastcombe, Northlew, Devon
Derrick and Carolyn Palmer, Kenilworth, Warwickshire
Revd John Peak, Northlew, Devon
Pearse family, Stockaton Farm, Mornick, Cornwall
Martin and Jane Perry, Elmfield, Northlew, Devon
Malcolm Robin Pratt, Higher Eastcott, Northlew, Devon
Reverend Jack and Mrs Vera A. Reason, Bideford, Devon
Paul and Heather Richards, Howards Gorhuish, Northlew, Devon
Mary Elizabeth Richards, Highampton, Devon
Valerie and Fred Riley, Shaldon and Northlew, Devon
Mrs Pat Roberts, Whaley Bridge, Derbyshire
Valerie D. Roberts, Okehampton, Devon
Mr C.H. Roulstone, Torquay, Devon
Mr and Mrs Fred Rundle, Northlew, Devon
Patricia Rundle, Exeter, Devon
Mark Rundle, Northlew, Devon
Alison and Steve Shelton, Crowden, Northlew, Devon
B.R. and M. Singleton
Kevin B.R. Singleton
S. Smale, Beer, Devon
N. Smale, Farnham, Surrey
C. Smale, Farnham, Surrey
Derek Smale, formerly Black Torrington, Devon
David and Geri Sperring, Northlew, Devon
Ruth and Tony Squire, Northlew, Devon
Mrs Phyllis M. Squire, Northlew, Devon
Christine N. Stacey, Sidford, Devon
Tim and Carole Stanleick
Mrs Avril Stentiford, Exeter, Devon
Sylvia Strauss, Trumansburg, New York, USA
Celia Stuart, Exeter, Devon
John and Celia Sturgeon, Lower Whiddon, Northlew, Devon
Peter and Heather Tapp, Little Hayes, Jacobstowe, Devon
Maurice Thomas, Burdon, Highampton, Devon
Beryl O. Tonkins, Newton Abbot, Devon
Geoff and Elspeth Tuke, Beaworthy, Devon
Rachelle and Richard Voaden, Nether Wallop, Hampshire
Francis W. Voaden, Northlew, Devon
Edward Charles Voaden, Northlew, Devon
Gary and Sylvia Voaden (née Curtis), Bolland Farm, Northlew, Devon
The Revd Ray and Mrs Jenny Voden, Harrowbarrow, Cornwall
Mr S. Voden, North Cornwall
John F.W. Walling, Newton Abbot, Devon
Christopher, Andrea, James and Victoria Ware, Crowden, Northlew, Devon
Norman Webster, Leeds, Yorkshire
Gregory D. Westbrook, South Kensington, London
Sarah L. Westbrook, North Tawton, Devon
Richard and Kay Westbrook, Northlew, Devon
Julian Wilkins, Northlew, Devon
Helena Williams, Northlew, Devon
Mrs R.F. Williams, Northlew, Devon
Mr and Mrs E.W. Williamson, Ashbury Court, Okehampton, Devon
Pip Wilson, Loveland Farm, Northlew, Devon
Lady Wilson, Child Okeford, Dorset
Revd Stuart Wilson, Bratton Clovelly, Devon
Morgen Witzel, Northlew, Devon
Simon Wood, Brockfield, Yorkshire
Wood family, Fourwoods Cottage, Northlew, Devon
Nicholas Woollcombe, Fulham, London
Lizzy Woollcombe, Melbourne, Australia
Amy Woollcombe, Melbourne, Australia
J.H.G. Woollcombe, Hemerdon House, Plympton, Devon
Hilary and Mike Wreford, Okehampton, Devon
Mr and Mrs F.W. Yelland, Northlew, Devon
Mr and Mrs M. Yelland, Northlew, Devon
Philip and Traci-Ann Yelland, Northlew, Devon
Brenda Zielinska

## Titles from the Series

*The Book of Addiscombe* • Various
*The Book of Addiscombe, Vol. II* • Various
*The Book of Bampton* • Caroline Seward
*The Book of Barnstaple* • Avril Stone
*Book of Bickington* • Stuart Hands
*Blandford Forum: A Millennium Portrait* • Various
*The Book of Bridestowe* • R. Cann
*The Book of Brixham* • Frank Pearce
*The Book of Buckland Monachorum & Yelverton* • Hemery
*The Book of Carshalton* • Stella Wilks
*The Parish Book of Cerne Abbas* • Vale & Vale
*The Book of Chagford* • Ian Rice
*The Book of Chittlehamholt with Warkleigh & Satterleigh* • Richard Lethbridge
*The Book of Chittlehampton* • Various
*The Book of Colney Heath* • Bryan Lilley
*The Book of Constantine* • Moore & Trethowan
*The Book of Cornwood & Lutton* • Various
*The Book of Creech St Michael* • June Small
*The Book of Cullompton* • Various
*The Book of Dawlish* • Frank Pearce
*The Book of Dulverton, Brushford, Bury & Exebridge* • Various
*The Book of Dunster* • Hilary Binding
*The Ellacombe Book* • Sydney R. Langmead
*The Book of Exmouth* • W.H. Pascoe
*The Book of Grampound with Creed* • Bane & Oliver
*The Book of Hayling Island & Langstone* • Rogers
*The Book of Helston* • Jenkin with Carter
*The Book of Hemyock* • Clist & Dracott
*The Book of Hethersett* • Various
*The Book of High Bickington* • Avril Stone
*The Book of Ilsington* • Dick Wills
*The Book of Lamerton* • Ann Cole & Friends
*Lanner, A Cornish Mining Parish* • Scharron Schwartz & Roger Parker
*The Book of Leigh & Bransford* • Various
*The Book of Litcham with Lexham & Mileham* • Various
*The Book of Loddiswell* • Various
*The Book of Lulworth* • Rodney Legg
*The Book of Lustleigh* • Joe Crowdy
*The Book of Manaton* • Various
*The Book of Markyate* • Various
*The Book of Mawnan* • Various
*The Book of Meavy* • Pauline Hemery
*The Book of Minehead with Alcombe* • Binding & Stevens
*The Book of Morchard Bishop* • Jeff Kingaby
*The Book of Newdigate* • John Callcut
*The Book of Northlew with Ashbury* • Various
*The Book of North Newton* • Robins & Robins
*The Book of North Tawton* • Various
*The Book of Okehampton* • Radford & Radford
*The Book of Paignton* • Frank Pearce
*The Book of Penge, Anerley & Crystal Palace* • Various
*The Book of Peter Tavy with Cudlipptown*• Various
*The Book of Pimperne* • Jean Coull
*The Book of Plymtree* • Tony Eames
*The Book of Porlock* • Denis Corner
*Postbridge – The Heart of Dartmoor* • Reg Bellamy
*The Book of Priddy* • Various
*The Book of Rattery* • Various
*The Book of Silverton* • Various
*The Book of South Molton* • Various
*The Book of South Stoke* • Various
*South Tawton & South Zeal with Sticklepath* • Radfords
*The Book of Sparkwell with Hemerdon & Lee Mill* • Pam James
*The Book of Staverton* • Pete Lavis
*The Book of Stithians* • Various
*The Book of Studland* • Rodney Legg
*The Book of Swanage* • Rodney Legg
*The Book of Torbay* • Frank Pearce
*Uncle Tom Cobley & All: Widecombe-in-the-Moor* • Stephen Woods
*The Book of Watchet* • Compiled by David Banks
*The Book of West Huntspill* • Various
*Widecombe-in-the-Moor* • Stephen Woods
*The Book of Williton* • Michael Williams
*Woodbury: The Twentieth Century Revisited* • Roger Stokes
*The Book of Woolmer Green* • Various

## Forthcoming

*The Book of Bakewell* • Various
*The Book of Barnstaple, Vol. II* • Avril Stone
*The Book of Brampford* • Various
*The Book of Breage & Gurmoe* • Stephen Polglase
*The Book of the Bedwyns* • Various
*The Book of Bideford* • Peter Christie
*The Book of Bridport* • Rodney Legg
*The Book of Buckfastleigh* • Sandra Coleman
*The Book of Carharrack* • Various
*The Book of Castleton* • Geoff Hill
*The Book of Edale* • Gordon Miller
*The Book of Kingskerswell* • Various
*The Book of Lostwithiel* • Barbara Frasier
*The Book of Lydford* • Barbara Weeks
*The Book of Lyme Regis* • Rodney Legg
*The Book of Nether Stowey* • Various
*The Book of Nynehead* • Various
*The Book of Princetown* • Dr Gardner-Thorpe
*The Book of St Day* • Various
*The Book of Sampford Courtenay with Honeychurch* • Stephanie Pouya
*The Book of Sculthorpe* • Garry Windeler
*The Book of Sherborne* • Rodney Legg
*The Book of Southbourne* • Rodney Legg
*The Book of Tavistock* • Gerry Woodcock
*The Book of Thorley* • Various
*The Book of Tiverton* • Mike Sampson
*The Book of West Lavington* • Various
*The Book of Witheridge* • Various
*The Book of Withycombe* • Chris Boyles

For details of any of the above titles or if you are interested in writing your own history, please contact: Commissioning Editor Community Histories, Halsgrove House, Lower Moor Way, Tiverton Business Park, Tiverton, Devon EX16 6SS, England; email: naomic@halsgrove.com

In order to include as many historic photographs as possible in this volume, a printed index is not included. However, the Community History Series is indexed by Genuki. For further information and indexes to volumes in the series, please visit: http://www.cs.ncl.uk/genuki/DEV/indexingproject.html